Testimonials for
The Procrastinator's Guide to Marketing

"This is an incredible book, a virtual bible for getting more customers, making more sales and increasing profitability. Every business owner should read and apply these great ideas."

—BRIAN TRACY, AUTHOR OF
THE WAY TO WEALTH AND *MILLION DOLLAR HABITS*

"Business owners in every industry should add The Procrastinator's Guide to Marketing *to their reference library. Written in the same spirit as Jay Conrad Levinson's* Guerrilla Marketing *book series, it provides a similar relevant context for solid marketing strategies and practical tactics. Mary and David Scarborough approach the tricky topic of marketing plans armed with years of study and experience as well as good old-fashioned common sense—a winning combination! Read it, absorb it, and most of all, apply it."*

—MITCH MEYERSON, PRESIDENT OF GUERRILLA MARKETING COACH AND
AUTHOR OF *SUCCESS SECRETS OF THE ONLINE MARKETING SUPERSTARS*

*"*The Procrastinator's Guide to Marketing *is a good one. What a superb, in-depth general guide. Congratulations. It's the kind of mainstay resource that any small business owner should keep prominently close to hand on their work desk. Well done."*

—JAY CONRAD LEVINSON, AUTHOR OF THE *GUERRILLA MARKETING* BOOK SERIES

"Think of something dependable, practical, and reliable, something you can count on . . . you've just thought of this book. Simply put, it's a problem-solving tool. If you're a procrastinator, or you've got marketing problems, this book is your solution. It's clear, simple, and succinct."

—MICHAEL PORT, AUTHOR OF THE NATIONAL BESTSELLER, *BOOK YOURSELF SOLID*

"The Procrastinator's Guide to Marketing *is an excellent and truly unique new book written in an easy-to-read style by authors Mary and David Scarborough.*

"After reviewing this practical, how-to gem, I'm reminded of the wonderful quote from Bill Bradley: 'Ambition is the path to success. Persistence is the vehicle you arrive in.' With that in mind, I would add, 'The Procrastinator's Guide to Marketing *is how you can get there.' It's really, really good—and I don't say that lightly!*

"This is a true marketing guide based on hard won, practical experience combined with smart marketing techniques that work today. When I'm going off course, it gently pulls me back on route, so that I can get done sooner, better, and spend more time and focus on my core activities.

"As you read this book and start using the templates, you almost feel like you have these two expert, approachable authors standing over your shoulder, advising, helping, encouraging, giving you a little push when you need it, so you need never feel stuck at any time.

"So there you have it. The Procrastinator's Guide to Marketing *gets my highest recommendation: don't waste another second floundering around in confusion: choose clarity and invest in* The Procrastinator's Guide to Marketing *right now while the templates are still included free, and set yourself back on the path to power, success, and achievement."*

—BRIAN AUSTIN, AUTHOR/WEBMASTER, INTERNETTIPS.COM

The PROCRASTINAT⏳R'S GUIDE to MARKETING

(Or:
How to Get Off Your Butt and Develop Your Marketing Plan!)

*Mary Eule Scarborough and
David A. Scarborough*

Entrepreneur
Press

Editorial Director: Jere L. Calmes
Cover Design: Beth Hansen-Winter
Production and Composition: Eliot House Productions

This publication is designed to provide accurate and authoritative information in regard to the
subject matter covered. It is sold with the understanding that the publisher is not engaged in
rendering legal, accounting or other professional services. If legal advice or other expert assistance is required, the services of a competent professional person should be sought.

Library of Congress Cataloging-in-Publication Data
Scarborough, Mary Eule.
  Procrastinator's guide to marketing/by Mary Eule Scarborough and David A.
Scarborough.
    p.   cm.
  ISBN-13: 978-1-59918-144-8 (alk. paper)
  ISBN-10: 1-59918-144-4 (alk. paper)
  1. Marketing. I. Scarborough, David A. II. Title.
HF5415.S285 2007
658.8—dc22   2007021487

Printed in Canada
12 11 10 09 08   10 9 8 7 6 5 4 3 2 1

CONTENTS

Chapter 6

Step 2: Shaping Your Identity, Mission, and Vision   89

Chapter 7

Step 3: Choosing Your Products and Services _____ 103

Chapter 8

Step 4: Identifying Your Target Market _____ 125

Chapter 9

Step 5: Turning Features into Benefits _____ 145

ACKNOWLEDGMENTS

First we'd like to thank our family and friends—those who lovingly gave us what every first-time writers need most—enthusiasm and support. We'd particularly like to express our gratitude to those who generously made time to read our initial manuscript and provide us with their honest and open feedback: Tom Eule, Suzanne Daughters, Zach and Tiffany Guerra, Stan Parker, Bob Walsh, Chelsea Guerra, Tennie and Harold Fletcher, Bob Parker, Randy Miller, and Stan Salter.

We'd also like to thank Rita, Joe, Tara, and Lewis Scarborough who supported us in many, many loving ways throughout our journey. And then there's the newest addition to our family, Zach and Tiff's beautiful little daughter, Sevilla—whose big blue eyes and seriously silly smile brightened many of our most frustrating days. We love you all very much.

And Chelsea, how can we forget your never faltering calls every Monday and Wednesday night? You have no idea how two tired writers came to rely on your consistent reminders to take a break and enjoy life's simple pleasures. You're pure joy. And thanks also to Shane Baxter for his patient answers to our many questions.

We'd also like to extend our infinite appreciation to our agents, Alana and Michael Lennie. The successful completion of this book is a clear reflection of their leap-of-faith belief in the project, attention to detail, unparalleled professionalism, keen insights, dogged tenacity, and most importantly, extraordinary kindness.

We would also like to thank Jere Calmes, our editor at Entrepreneur Press, whose rare talent is only exceeded by his boundless energy and kind spirit, and his assistant, Karen Thomas. Also, thanks to Karen Billipp for her outstanding work. It's a tough job but her diligence paid off.

And, of course, thanks to Keith Ferrazzi, who is living proof that you can be incredibly successful and busy beyond reason yet still find time to share your abundant good fortune with others.

Last, but not least, we'd like to thank Graham Guerra. The book that you now hold in your hands is in large part a result of his unbridled interest, thoughtful suggestions, ongoing attentiveness, and steadfast encouragement.

FOREWORD
by Keith Ferrazzi,
CEO of Ferrazzi Greenlight and best selling author of Never Eat Alone

You now hold in your hands the marketing book you've been looking for. It is a recipe for your achievement. Embrace it. Learn from it. Apply it.

After my first book, *Never Eat Alone*, was published in 2005, I was asked to serve as the keynote speaker at a Yale University alumni seminar in Washington, DC. This is where I met Mary and David Scarborough.

Over breakfast we discussed their ideas for this very book. I had dozens of questions and comments for my new acquaintances, and they patiently answered them as we talked about the world of marketing. Later, after reading and rereading their manuscript, I became increasingly impressed with its content and scope—so much so, that I incorporated it into new employee training at my consultancy, Ferrazzi Greenlight. So, when David and Mary asked if I would write the Foreword, it was an honor and I gladly took on the task.

A brief "thumbing" through the Table of Contents will quickly reveal the book's worth. You'll find everything you need to remove any fear or intimation you may be experiencing regarding the most dreaded four-letter marketing word: *plan*. Not only is their systematic approach comprehensive, well-thought-out, and rock-solid, but they have a knack for presenting it in clear and concise language.

Entrepreneurs must maneuver in a dynamic, worldwide, rough-and-tumble marketplace, something that spells doom for business people who lack know-how and expertise. In order to be successful you must gain mastery over certain fundamental skills, because they do not come naturally, or overnight, regardless of what you've heard.

For most, marketing proficiency is earned only after a great deal of effort and years of practice. But, once mastered, you can apply its principles many times in the future and under widely varying circumstances.

First, however, you must stop dreaming about your business's happy ending and shift your perspective by defining your life's vision and goals; facing the brutal facts of reality (while remaining optimistic); and objectively assessing your strengths and weaknesses.

Only then can you plan your journey by selecting the places, tools, and most importantly, the people who will help you achieve your mission. All this takes work and involves a lot of sweat equity.

That's why I strongly recommend that you use David and Mary's trustworthy expertise and legwork to shorten your learning curve. In addition to their rock-solid advice, brilliant templates, and step-by-step guides, you'll experience an enjoyable ride through their (and others) "real-life" lessons learned, stunning successes, and vivid disappointments.

Yet, while I acknowledge that these elements help solve a largely unmet challenge for today's small businesspeople, my chief interest in this book lies elsewhere. And although my perspective may understandably be viewed as biased, I state it without reservation. That is, this book reveals something more because it embodies several of the central tenets I introduced in *Never Eat Alone*.

And at every stage of my own career, I sought advice from the most successful people around me—those who could help me make more of myself. Like other accomplished people, my eventual successes were due, in part, to their kind and patient support . . . a "secret" rarely recognized, much less discussed, by business professors, career counselors, or therapists.

Simply put, real "networking" is about finding ways to make other people prosper. It's about working hard to give more than you get.

And since today's primary currency is information, a wide-reaching network of respected colleagues, mentors, and friends is more critical than ever and one of the surest ways of becoming and remaining successful.

Savvy consumers enjoy a new and ever growing abundance of choice. They have grown tired and suspicious of the plethora of self-proclaimed marketing "gurus" and entertaining "tricks" and tactics hyped on the internet and elsewhere. Smoke screens and latest diversionary "get-rich-quick" schemes aren't making it anymore.

Information is everywhere.

Competent, creative, and well-thought-out content is hard to find.

This time, you're in luck. David and Mary, unassailable marketing experts and thought leaders in their industry, genuinely and generously share their keen insights and intellectual property here as well as in their seminars and speaking engagements. They consistently over-deliver and won't let you down.

In the end, life is short and our opportunities are limited by time. So never waste one hour. Reach out to others. Develop a group of trusted colleagues, friends, and mentors to lean on. Your long-term success depends upon it.

And David and Mary are very good company.

—*Keith Ferrazzi*

PREFACE

According to a June, 2004 survey by the Small Business Administration (SBA) America's more than 25 million small businesses (defined as companies with fewer than 100 employees) employ half of all private sector workers; they account for between 60 and 80 percent of all new jobs annually, pay more than 44 percent of the country's total private payroll, and contribute approximately $6 trillion annually to the country's Gross National Product (GNP), making them truly the backbone of the American economy.

> *The person who wakes up and finds himself a success hasn't been asleep.*
>
> —WILSON MIZNER

Moreover, America's entrepreneurs are responsible for developing many of the most ground-breaking and far-reaching inventions in the past century—the airplane, aerosol can, heart valve, soft contact lens, cotton picker, and frozen foods, just to name a few. To many, their pioneering fortitude and action-oriented nature symbolize the true American spirit.

Sustainable Small Businesses: The Uncommon Thread

Now consider this: The US Department of Commerce estimates that 62 percent of all American businesses, regardless of size, fail within the first six years. Forty percent of small companies go under before their first anniversary, and 80 percent of the first-year survivors fail within five years.

Even worse, 85 percent of the 1 in 25 small businesses that *do* survive for ten or more years never reach $1 million in annual revenues and only 5 percent of *those* hit the $5 million mark!

These grim statistics point to the serious challenges entrepreneurs face, even though the United States still offers the world's best environment for small businesses.

Exploring these incongruities—the "whys" and eventual solutions—served as the foundation for writing this book. Like other American businesspeople we were seeking answers, and after years of observations and research we uncovered what we feel is the genuine truth.

America's small businesses are failing in record numbers because their founders, owners, employees, or managers do not understand that:

- *First-rate marketing is the only leverage they have for growing a healthy business*; it is about taking limited assets and achieving the best possible outcome.
- *"Marketing" means something different from what many people assume*; this misunderstanding is killing their businesses.
- *Success is in the plan.* Without a marketing plan there are no strategies; without strategies, there is no sustainable business.
- *Excellent marketing cannot be accomplished on a wing and a prayer.* It comes only with study, practice,1 and perseverance.

- *Superior marketing has more to do with passion, know-how, time management, energy, and action, than money.*
- *No one can make it alone.* We all need the help of others.

An expert is a person who has made all the mistakes that can be made in a very narrow field.

—NEILS BOHR

Why Do We Think We Can Help You?

As entrepreneurs, consultants and coaches, and former executives, we have been working professionally with the subject of marketing for nearly three decades. In addition to our latest search for answers, each of us—since the beginning of our careers—have at various times thought about writing a practical book, a marketing game plan. We knew it would be helpful to almost anyone—small business owners, independent professionals, marketing directors, and sales professionals—searching for proven ways to attract more new customers, sell more to existing customers, and bring back those customers more often, with less effort, no matter what product or service.

We have worked hard to write the most comprehensive, yet practical, how-to book on this subject and crammed it full of simple, yet proven, ideas that will make a big difference in any business person's life. Each of us has personally read dozens of books on sales, advertising, marketing, management, and leadership. We have subscriptions to the most current business magazines; reviewed college-level teaching materials; enrolled in dozens of additional classes presented by the world's most respected experts (and a few who are not); developed and presented our own marketing seminars; lectured and taught business college level courses; and worked with hundreds of entrepreneurs. We have individually and/or collectively, developed marketing campaigns for small and medium-sized businesses, large corporations, organizations, and educational institutions.

This book, then, includes the most useful ideas from all of these venues. But just as important it is based on our own observations and experiences, those hard-earned wisdoms, real-life lessons learned, objective assessments, our own creativity, and of course, subjective judgments.

We have designed this in-depth guide to include templates, worksheets, advice, practical tips, examples, stories, and analogies to help you learn, or rediscover, all the things you need to achieve your most important lifestyle goals.

Together, we will:

- Convince you that a marketing plan is your business's best friend, and there's no good reason to "wing" it.
- Take the mystery and guesswork out of the equation so you're less likely to procrastinate and start planning today.
- Teach you a tried-and-true approach—a line of attack—that you can use to achieve *any goal*, big or small, complex or simple, personal or business, regardless of your industry, products, services, the marketplace, you name it. As with many things, the journey, or the process you'll use to complete your plan, is as valuable as the result.
- Help you create your own comprehensive, easy-to-understand marketing plan; one that will use your limited resources (time, people, and money) to achieve the best possible outcome.
- Teach you how to ask the right questions and make sure you know what to do with the answers you receive.
- Ensure that you're making decisions based on careful research and time-tested methods, not the latest hype, and explain why it's so important to become an ardent life-long student of business.
- Help you achieve sustainable, profitable business growth by attracting more qualified prospects, converting them into profitable customers, and turning them into raving fans.

We hope our advice will make a significant difference in your personal and professional lives.

How Will We Work Together to Accomplish These Goals?

Simply put: a little bit at a time.

We will provide you with solid direction, sound advice, and clear guidance, in the form of:

- Worksheets that will help you collect the information you need.

- Examples of what to do and what to avoid.
- Fill-in-the-blank templates and outlines that take the worry out of starting from scratch.
- Tips, advice, and cautions that alert you to common errors beforehand.
- Resources, so you'll know where to get more information or help.
- Analogies/stories that help make unfamiliar material more friendly.

And most importantly, we'll share our own lessons learned. You see, one of the reasons we are allowed to call ourselves marketing experts is that collectively, or individually, we have made just about every mistake possible—at least twice. So, in addition to our graduate degrees we have two diplomas from The School of Hard Knocks.

Is this Book for You?

We do not intend this book to be all things to all people. In order to stay focused, provide essential information, and offer enough details on the critical elements for creating a sound strategic and tactical marketing plan, we are offering content that is most useful to:

- entrepreneurs, "solopreneurs," small- and medium-sized business owners or managers;
- nonprofit employees;
- service providers;
- marketing managers or directors;
- business or marketing students; and
- people starting a business, or considering it.

These categories alone do not properly describe our targeted readers or their motivation for purchasing this book. More significantly they are intelligent and inspired everyday folks who are as diverse as people worldwide. Their current financial status, age, industry, education, geography, beliefs, passions, race, gender, and more run the gamut, but they all have one thing in common with you: *they need marketing help*. If you recognize yourself in the following scenarios, we are here to help:

You are

- Tired of slogging through mounds of marketing information and theories to pick out the most relevant content.
- Worried that you won't be able to attract investors or obtain a much-needed business loan without a solid marketing plan.
- Uneasy because you've been hired to market and aren't sure what that really entails.
- Ready to start a new business or change career and have no idea where to begin.
- Bewildered by intimidating business and marketing jargon and searching for clear, simple, and practical answers.
- Confused by all the different marketing theories and unsure whom to trust for good advice.
- Uncertain whether you have the ability to manage a successful small business.
- Panic-stricken: Your business is headed for extinction and you need to stop the bleeding.
- Seeking solutions for growing your business to the next level and/or increasing profits.
- Frustrated after one, or more, unsuccessful attempts at trying to buy advertising, a web site, or other types of marketing communication.
- Stressed because you need, or have been asked to write a marketing plan and have no idea where to begin.
- Scared that your business is failing and you don't have the knowledge or wherewithal to fix it.
- Frazzled, because even though you always *intended to write a marketing plan, you did not.*

Throughout the book, we'll continue to delve into this subject as well as the other roadblocks that may be standing in your way. We'll help you identify your own and offer ways for overcoming them. We hope our guide becomes one of your favorite business tools. Please dog-ear pages, write notes in the margins, and use a bright yellow highlighter to underscore points of interest.

And as part of our commitment to provide you with time- and money-saving tools, we've included our SMA Marketing Template Library in the price of this book. In order to access our full array of over 100 templates, go to: www.**TheProcrastinatorsGuideToMarketing**.com or www.TPGTM.com. Once there, you'll be asked to register and given instructions for downloading.

So, grab your favorite drink, sit down, relax, and get ready to take this journey with us. Although the road has some patchy spots and hairpin turns, we'll be there to help you navigate through them safely. So hang on and enjoy the ride!

To Your Bright Future,
Mary and David

If we could sell our experiences for what they cost us,
we'd all be millionaires.

OSCAR WILDE

1

MIND OVER MATTER

It's All in Your Head

In Jim Collins' brilliant book, *Good to Great* (HarperCollins, 2001), he discusses Isaiah Berlin's famous allegory about certain types of people. Even if you've heard this story, it bears rereading:

> *I couldn't wait for success, so I went ahead without it.*
>
> —JONATHAN WINTERS

Once upon a time, there was a fox. This particular fox was a very sly and cunning creature, and a rather intelligent one as well. Each day he schemed, invented, and reinvented complicated strategies—all devised to outwit and attack the hedgehog. Then, as soon as he was satisfied with his latest brilliant plan he would pay a visit to the hedgehog's den and circle it continuously, until the perfect moment arrived for him to pounce. And from an outside vantage point, he had every reason to be confident. After all, he was fast, sleek, crafty, sure-footed, and striking. He looked like a champion, especially compared to his prey.

The hedgehog, a funny creature with an odd appearance (part porcupine and part armadillo) enjoyed his simple life: waddling around searching for food, taking care of his home, and resting.

One day as he went about his routine, the little hedgehog crossed directly in front of the fox—who all along had been waiting in cunning silence. "Aha" the fox thought, "I've got you now!" With that, he leapt out and with lightning-fast speed ran straight for the hedgehog. The hedgehog, sensing danger turned around and saw the fox and thought, "Here we go again. Will he ever learn?" Rolling up into a perfect sphere, he became a ball of sharp spikes. As the fox drew closer he saw the hedgehog sticking out in all directions and called off the attack, vowing to devise a new plot to get him.

Each day for the rest of their lives some form of this battle took place, and despite all of the fox's wiles the hedgehog always won.

What Does this Story Have to Do with Marketing Your Business?

Everything. Berlin argues that, like the fox, some people choose to chase too many things at the same time. Because they view the world as excessively complex, they never shape a single unified philosophy or vision. So, they operate on too many levels and simply cannot manage it all. For example, these are the folks who:

- Waste precious time unnecessarily reinventing the wheel whenever they're called upon to perform a task;
- Use ten words when three would suffice;
- Avoid making decisions because it never seems like the right time;
- Worry excessively about "what-ifs" down the road;
- Over-analyze things until they feel paralyzed;

- Jump at every opportunity instead of focusing on their most important strategies.

The end result? They're confused, overwhelmed, distracted, frustrated, and stressed. Their personal lives take a big hit and their businesses suffer. In short, they are opportunists instead of true entrepreneurs.

In contrast, "hedgehogs" are adept at taking complicated concepts and condensing them into their most elemental parts. Their methodology for unraveling any challenge is therefore quite simple. They identify the most important components needed to solve their problem (i.e., ingredients and procedures) and focus their efforts there.

They understand that true genius—and the ability to get things done—relies upon making things simpler, not more complex. (And what better example of this is there than Einstein's Theory of Relativity formula, "$e = mc^2$"?)

Mistakes are the portals of discovery.

—JAMES JOYCE

As a general rule, hedgehogs do not place worth on anything that doesn't materially add value to their focused ideology, and thus are masters at shortening their learning curves by developing dependable problem-solving methods and tools.

Therefore, we've written this book as a hedgehog would: clearly, simply, and succinctly. Additionally, we've constructed concise models that represent multifaceted concepts and procedures and demonstrate how to write a comprehensive strategic and tactical marketing plan!

So, we'll begin by introducing you to a useful tool that you can use to approach any challenge and/or achieve any objective. It will serve as a building block for the rest of your plan and may even clear away the lingering fog in your brain.

 ## The Million Dollar Question

In an interview Thomas Edison, was asked how many times he tried, and failed, to invent the light bulb. He patiently replied that he did not consider his more than 800 attempts as failures, rather he had learned more than 800 ways *not* to make a light bulb! Thomas Edison's mindset ensured his success.

Like a hedgehog, he had one clear goal—to invent a light bulb. He started there and then asked himself the only right question:

"How do I do this?"

This is where all winning entrepreneurs begin. It is the question that ignites ideas and helps develop the solution-oriented mindset of successful people!

Then he acted. Thomas Edison focused and persevered until he cracked the code. He understood that a well-thought-out plan combined with action, failure, action, failure, action, more failure, and more action would eventually result in success. So, he never allowed himself to wonder if he would figure it out; it was merely a question of when.

Think of his sage advice if you find yourself wondering why so many successful people feel compelled to recount their list of failures. Then remember that every disappointment is chock-full of valuable lessons and it's up to you to reach into your "baggage" and use its content wisely.

You can only succeed by failing! If you never fail, you never act.
If you never act, it's impossible to succeed.

The Bottom Line
Set Goals ⇨ Ask: How do I do it? ⇨ Take Action ⇨ Fail ⇨ Ask: How do I do it better? ⇨ Take Action ⇨ Succeed

Assessing Your Mindset

- What are your conscious, and unconscious, beliefs?
- What do you value?
- What are your blind spots, the ones preventing you from achieving your goals?
- Will your state of mind help, or hurt, your ability to succeed?

We are guided by a passionate belief in a set of exceptional, fundamental principles regarding the huge impact that our state of mind has on every aspect—personal and professional—of our lives.

These tenets serve as our philosophical foundation and shape our approach to all situations and challenges. We were first introduced to the concepts by a mentor of ours, Jim Rohn, an American icon and leading business philosopher (www.myJimRohn.com). They can be summarized with the mnemonic device PADAR:

- *Philosophies* (truths, ideology, or "givens")—those beliefs that you know to be true—*determine your*
- *Attitudes* (opinions, feelings, outlook), *which determine your*
- *Decisions* (conclusions, assessments, choices), *which determine your*
- *Actions* (behaviors), *which determine your*
- *Results*

And just like dominoes they all fall in line, one after the other. The good news is that if you begin with the "right stuff"—facts, healthy beliefs—you're more likely to end up with great results. Alternatively, if you start the process with half-truths, misassumptions and/or outright fabrications, then you're headed for a train wreck. (The computer science world came up with their own acronym for this—GIGO—which means "garbage in, garbage out.")

So, before beginning your marketing plan, check and recheck your "givens." (Mary's Lesson Learned on page 6 will help to illustrate this.)

This undemanding analogy points to a profound reality: when you fail to check the validity of your truths you substantially increase the odds that the outcome you desire will be jeopardized. It is also a reminder about how powerful misunderstandings can be, and if you're truly interested in growing and maintaining a successful business you must be willing to:

- *Candidly assess your own strengths, weaknesses, skills, and knowledge.* Brilliant marketers are not born, they are made. Marketing is a teachable skill that starts in your brain. You can choose to be your best, mediocre, or worst self.

> Never build a business, or anything else for that matter, around an assumption until you've tested it. This is far less risky and costly than moving forward and finding out later that you were wrong. Yes, you may have to move a bit slower, but the time you spend getting this information will be more than worth it.

Mary's
Lesson Learned:

Challenge Your
Own Beliefs

Several years ago I was hired to help a medium-sized telecom reduce their tremendously high call-center-abandon rates—how many times callers hung up before they were connected to a sales representative. The company was conducting a direct-mail campaign that invited prospects to dial their toll-free number to learn more, or sign up for local and/or long-distance phone service. Although they were pleased with the overall response rate (the total calls into the center), 12 percent of the callers hung up before speaking with anyone and another 5 percent hung up just after being connected to a consultant! Since this situation was seriously affecting their sales rates, they wanted it fixed yesterday.

Company executives were sure of two things: the letter copy and their sales consultants were at the heart of the problem. They surmised that interested folks picked up the phone to find out more. Then, while on hold waiting to speak to a representative, they reread the letter, found it lacking, so hung up. I was asked to come up with the magic words that would keep those prospects interested. Moreover, the company wanted me to write new scripts for and/or retrain their sales consultants, since it was clear that they must be saying something wrong if so many people simply hung up after speaking with them for less than 30 seconds!

However, after many years of experience, I knew I first had to verify their "givens" in order to uncover the root causes of the problem. So, I did something very simple. I phoned their call center to find out exactly what their prospects were experiencing.

Picture this: My call was answered by a voice response unit (VRU) and before I was ever afforded the option to speak to a human being I had to dial in my telephone number and respond to an additional 22 prompts. Then, I was placed in a queue to wait. Even worse, after remaining on hold for more than five minutes my call was answered by a very nice representative who asked me four of the questions I had already dialed into their system.

No wonder people were hanging up!

The fix? I helped the company change the scripting and call flow so callers were efficiently directed to a live service representative after two or three prompts. What's more, the technology used to achieve this improvement was sitting in their system, ready to work; they just weren't using it! This seemingly small—even obvious—solution resulted in a 35 percent decrease in abandoned calls, a 25 percent increase in sales in less than one week, and hundreds of thousands of dollars in additional revenues.

But why didn't these very intelligent people figure this out themselves? The answer is profoundly simple—they were blinded by their own "truths" and never challenged them.

- *Actively seek objective and open feedback* and suggestions from customers, employees, family, friends, and even your competitors.
- *Conduct objective research* and use it to help make more informed decisions.
- *Challenge your own beliefs and police yourself.* Make sure that your truths are just that. For example, just because you believe that people in Cincinnati need/want your widget and will pay you $35 each doesn't mean it's *true*.
- *Get a coach.* Guess what Michael Jordan, Oprah Winfrey, and Lance Armstrong all have in common? The vast majority of highly successful people have mentors who ask them tough questions, push them to be their best and help them keep the promises they made to themselves and others.
- *Get "undiscussables" out on the table.* We've noticed that very few gurus spend much time here. Yes, a mindset that allows you to believe in success, picture your dreams, and have a positive attitude is important, but it's

Too many people have one foot in yesterday, the other in tomorrow, and are going nowhere today. A better way would be to learn from yesterday, plan for tomorrow and make the best of today.

—DAVID A. SCARBOROUGH

not enough. You have to face reality and all its warts, if you are serious about managing a thriving business.

Character Traits that Improve Your Chances of Achieving Your Goals

After years of working with small-business owners and managers, we developed our own list of personality traits commonly held by people who are successful in life and business. These are:

- *Passion*. Successful people love their chosen career and can't think of anything else they'd rather do.
- *Willingness to learn*. They are endlessly inquisitive and committed to becoming and/or remaining life-long students of business and marketing.
- *Clear perception*. They understand that perception is reality.
- *Patience*. They know that get-rich-quick schemes are hooey.
- *Preparedness*. They've done their homework and are poised and ready for opportunity when it comes knocking.
- *Tenacity*. They have a long-term perspective and are willing to stay the course.
- *Optimism*. They face the brutal facts of reality but choose to maintain a positive attitude.
- *Presence in the moment*. They repeat their past successes and don't dwell on yesterday's mistakes.
- *Reliability*. They keep their promises and do what they say they're going to do.
- *Honesty and trustworthiness*. They understand how long it takes to develop a great reputation and how quickly it can be destroyed.
- *Attentive*. Successful people understand that their best marketing tools are their ears.
- *Willingness to change*. They modify their behaviors, beliefs, and attitudes after gaining knowledge that effectively disputes previous notions.
- *Accountability*. They accept responsibility and take ownership for their behaviors and actions and never look to blame others.

David's Lesson Learned: Your Baggage Is Filled with Insights

Wise people recognize that time is their most precious asset. I've never heard of, or met, anyone who has managed to escape life's disappointments. It's true: life is not always fair. Believe it and move on.

What happens to you is far less important than your reaction. Attitude is not something that just happens, it's something you choose.

In other words, "Face it, trace it, and erase it." And while you must confront the brutal facts of reality, reach into your baggage and pull out the valuable lessons you've learned from your mistakes, disenchantments, frustrations, and the like.

One of America's most successful businesspeople, Brian Tracy, says, "All the good ideas have already been found. It's up to you to apply them. Don't worry about the stuff you can't do anything about. Let go of the past. Stop the, 'if—onlys.' The only good thing about the past is that it teaches you how to be successful in the future."

How Can You Apply this in the Real World?

Use the following five-step process to guide your important decisions, actions, and results.

Step One: Define and Write Down Your Goals

Know what you want coming out, before you ever go in. It doesn't matter if you're planning for a year, a day, or a minute, your goal(s) should be specific, well defined, and written down.

Step Two: Check Your Givens (Police Yourself)

Make sure that your truths are factual. Don't assume anything is true unless you've verified it—test, question, and research. And while it might take you a little longer to get moving, it will be well worth it.

Step Three: Plan

After you complete steps one and two, you'll have already substantially reduced your chances of making poor decisions. So start planning!

Step Four: Act

Put your plan to work. Creating a plan and not using it will get you to the same place as not creating a plan at all: in trouble. But prepare for the unexpected and stay flexible.

Step Five: Track, Measure, and Evaluate

Monitor your activities and objectively assess your results. Then adjust accordingly.

Before you can even begin with Step One, you'll need to take a closer look at your attitudes and how they may help or hurt your ability to attain your goals. Take a look at Figure 1.1, the Mindset Self-Assessment.

 Overnight Sensations?

Want to be let in on the secret to overnight success? Well, listen up, because here it is:

1. Devote yourself to learning from other experts in your field.

2. Master a skill or subject: Experts agree that in a year's time you'll be quite capable, by three years you'll be very proficient, and by year five you'll be an expert.

3. Remain poised and ready when opportunity knocks.

You will know that it took time, patience, perseverance, and a lot of hard work, but others will view you as an overnight success.

FIGURE 1.1: **Mindset Self-Assessment**

How Do You Stack Up?

Directions: Rate yourself on the following 12 essential characteristics on a scale of 1–10 (1 is least applicable, 10 is most). Over the next several weeks, work on improving the ones that concern you the most.

Essential Characteristic	Rating
1. I maintain healthy relationships with others, including those who have different opinions and perspectives.	
2. I give and ask for constructive feedback.	
3. I listen to others carefully and then respond.	
4. My friends, co-workers, employees, customers, and family members know that they can count on me to keep my word.	
5. I share my time, talent, and knowledge freely with others.	
6. I am committed to life-long learning and actively seek out information on a variety of topics.	
7. I accept responsibility for my attitudes, decisions, and actions.	
8. I organize and prioritize my time and tasks.	
9. I generally focus on why things will work, rather than why they won't.	
10. I am not afraid to uncover and work on my own "blind spots."	
11. I am a resourceful and innovative thinker.	
12. I understand that building a business takes time, energy, planning, and hard work.	

Chapter 1 Snapshot

Before moving on to Chapter 2, let's take time to review several of the most important take-aways from this chapter.

- You can only succeed by failing! If you never fail, you don't act. If you don't act, you can't succeed.

- When you fail to check the validity of your truths you substantially increase the odds that the outcome you desire will be jeopardized.

- Your philosophies and attitudes determine your decisions, actions, and results.

- To be truly successful you must be disciplined, focused, and committed to achieving your goals.

None of us has gotten where we are solely by pulling ourselves up from our own bootstraps. We got here because somebody bent down and helped us.

—THURGOOD MARSHALL

MARKETING MYTHS AND THE BLUNDERS THEY CAUSE

Ninety-five percent of America's small companies do not make it past their fifth year. And although some of these business owners leave in a blaze of glory after years of sustainable growth, more cease to exist for other reasons.

Most exit bone weary and confused. They worked hard and stayed busy, and can't figure out why they have so little to show for their efforts. They're dog-tired from doing "everything" because they couldn't trust their unmotivated employees. Many are frustrated and certain that given more

> *The greatest enemy of any one of our truths may be the rest of our truths.*
>
> —WILLIAM JAMES

time and money, they could have turned things around. And unfortunately, all too many are close to financial ruin.

They are your best friends, brothers, sisters, aunts, cousins, parents, sons, and daughters; intelligent, energetic people with great ideas and innovative products and services. So, why is it that so many of them just can't make it?

This question is a bit like asking a coroner why someone died. While the bottom line is that his/her heart stopped beating and/or brain stopped functioning, there are hundreds of potential underlying root causes.

So it is when businesses expire. The simple answer to the question is that one, or more, people goofed. Things went wrong. Mistakes were made.

But regardless of "the official cause of death," such as:

- inadequate funding
- an unfortunate location
- increased fuel prices
- worker's compensation costs
- supplier problems
- untrustworthy employees
- unexpected competition
- seasonal slow downs

businesses rarely go under because of one catastrophic event!

It happens because everyone involved in the company (owners, executives, and managers) commit many seemingly small errors over a prolonged period of time. They're easy to ignore, because their effects don't cause pain right away. And when finally brought to light, the "cancer" is so widespread that it's almost impossible to contain and their "cure" is like putting a band aid on a gaping wound.

So, the very best way to avoid this fate is to prevent the disease. However, if you're already on your way there, it's time to stop the bleeding! You only have two choices: Keep doing what you're doing and suffer the same results, or change.

We think business blunders begin "in the head" with a firm belief in mis-assumptions, half-truths, misinformation, outright lies, misunderstandings, or myths. Once firmly entrenched, they set in motion their believers' attitudes, decisions, and actions—a recipe for disaster.

What Are Myths?

We like to think of them as commonly accepted, unverified, truths—except they're false. Like folklore stories, they're passed down from generation to generation and seldom debunked. As a result, many of us unquestionably alter our behavior because we believe them to be factual.

To make our case we conducted some nonscientific research. Our goal was to come up with a list of "wisdoms" that we, or various family members and friends, thought were true and find out if we were right or wrong. We hopped online and consulted several different resources. Here's what we came up with. Which ones do you think are true? (Hint: None of them.)

- Premium gas makes your car run better.
- You shouldn't go swimming for an hour after eating.
- If you cross your eyes they'll remain stuck.
- Cracking your knuckles will cause arthritis.
- Feed a cold, starve a fever.
- Spicy foods cause ulcers.
- If you go outside with wet hair, you'll catch a cold.

Now, based on years of experience consulting with entrepreneurs, we have compiled our list of the worst-of-the-worst marketing myths—ones so dangerous that believing in them could kill your business.

Myth #1: "Marketing" Is Another Word for "Advertising"

This is perhaps the most prevalent of all marketing myths and one of the toughest to dispel because the folks who believe it's true, can still do well . . . at least for a while.

They see marketing as a tactical role rather than the series of multifaceted activities that it really is. Yes, advertising (marketing communications) is an essential component of your overall marketing plan, but it is not *the* penultimate plan, and ideally should account for only a small percentage of your entire marketing efforts.

Believers in this glitz-over-substance myth:

- think slick advertisements can make up for shoddy products or services.
- focus excessively on attracting new prospects, and ignore their current customers.
- throw money into advertising because they have no idea how to really grow a business.
- host meaningless "sales" such as, "Mid-Summer-Red-Dot Big Sale."
- enforce restrictive guarantee policies.
- publish screaming ads with lots of fine print.
- underestimate the intelligence of consumers.
- use "get-rich-quick" tactics.
- have no idea what it costs them to get a new customer or what it costs them to lose one.

All this results in:

- wasting money, because it costs between four and nine times more to obtain a new customer than to keep one.
- overspending on costly advertising that doesn't work.
- overlooking other highly effective, low-cost strategies and tactics.
- losing credibility and tarnishing their reputations with employees (resulting in higher employee turnover), customers, prospects, and competitors.
- experiencing higher-than-average product returns and refunds.

OK, What's the Truth?

Marketing includes every contact and aspect of the publics' experiences, such as the way you answer their calls; how you "make good" when something goes wrong; how well you help them solve their most pressing problems, and your employees' attitudes, dress, and demeanor.

It is about building sincere and profitable long-term relationships with prospects and customers (as well as employees, suppliers, and even competitors). Entrepreneurs who focus on advertising, lead generation, and sales often

Strategic Marketing Is the Party—Advertising Is Only the Invitation!

Imagine, if you will, sending out formal invitations to all of your family and friends for a holiday party at your home. When your guests arrive, however, they discover that your house is a mess; you're still in the shower; the food is not prepared; and there's only water to drink. The moral of the story is obvious. You shouldn't invite people into your home if you're not prepared. It is no different for companies. One of the quickest ways to go out of business is to advertise a bad product or company!

overlook this and therefore lose their credibility, and it's not long before people take their business elsewhere.

Remember, no amount of advertising, no matter how slick, will make up for such things as shoddy workmanship, rude employees, or hucksterism.

It's like building a house of cards, it may hold up awhile, but will eventually come tumbling down.

Making Good on a Promise

Want to get in on a really big secret? A hush-hush tactic guaranteed to substantially increase your revenues and dramatically decrease your advertising expenses? An underground tip that will help catapult you into a very small but elite group of like-minded—and extremely successful—businesspeople?

Even better, what if you knew it wouldn't cost you a thing?

We're about to tell all—let the cat out of the bag—drum roll please!

Ready?

Sure?

OK, OK, enough fun.

The secret is:

Do what you say you're going to do when you say you're going to do it.

We repeat:

Do what you say you're going to do when you say you're going to do it.

Huh? Is that all? We must be kidding, right? Wrong. Think about your own consumer experiences:

- The roofer who shows up three days late;
- The real estate agent who didn't return your calls or e-mails;
- The physicians who left you waiting for hours;
- The electrician who drops out of your life after promising to fix your ceiling fan;
- The online marketer who got busy and forgot to mail your next-day air package;
- The consignment retailers who conveniently forgot to pay your commission;

and the many others who disappointed you.

Unfortunately, we have all been there. And, sadly, these behaviors have become the norm, not the exception. When someone actually delivers on their promises, we're thrilled and we tell our friends, family members, co-workers—even complete strangers! Word spreads fast and before you know it, *voila!* you'll have more business than you ever imagined possible.

> *There is no truth.*
> *There is only perception.*
>
> —GUSTAVE FLAUBERT

But remember, the reverse is also true. When you let people down, they'll tell four people, who will tell four more, who will tell four more, and soon your reputation is shot.

The Bottom Line
Time will either promote you or expose you.
—JIM ROHN

Myth #2: Perception Is Not Reality

The concept that what others perceive—especially when it's their prospects and customers—is more important than what is factual is one of the hardest tenets

David's Lesson Learned: Things Aren't Always What They Seem

I recently heard a story about the famous concert violinist, Joshua Bell, an extremely popular and recognizable artist who fills concert halls with $100-per-piece ticket holders. One day he was approached by a writer from the Washington Post newspaper who asked him to give a free, live performance in a DC metro station. Bell agreed and played his $3.5 million Stradivarius for almost an hour. But very few people stopped long enough to listen. He collected $32 in tips.

After reading the subsequent news story (you can read a copy on our web site, www.StrategicMarketingAdvisors.com/articles/marketing-myths/perception-is-not-reality) many of the people who had ignored the master were understandably unsettled and disappointed.

This simple experiment in perception is really quite profound. You see, although Bell is one of the world's most renowned violinists, *he didn't appear to be*. Onlookers perceived that his talent matched his environment, and rewarded him accordingly.

for business owners to accept. However, if your goal is to sustain a profitable business, you must accept it. If not, you'll likely end up committing serious blunders.

Remember, consumers make their buying decisions based on their own "givens" and attitudes, and as we all know, they're not always accurate! Additionally, everyone has their unique perspectives, and if you've ever asked three people to relate the same story, you know what we mean.

Believers in this pervasive myth:

- waste countless hours trying to convince unyielding clients to accept their version of reality.
- rarely ask their customers for feedback.
- make sure the facts fit their beliefs.
- assume that a good product at the best price wins.

- use meaningless platitudes (e.g. *"Best Anywhere" "Friendly Service," "Quality Products"*) to describe their products or services.
- force consumers to choose them based on price or convenience alone.
- ignore the importance of contact personnel, environment, and other customer touch points, particularly in professional service companies.

All this results in:

- never earning a substantial income, let alone what they're worth.
- more disgruntled customers who are unhappy about unfixed product or service flaws.
- missed opportunities.
- being forgotten or lumped together with everyone else—good or bad.

Tiffany, a savvy marketer, believes businesspeople should ask their prospects and customers for their candid feedback and make sure they don't pretty it up! This is the first step in making sure you don't get lumped into the commodity pot.

The worst (or best?) thing you'll discover may be that your customers and prospects do indeed see you as similar, or identical, to others. Once you obtain this vital information, identify specific areas where your inside reality does not match outside perceptions. For instance, you may need to do a better job of educating the public about your exceptional qualities (service, delivery, product benefits, etc.), or conversely, you may need to fix inconsistencies.

OK, What's the Truth?

The following is a good illustration of how this might look in the real world.

Let's assume that George is the most knowledgeable, educated, and competent financial advisor in his area, having consistently earned and saved his clients a great deal of money over the years.

At a networking event, he schedules an initial consultation with a qualified prospect, Jane, who is in need of his services. However, upon arrival, she's greeted by a bland waiting room with a threadbare sofa, a curt receptionist, and dirty rest rooms.

After inviting Jane into his office, George shares his stellar track record and reiterates his professionalism: careful attention to details, reliable service, and thoroughly researched advice. Yet, as she's about to leave he has trouble finding her forms because they're buried underneath mounds of other paperwork on his desk.

George, confident of his ability to help Jane, is baffled when he learns that she's chosen another firm. You see, he didn't understand that there was a serious gap between his words and his office's environment and staff: one said "excellence and professionalism" while the other said "mediocre and fly-by-night!" Whether consciously or otherwise, Jane probably surmised that George would treat her money the same way he treated his office: carelessly.

> *It is the tragedy of the world that no one knows what he doesn't know. And the less a man knows, the more sure he is that he knows everything.*
>
> —JOYCE CARY

As the saying goes, "If it looks like a duck and walks like a duck, it's probably a duck." You can either argue that public perception doesn't affect sales all the way to the poor house, or do whatever is necessary to make sure that your inside reality matches outside perception.

This works the other way around, too. It's a great idea to ask your current customers what you do well. You may be surprised to learn how much they appreciate things that you take for granted. A man who owned an auto repair shop was reviewing his marketing strategy, and couldn't come up with one thing that he did better than his competitors. So, he asked his customers and was shocked to learn that many of them were loyal to his business because he always finished the job on time. Presto! A valuable differentiator handed to him on a silver platter!

The Bottom Line
Denial ain't just a river in Egypt. Take the time to see how you're viewed, fill in the gaps, become memorable, and then communicate your unique benefits—often!

Myth #3: Technical Expertise Guarantees Success
This is the most pervasive, far-reaching, and detrimental myth of them all! It is an equal-opportunity fantasy whose believers are corporate CEOs, entrepreneurs, male and female, young and old, rich and poor, tall and short, and moms and pops.

If you would like a free copy of Michael Gerber's book *The E-Myth Revisited*, please send an e-mail to SupportedStrategicAdvisors.com. Put E-Myth in the subject line and include your name, address, telephone, e-mail address, name of business, and type of business.

It is also the most difficult one to correct because the "patient" doesn't know he/she is ill! It serves as the foundation for prejudice, ignorance, and failure, and influences all of the sufferer's decisions and behaviors—personal and professional.

Ironically, this myth often serves as the very basis for becoming an entrepreneur in the first place. Michael Gerber, in his classic book, *The E-Myth*, says that most small businesses are started by technicians (folks who are proficient at a particular skill) with entrepreneurial seizures.

Believers in this unfortunate myth:

- think that being the most skilled computer wiz, cookie baker, financial planner, doctor, photographer, chef, hairstylist, CPA, packaged goods manufacturer, technician—whatever—makes them qualified to own and operate a small business.
- assume that if they can do something, they should.
- confuse least cost with best cost.
- latch onto "cool" products that nobody wants.
- keep little or no data on current, or past, customers.
- think all customers are worth getting and keeping so they over-serve low-value customers and under-serve high-value ones.
- reinvent the wheel, and don't know how, or refuse to, borrow effective strategies from others.
- base decisions on broad assumptions.
- conduct little or no research on customers, competition, and the marketplace.

Ninety-nine percent of the failures come from people who have the habit of making excuses.

—GEORGE WASHINGTON CARVER

All this results in:

- commiting avoidable mistakes which results in unnecessary rework.
- experiencing higher-than-average customer churn.

- wasting time (and money) dealing with unprofitable customers.
- achieving less-than-expected customer acquisition results due to poor targeting, communication, and follow-through.
- having low profits and incurring higher expenses.

Myths and creeds are heroic struggles to comprehend the truth in the world.

—ANSEL ADAMS

OK, What's the Truth?

Since advances in technology and affordable software make it tempting to try just about anything, you can easily get yourself in over your head, it's imperative that you know what you don't know.

For example, it's fairly easy to design a business logo. However, if you're not a skilled graphic designer, resist the urge to do it yourself!

Consider how important your logo is, or may become, to your company. It is your visual symbol, one that should be included on everything you develop. It communicates your attention to detail, professionalism, personality and industry, among other things.

It must be pleasing to the eye in color, black and white, and reverse type; it must be easily read in large or small print. Why risk having your logo scream, "We're sloppy amateurs"? Consult a professional. As they say, "If you pay an expert, you'll cry once, if you don't, you'll cry many times."

There are times, however, when it's perfectly fine, and actually quite smart, to do things yourself. For instance, if you've got better than average computer skills or design talents go ahead and create those logos and letterhead, but please, assess your skills honestly first. (Take a look at Mary's Lesson Learned on page 24, for another example of sticking to your skills.)

And, although we've said this before, it bears repeating:

> *Being skilled in the work of a business has nothing to do with being skilled at running a business that does that work!*

Even though most of us acknowledge that if we want to do something, anything, really well it pays to practice, practice, and practice some more.

I had no delusions that I was an expert in internet marketing right from the start. Yet, as I learned more about the process, I became increasingly panicked. Cyberspace jargon was a foreign language to me and the more I tried to do myself, the more lost I became. And it wasn't as though I didn't want the help! Quite the contrary, but I was so lost that I didn't understand what I really needed, let alone who to contact! Gratefully, I used the tried-and-true methodology and "baby-steps" process presented in this book and found a wonderful coach who made all the difference!

The philosophical concept is not difficult to grasp, but identifying our own level of incompetence is another story all together. Like most things, it begins with an open mind and heart, insatiable curiosity, careful research, and a very large mirror! And what makes it even more challenging is that the opposite is also true: there are many marketing strategies and tactics that even a beginner can use successfully. You don't have to hire an expert for everything! However, first learn how to distinguish one from the other.

It's like trying to save a few bucks by changing your car's oil yourself. Now, this is not an overly complex task, but is it a smart use of your time? Think about what's involved: you drive to the store; wait in line; ask questions; look at the merchandise; select the oil, pan, funnel; wait in the check-out line; pay the cashier; drive back home; try to jack up the car so you can get underneath it to put the pan in place; undo the screw; get some oil in the pan; get most of the oil on you; get the funnel and fill it with the new oil; figure out what to do with the old oil; close everything down; throw your oil-laden shirt in the trash; and take a shower. The cost? $24.97 in stuff; $1.32 in gas; $25 for the ruined shirt; 3.25 hours of your time; and $1,000,000 in frustration. All of this, when you could have had it done for $25 or less!

Low cost is not always best cost! Oh, and by the way, never try to hang your own drywall, either! Trust me on this one.

Ironically, when it comes to owning and operating a small business, however, many entrepreneurs believe just the opposite, and "put out their shingle," certain they possess all of the business and marketing skills they need to be widely successful. After all, they reason, how hard can it be?

Unfortunately, these are the same people who finally figure out that technical know-how means little when it comes to running a well-oiled, profitable "machine." So, they end up trading lots of hours for very few dollars, and wasting a great deal of time and money learning the hard way. What's more, their businesses remain unprofitable and many do not earn a sufficient income, let alone one that allows them to enjoy the lifestyle they originally envisioned.

Being busy does not always mean real work. The object of all work is production or accomplishment and to either of these ends there must be forethought, system planning, intelligence, and honest purpose, as well as perspiration. Seeming to do is not doing.

—THOMAS EDISON

If you want to see this at work, go online or look at the "Help Wanted" ads in your local newspaper. Assisted-living facilities are searching for nurses; construction companies are looking for carpenters; accounting firms want CPAs *to run their marketing departments*. Then after they're hired, these employees are understandably panicked because they have no idea what's involved in marketing beyond creating brochures or mailing sales letters.

In other words, starting, growing and/or maintaining a profitable business requires that you study, learn, and practice mandatory business and marketing concepts, strategies, and tactics that are relevant *regardless of industry*.

That's why it's imperative that you find out what's in your own skills tool box and add missing ones to fill in the gaps . . . or let others help you out.

Myth #4: Life Happens While We're Busy Planning

By nature, entrepreneurs are more action-oriented than others. They can't wait to roll up their sleeves and get to work. And for the most part, this is an exemplary trait unless, of course, it crosses the line.

Like most people, entrepreneurs have a lot on their plate. However, unlike others they often lack "break lights" and keep moving, convinced that if they just work harder and longer, they'll reap the rewards. So they remain in a constant motion and convince themselves that this is time well spent. They equate planning with a halt or slow-down of progress and assume it's a luxury that only highly-paid executives can afford. But they're wrong and usually end up in the all-too-common "*doing-it, doing-it, doing-it*" rut.

Believers in this perpetual mortion myth:

- wear their long hours like a badge of honor.
- have very long to-do lists and no not-to-do list.
- never say "no" to any business opportunity.
- live from job to job, never sure of their next move.
- appear distracted and overwhelmed.

All this results in:

> *To get what you want,*
> *stop doing what isn't working.*
>
> —DENNIS WEAVER

- stress, burn out, and brain clutter.
- missed opportunities.
- lack of a competitive edge.
- wasting time and money on disjointed advertising aimed at seeing what sticks.

We're not advocating a get-wealthy-without-working plan or an overnight-success scheme. Far from it. Successful entrepreneurs know that hard work is essential, so long as the effort is expended where it counts.

What we are suggesting is that you, your family, friends, and business would be far better off if you focused your attention and channeled your energies into actions that matter. Regardless of whether you work hard on the "wrong" things, or put little effort into the "right" things, you'll end up in the same spot—bankrupt, in more ways than one.

The Bottom Line

The worst way to get a glass full of water is with a garden hose turned on full power. The water will certainly come out fast and hard, but you'll end up with very little in the glass. However, if you turn it down to a trickle it will be more manageable and you'll get exactly what you need.

That's how you should think of applying your focus and resources: steadily and with clear intentions.

David's Lesson Learned: Nobody Gets More than 24 Hours a Day

Most small-business owners and managers are convinced that the more they do, the more successful they'll be. If you agree, get rid of this notion right now! It couldn't be farther from the truth, even though many of us wear it like a badge of honor. The next time you ask someone what they do, beware of those who answer, "Well, I've just opened a car wash on Rt. 95 to go with my pharmacy and financial planning web site. Then I got my wife running my lawn care company. We're working 14 hours a day, but one day it's all going to be worth it."

Although this is exaggerated to make a point, it's not uncommon to meet entrepreneurs who have three or more business cards. Trust me; this is not good! Ultimate success has to do with focus and prioritization. Not very glamorous, eh? Well, when you begin to work smarter, not harder—to do less, yet earn more—you will be happy you did away with the super-human routine! That goes for the tips you'll find in this book, as well. Don't try all of them. Use the ones that are most suitable for your business, resources, industry, and time. Remember, nobody gets more than 24 hours a day. Time is your most valuable resource, so use it wisely.

> *Planning is bringing the future into the present so that you can do something about it now.*
>
> —ALAN LAKEIN

Schedule time to write and update your marketing plan regularly. *It is the single most important thing you can do to increase your chances of success.* Although estimates vary, many business analysts claim that the mere act of writing a marketing plan makes a company between 15 and 31 percent more likely to succeed than those that do not.

And, by the way, it has nothing to do with the plan's length, ink color, or authors' writing skills.

The Bottom Line

The "planning" is far more important than "the plan."

Myth #5: Before Taking Action, Wait for the Perfect Moment

What? Didn't we just say that it is unwise to leap into action before taking time out to plan? Aren't we contradicting ourselves?

The simple answer is, "No." Even though the very foundation of this book rests on the importance of planning, you'll wait a lifetime if you hold out for perfection.

You probably know men and women who have lots of great ideas but never do much. Instead they make excuses like this:

> *My industry is different, and nobody understands how hard it is, and it won't work for me anyhow 'cause I tried it once, and it turned out awful 'cause that stuff just doesn't work, and I'm doing OK without it, anyway, so who needs more problems? Thank you very much, and besides which, money is tight, and my sister is having her baby soon, so I should probably put that on the back burner just in case she needs my help, because goodness knows, nobody else is going to be there for her, which means I won't have time to take that computer class either, 'cause they're on Wednesday nights, and I have to be in the shop then 'cause I can't trust George to take over since he's unreliable . . .*

Does this sound familiar? If so, you're not alone. Most of us are guilty of putting things off, even if we acknowledge that doing so may hurt us, physically, emotionally, mentally, financially, or otherwise.

However, for some people, procrastination is a way of life, and if left unchecked will prohibit the creation of a profitable business. That's why it's imperative to uncover the reasons for procrastination and learn ways to end it once and for all. And while they vary, professionals believe that people are more likely to put work off

> *Myth is the hidden part of every story, the buried part, the region that is still unexplored because there are as yet no words to enable us to get there. Myth is nourished by silence as well as by words.*
>
> —ITALO CAVINO

when they are uncertain about their ability to get the desired results; unclear about the process; view the task as dull, time-consuming, or irrelevant; or feel that they lack the necessary skills, knowledge, or tools to complete it.

Believers in this perfect timing myth:

- put things off, and off, and off.
- invent excuses for avoiding action.
- feel more comfortable talking, than doing.
- worry obsessively about things in the future over which they have little or no control.
- exhibit conflicting intentions.

All this results in:

- stagnation and performing work quickly and sloppily, which often creates unnecessary rework.
- stress due to last-minute emergencies.
- missed opportunities.
- an escalating lack of confidence.

In this rough-and-tumble business world, it is common to find people who put things off because their ability to achieve their goals are misaligned with the amount of effort and resources they're willing, or able, to donate. These conflicting intentions cause inertia. An example of this is someone who desires $100,000 in profits during their first year in business, but wants to work only two hours a day. You get the idea.

A great way to begin overcoming procrastination is to promise yourself that you will stop making excuses, and act. Ask a trusted friend or family member to become your accountability partner, define more acceptable standards of performance, and get organized—eat those elephants one bite at a time!

> Even though you may already agree with what you've read so far and discover the rest of the book contains useful information and tools, you might still find it difficult to take action. If so, don't feel discouraged. Making positive changes to your attitudes and behaviors takes time, so don't be too hard on yourself. No one can accomplish this by attending a workshop, enrolling in a seminar, or reading a book—even this one! So, throughout the process remember to celebrate your achievements before moving on to your next challenge. Then, roll up your sleeves and get to work!
>
> Decide, at last, that your inaction and procrastination is hurting you, and if you have to choose between doing nothing and doing something—no matter how small—choose the latter! This book is chock-full of wonderfully effective and inexpensive ways to attain your dreams by investing more time, energy, and imagination, and less money. *However, it's up to you to make it happen!*

Chapter 2 Snapshot

Before moving on to Chapter 3 let's take time to review several of the most important take-aways from this chapter.

- The majority of small-business failures can be traced back to their founder's mindset, which is usually exacerbated by one or several of the five deadliest marketing myths.

  1. Marketing is another word for advertising.
  2. Perception is not reality.
  3. Technical expertise guarantees success.
  4. Life happens while we're busy planning.
  5. Before taking action, wait for the perfect moment.

- Avoid becoming a commodity; never compete on price alone.

- Make sure that your attitudes and decisions are based on truths, not myths!

Understanding these myths and how they can affect your business is an important first step to a successful business.

Now that we've discussed what not to do, it's time to learn how to get it right.

The great enemy of the truth is very often not the lie,
deliberate, contrived, and dishonest, but the myth,
persistent, persuasive, and unrealistic.

—JOHN F. KENNEDY

GETTING IT RIGHT

What Marketing Really Means

W hat does the word "marketing" really mean? You'll find dozens of answers to this question in business magazines, internet white papers, academic journals, and marketing textbooks. They vary in length and breadth, but one thing is certain—you won't find two that are the same. And there's a better-than-even chance that you'll have to consult a dictionary in order to interpret the bureaucratic terminology, industry jargon, and fashionable buzzwords used in the definition. Marketing

> *Things may come to those who wait, but only the things left by those who hustle.*
>
> —ABRAHAM LINCOLN

books and articles are filled with the latest gee-whiz industry catchwords, and tactics purported to be hottest new discoveries.

Even worse, with over one million marketing web sites on the World Wide Web, how is the average person to know whom to believe? We're going to clear up that confusion in this chapter.

The Definition

Over the span of our careers, we've come across hundreds of definitions for the word "marketing." According to *Contemporary Marketing Wired* (Dryden Press, 1998) by Boone and Kurtz, "marketing is the process of planning and executing the conception, pricing, promotion, and distribution of ideas, goods, services, organizations, and events to create and maintain relationships that will satisfy individual and organizational objectives."

Marketing Management by Philip Kotler and Kevin Keller (Prentice Hall, 2005), defines marketing as a "social and managerial process by which individuals and groups obtain what they need and want through creating, offering and exchanging products of value with others."

The late business and management leader, Peter Drucker, said in *The Essential Drucker* (Collins, 2007) that "marketing and innovation are the two chief functions of business. You get paid for creating a customer, which is marketing. And you get paid for creating a new dimension of performance, which is innovation. Everything else is a cost center."

The Small Business Administration (SBA) succinctly defines marketing as "the commercial functions involved in transferring goods from producer to consumer."

We think the best way to summarize all of these is:

> *"marketing is the art and science of getting and keeping profitable customers."*

We think this says it all, in a simple and clear manner. It says that marketers must be creative, imaginative, and innovative while being objective, curious, precise, and methodical.

In other words, marketing is the heart and soul of every business. It sets the stage for everything else and, when planned and executed flawlessly, makes the sales function redundant. At the beginning of our seminars we ask our students—mostly small- and medium-sized business owners and managers, and nonprofit employees—to introduce themselves and answer the question, "What business are you in?" Invariably we end up with a multitude of different replies, such as, "I am in real estate," "health care," "web site development," and so on. We inform them that the right answer is, "I'm in the marketing business, which means engaging in the art and science of getting and keeping profitable customers." And even though our main goal is to get our students talking, this topic is worthy of serious discussion, because anyone with direct, or indirect, responsibility for growing or maintaining a business or organization is a marketer.

The Art in Marketing

A good strategic marketer uses his or her creative talents to design and develop the company's marketing collateral—brochures, signs, ads, direct mail program, etc. A marketer must create innovative solutions and work around sticky situations such as those involving politics and even legal matters.

Moreover, the word "art" suggests that marketers master and hone their skill with study, practice, and observation. As we've already said, superior marketing skills are not a birthright, no one is a born marketer! Regardless of what you've heard, or how easy it appears, it takes knowledge, time, and experience to do it right. When Tiger Woods swings a golf club, it looks easy. But if you've ever tried it, you know how hard he's worked to develop his muscle memory. Also, since art is created by humans, the finished "piece" is judged subjectively based on the audience's personal perspective, likes and dislikes, history, environment, and background.

This is particularly relevant for marketers when they communicate with the public. Elements such as web site copy, brand image, and product positioning and messaging must be developed with the company's target audiences preferences and personalities in mind.

The Science of Marketing

Marketing expertise is based on obtaining objective knowledge and using it to develop sound strategies, choose the right tactics, and take appropriate action. It begins with gathering, managing, organizing, and analyzing information.

Therefore, the word "science" aptly reminds us that first-rate marketers do their homework by researching the marketplace, competition, and customer preferences, just to name a few. It's the best way of turning a crap shoot into an informed decision. There will still be risks, but the odds of failing will be greatly reduced.

If you're a more advanced marketer or interested in learning more about marketing research visit our web site at: www.StrategicMarketingAdvisors.com and look under the section titled, "Marketing Research."

Getting Customers

All businesses obviously need new customers; this hardly requires further explanation. However, it's also important to understand the conscious and subconscious psychological and emotional factors behind a consumer's first buying decision. Simply put, prospects become customers based on:

- *How they experience your company*. This includes how you, your employees, your products, your environment, your web site, your service, and your location make them feel.
- *Your product and service benefits*. Prospects seek to increase pleasure (glowing health, sex appeal, entertainment) or reduce pain (less stress, fewer financial worries, smaller problems), not features.
- *Your trustworthiness and honesty*. Your credibility, plausibility, and truthfulness will win more customers than will exaggerated claims.
- *Value*. This means the difference between what something costs and what it's worth to consumers.
- *Safety, security, and freedom from risk*. These are made possible by your product and service guarantees, privacy policies, and secure payment procedures.

- *Reliability and consistency.* Prospects need to know they can count on you every time.
- *Expectations.* The likelihood that the benefits you promised will be delivered is a big factor.
- *Convenience.* Your location, payment policies, contact information, and availability can make all the difference.
- *Product or service selection and quality.* How these compare with your competitors is always important to prospective customers.

> *The sale merely consummates the courtship. Then the marriage begins. How good the marriage is, depends on how well the relationship is managed by the seller.*
>
> —THOMAS LEVITT

Taking a systematic approach and working with these factors to help prospects make that buying decision is the science and art of marketing, but it doesn't end there. It is a constant process of identifying your most valuable customers and making sure your products or services meet their needs, over and over again.

Keeping Customers

Small-business owners' most important assets are their customers. Because entrepreneurs are constantly looking for new purchasers, they often, unfortunately, stop developing their existing customer relationships, even though it costs an average of four to nine times more to acquire a customer than retain one.

In the next chapter we'll go into this in greater detail, but for now we ask that you accept this tenet: There are *only four ways to grow any business* geometrically, and three of them have to do with nuturing long-term and profitable relationships with current customers.

Having said this, we understand that every business gains and loses customers. While some losses are unavoidable (due to a death, move, or lifestyle change), most are entirely preventable, ranging from the average 15 percent who cite "product dissatisfaction" as their primary reason for leaving, to a whopping 67 percent who leave due to "no ongoing contact."

In later chapters we will provide you with specific communication tactics designed to help you retain more customers. But for now, read the following list of factors that consumers use to decide whether or not they'll continue to do business with a person or company. You can cultivate customer loyalty if you:

- *Are focused on providing an outstanding overall experience*, not just once, but every time.
- *Make good when something goes wrong* and do whatever it takes to right a situation and empower your employees to do the same.
- *Stay in touch by communicating regularly* with welcome letters, personal calls, surveys, cards, and the like.

> *In business, words are words; explanations are explanations; promises are promises, but only performance is reality.*
>
> —HAROLD S. GENEEN

- *Reward them for their loyalty* in a heartfelt manner and with no-strings-attached gifts.
- *Get to know and remember them*, take the time to anticipate their needs, and greet them personally.
- *Behave ethically and honestly*—people like to keep company with reputable businesses.
- *Are reliable* and do what you say, just as you've promised.
- *Concentrate on solving their problems*, not selling them something.
- *Respect their intelligence, ideas, and personalities*, because consumers are your moms, dads, aunts, cousins, best friends, co-workers, wives, and husbands—not statistics.

Recognizing Profitable Customers

Every customer is an asset, so long as they're *profitable*. This is an extremely important distinction and one that is horribly overlooked in most small and medium-sized businesses. And while it's true that a customer-focused company is essential in today's marketplace, it must be balanced with maintaining profits—unless it's a nonprofit or government agency!

Simply put, some customers are more valuable than others. And if you're not careful a few may even be *costing you* time, money, or both. We are not suggesting that you judge anyone's intrinsic worth. Rather, we ask that you assess, if appropriate, your current customers based on pre-determined, subjective and objective criteria. And if they don't measure up, "fire" them!

"What," you say incredulously, "fire a customer?" Yes.

When to Fire a Customer

You might need to fire a customer if he or she has you saying anything like the following:

- "They usually pay me, but never on time… I have to send them a minimum of three invoices before I receive their check."
- "That woman calls me every day and ties up the phone for hours. She complains about everything we do one day, and then sings our praises the next. And since we never know what mood she's going to be in, no one in the office wants to answer the phone when she calls."
- "He's a nice enough guy, but he quibbles over every charge and makes us feel rotten for making an honest profit. So he calls every month when his bill arrives, and we have to go over it again and again. We usually end up giving him credits, just to get off the phone. And it's not like he's even a big spender."
- "I couldn't get over to Mrs. Smith's house to finish her renovation because Mr. Jones insisted that I come to his store right away to hand deliver the blueprints he forgot to take with him last night. He even threatened to look for another contractor if I couldn't make it right then."

You get the idea. Commerce is a two-way street, give and take. And if certain customers—and it's usually no more than a small percentage your total base—are draining you emotionally, financially, mentally, or physically, ask them politely to take their business elsewhere.

The 80/20 Rule and Customer Value

The essential take-away from this little story is that the 80/20 rule is alive and well. That is, 20 percent of your customers will cause 80 percent of your

David's Lesson Learned: Don't Wait Too Long to Fire Unpleasant Customers

My first experience with "the customer from hell" came at an early age. I was eleven years old and delivered newspapers in my neighborhood on the outskirts of Detroit, Michigan.

No matter how I tried to please her, Mrs. Unpleasant (not her real name) complained about something every week. Even though I delivered her paper on time, rain or shine, month after month, she was never happy. Worse yet, she usually paid me two to three weeks late. But when I would discuss my frustrations with my mother, she would kindly say, "But David, the customer is always right." So this pattern continued for years. Mrs. Unpleasant would bully me and I would take it. Eventually, I moved on to another career (stock boy at the local grocery store) and was relieved to end our "dance."

In hindsight, however, I should have fired Mrs. Unpleasant years earlier. Yes, customers are always right, unless they're abusive or unprofitable. She was both.

But like many, my Mom agreed with the long-accepted principle made famous by Stew Leonard, who etched the following two rules on granite outside of his business:

Rule #1: The customer is always right.

Rule #2: If the customer is ever wrong, reread Rule #1.

And even though I agree with Stew Leonard for the most part, I would revise his rules to read:

Rule #1: Pleasant and profitable customers are always right.

Rule #2: If a pleasant and profitable customer is ever wrong, reread Rule #1.

Rule #3: If a customer is neither pleasant nor profitable, fire them.

problems. Conversely, 20 percent of your customers probably contribute 80 percent of your profits. And if you're spending 80 percent of your time dealing with the 20 percent who are draining your profits, then you'll have far less time to spend with the 20 percent who really matter! See? It's easy!

That's why a customer database is worth its weight in gold, yet fewer than 10 percent of America's small businesses even have a customer mailing list! And in today's marketplace, that isn't going to make it. The only way to build relationships is to engender trust, which happens faster when you know someone. And you'll find it's much easier to get to know your customers if you find out more than just their names, phone numbers, and e-mail addresses! Ask them to share information about their interests, families, careers, and concerns. Then track behaviors such as their average transactions amount, how often they purchase, or how they pay their bills. This will provide you with a great foundation for locating your high, medium and low-value customers. Then use this information to guide your retention and targeting efforts.

Progress isn't made by early risers. It's made by lazy men trying to find easier ways to do something.

—ROBERT HEINLEIN

In the next chapter, we'll show you how to calculate a critical business metric—customer lifetime value, or CLV—your average customers' revenue contributions during the time they remain loyal to your business. Without understanding what a customer is worth to your business, all of your advertising and marketing efforts will be handicapped, because you won't know what you can spend to acquire a new customer.

And remember GIGO (garbage in, garbage out)? The best way to ensure that your CLV is accurate is by keeping track of your past and current customers' actions! Keep in mind that the *best predictor of future behavior is past behavior*. If your business is new, start collecting this data right away. We've looked and looked but haven't found any reliable industry resources for obtaining this type of information.

What Is the Marketing Function within Any Business?

Marketing is the hub of every company, an ever-changing orchestration of all the activities needed to accomplish a business's or organization's overall strategies and objectives, especially those that touch prospects and customers.

For example, let's assume that you're marketing for a company that sells how-to home decor books and CDs. You've just sent 100,000 direct mail letters to your targeted audience, inviting them to call your company's toll-free number if they need more information or want to place an order for one or more of your six product packages. In this case, your job entailed creating the letter and making sure it was mailed to the right prospects, correct? Wrong.

It would be a waste of time to send out the direct-mail pieces if:

- No one answers the phone when the targeted audience responds.
- Callers are placed on hold for long periods because the company's phone lines are overloaded.
- Service representatives can't answer simple questions.
- Many of the books and CDs are out of stock.
- The sales prices are so low they're unprofitable.
- The letter recipients are not interested in home decor.
- The company can't accept credit cards over the phone.

> *Management is efficiency in climbing the ladder of success; leadership determines whether the ladder is leaning against the right wall.*
>
> —STEPHEN COVEY

The list goes on, yet in this uncomplicated example it's easy to see how one function relies on the other. When "operations" doesn't communicate with "sales," who isn't talking to "human resources," who forgot to check with "marketing," unnecessary problems arise.

Marketers are responsible for researching and communicating to company officers and colleagues marketplace wants and needs; creating and implementing programs that support company objectives; and ensuring that all functional units are prepared to deliver the promised prospect and customer experience.

Culture and Leadership Styles

As we've said many times, superior marketing doesn't just happen. In addition to practiced skills and knowledge, it emerges in companies whose owners or founders have created environments where it can be developed and nurtured.

Anybody, Everybody, Nobody

Here is a wonderfully clever poem which serves as a great reminder that winners don't wait to be asked, they act. Enjoy!

A Poem about Responsibility

Attributed to Charles Osgood

There was a most important job that needed to be done,
And no reason not to do it, there was absolutely none.
But in vital matters such as this, the thing you have to ask
Is who exactly will it be who'll carry out the task.
Anybody could have told you that Everybody knew
That this was something Somebody would surely have to do.
Nobody was unwilling. Anybody had the ability.
But Nobody believed that it was his responsibility.
It seemed to be a job that Anybody could have done.
If Anybody thought he was supposed to be the one.
But since Everybody recognized that Anybody could
Everybody took for granted that Somebody would.
But Nobody told Anybody that we are aware of,
That he would be in charge of seeing it was taken care of.
And Nobody took it on himself to follow through,
And do what Everybody thought that Somebody would do.
When what Everybody needed did not get done at all,
Everybody was complaining that Somebody dropped the ball.
Anybody then could see it was an awful crying shame,
And Everybody looked around for Somebody to blame.
Somebody should have done the job
And Everybody should have,
But in the end Nobody did
What Anybody could have.

And since there is widespread misunderstanding regarding the far-reaching role of marketing in many organizations, company leaders must act as catalysts for change by:

- Adopting and communicating an attitude of service;
- Demonstrating ideal behaviors and tolerating nothing less;
- Understanding and encouraging healthy conflict;
- Creating a climate where honesty is heard and valued;
- Confronting the brutal facts of reality;
- Making sure the *right* people are hired, not just people;
- Placing their employees' ambitions over their own;
- Becoming and staying constantly curious;
- Never forgetting their passion and vision.

And just for fun, we've included our own list of the ten most fundamental and fantastic leadership traits.

1. *Fair*. They supply their subordinates with the tools, training, and direction they need to "win" and judge their performance accordingly.
2. *Friendly*. They foster good relationships with colleagues, vendors, customers, and employees.
3. *Focused*. They set clear goals and differentiate between long- and short-term objectives.
4. *Firm, but kind*. Leaders get the behavior they exhibit and tolerate.
5. *Feedback providers*. They offer continual, specific feedback (whether positive or negative).
6. *Follow-throughers*. They take a hands-on approach to ensure that agreed-upon milestones are reached.
7. *Fit*. They are competent physically, mentally, and emotionally for their job's responsibilities.
8. *Flames*. They are passionate about achieving their vision and are beacons of energy and enthusiasm. They are the light that ignites others into action.
9. *Fun*. They take their work seriously—not themselves—and recognize the beneficial effects of laughter in the workplace.

10. *Flexible.* They welcome change and prepare for it. Stuff happens!

Now that you've gained a new perspective on what the word "marketing" really means and how you can make it work for your business, it's time to apply these insights and begin creating your marketing plan.

 Chapter 3 Snapshot

Before moving on to Chapter 4, let's take time to review several of the most important take-aways from this chapter:

- Marketing is the art and science of getting and keeping profitable customers.

- First-rate marketers do their homework by researching the marketplace, competition, and customer preferences.

- Some customers are more valuable than others. Focus on the 20 percent who are contributing 80 percent of your profits.

- The best predictor of future behavior is past behavior.

- Our revision to Stew Leonard's rules:

  Rule #1: Pleasant and profitable customers are always right.

  Rule #2: If a pleasant and profitable customer is ever wrong, reread Rule #1.

  Rule #3: If a customer is neither pleasant nor profitable, fire them.

The workplace should primarily be an
incubator for the human spirit.

—ANITA RODDICK

MARKETING PLAN OVERVIEW

B usiness owners and executives today tend to be less focused on marketing plans than on tactics such as internet advertising, sales brochures, and Flash animation. And although these devices are legitimate tools of the trade, they become temporary, patchwork fixes when substituted for implementing a well-thought-out plan. Invariably they work OK for a while, but over time companies run by these managers often get crushed under the weight of competition and go under.

> *Determine that the thing can and shall be done, and then we shall find the way.*
>
> —ABRAHAM LINCOLN

As a matter of fact, a 2003 U.S. Department of Commerce research study concluded that more than 80 percent of American companies of all sizes experience lower-than-anticipated marketing activity results and the vast majority of these do not have written marketing plans! This is not a coincidental relationship.

There are four main contributing factors that make writing a marketing plan seem daunting. Many people:

- Are uncertain what to include or how to format one;
- Lack confidence in their writing skills;
- Don't know where to begin or how to find the information they need;
- Think it's not necessary or irrelevant for their businesses.

But there's no longer a reason to feel intimidated. To address such concerns, we've devoted this chapter to an overview of what a marketing plan is, what it is not, what it's used for, and what's included. In subsequent chapters, we'll walk you through our nine-step system for gathering the information you'll need to enter either into the plan outline included in Chapter 13, or your own.

Marketing Plan 101

A marketing plan is a written roadmap that documents a company's short and/or long-term objectives, the strategies and actions necessary to achieve them, and the relevant data used to support its forecasts and conclusions. Among other things it includes a business's:

- Vision and mission
- Product and service offerings
- Targeted audience
- Pricing policies
- Sales, revenue, and profitability forecasts
- Distribution channels
- Communication strategies

Traditionally, marketing plans covered at least three years, but modern businesses increasingly opt for shorter cycles, which we recommend. In any case, the plan should be updated yearly. It can be for a single product, service, brand, or an entire product line. Simply put, its goal is to bring strategies to life and, as former Giants quarterback Fran Tarkinton said, "wrestle that bear to the ground."

What Is a Marketing Plan NOT

Although it should be a large part of a full-blown business plan, it is not a substitute for one. Business plans contain additional information, such as:

- Sources of funding
- Capital equipment lists
- Balance sheets
- Historical financial reports
- Copies of legal documents
- Income statements

Moreover, a business plan contains more detailed information on a company's resources, day-to-day management, operational activities, and capital investments, all of which either feed into, or from, the marketing process.

A *marketing plan* is not rocket science. A *marketing plan* is not at all similar to a Ph.D. dissertation. A *marketing plan* can be handwritten, and it can have typos. A *marketing plan* can be created with crayons. A *marketing plan* can be developed by anyone, as long as they can follow a simple recipe. Writing a *marketing plan* may not be your idea of fun, but spending more time with family and friends, and enjoying the extra money you'll make (because you wrote it, and it worked), is loads of fun. A *marketing plan* will help you save money and make money. A *marketing plan* means fewer headaches. A *marketing plan* is a vital, living document that can be dog-eared, written on, and highlighted. A *marketing plan* saves time, no matter how long it takes to write. A *marketing plan* has to-do lists and not-to-do lists. A *marketing plan* is your guide, your sanity check, your blueprint, your roadmap, and your business's best friend.

Good Reasons for Writing a Marketing Plan

The single best reason for writing a marketing plan is in the journey, not the plan. In other words, in order to end up at the final destination (i.e., the written plan) its author(s) must conduct relevant research; assess their own strengths and weaknesses; define their goals; set measurement standards, and the like. Thus, the *process itself* will provide you invaluable insights and incredible peace of mind.

Additionally, they're undertaken to:

- Set objectives as part of a yearly planning process;
- Assess the viability of new business ventures;

> *Failing to plan is planning to fail.*
>
> —IAN LAKEIN

- Include in an overall business plan, especially when a company is seeking investment capital;
- Introduce a new product; enter a new market; and/or grow an existing product or service line;
- Document specific, additional strategies for new products, projects, programs, market areas, etc.

Most importantly, however, they provide business people with far better odds of achieving their *goals*, a topic we'll cover in the next chapter. Just remember this for now: If you don't have goals, you don't need a marketing plan!

So, what do you hope to accomplish by writing your marketing plan? Please enter your answer in the space below.

```
I am (we are) writing this marketing plan in order to:



```

You'll include this in Part One of your marketing plan (Executive Summary, Section A: Purpose).

Goal Attainment = Inputs + Processes

Once you have defined your purpose in order to enjoy the journey and make the effort worthwhile, evaluate what you have to do to achieve it. As the saying goes, "Junk in, junk out" (a variation of GIGO). Simply put, your ability to achieve any purpose hinges on two things:

1. *Inputs.* The ingredients you use. In this case, they are your resources and assets, such as time, money, people, machines, and raw materials.
2. *Processes.* These are the systematized actions—decisions, tasks, behaviors, planning, brainstorming, purchasing, writing, and the like—you'll perform to complete the job.

Do not forget these—write them down on a Post-It™ note, tape them written backwards on your forehead, pin them on a bulletin board, and make them your screen saver.

The integrity of your marketing plan, which will play a large part in achieving your goals, depends upon the *quality* of your inputs and processes. That's why you should continually question and assess them to ensure that you're maximizing your chances for success.

And one of the best ways to do this is by developing systems, the bridges that connect your available resources (inputs) to your goal. Systems are really just standardized methods for solving problems. When they work well, you achieve predictable results. If not, your results will be disappointing. Figure 4.1 is a simple diagram that illustrates the concept.

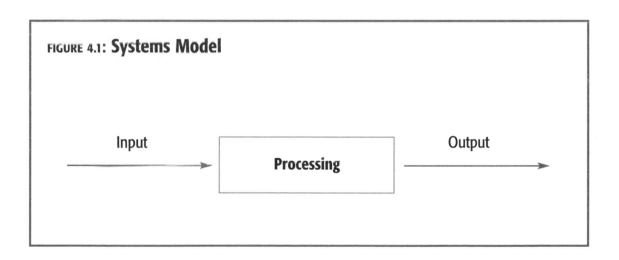

FIGURE 4.1: **Systems Model**

Input → **Processing** → Output

Here's a straightforward analogy of our model in action.

Let's assume our friend, Lucy, is hosting an informal dinner party for twelve of her friends on Sunday. After some thought, she decides to serve wild rice soup and, although she's never made it before, she understands that it's delicious and a perfect solution for small gatherings. Additionally, Lucy feels confident that she'll end up with a big pot of warm, scrumptious, and creamy soup for her friends.

So, in this case the following apply:

1. *The goal*: to make enough warm, scrumptious, and creamy wild rice soup to serve herself and 12 others by Sunday at 2 P.M.

2. *The inputs*

   - *The recipe*. This defines much of the process she'll use to make her soup.
   - *The ingredients*. 7 cups of cooked wild rice, 2 sticks of butter, 3.5 cups half-and-half, 2-3 grated carrots, two onions, one ham steak, 10 tsp. slivered almonds.
   - *Time requirements*. Half hour for preparation; 1 hr. for cooking.
   - *Equipment*. A large pot, functioning stove, 13 bowls, 13 spoons.
   - *Labor*. Someone to prepare the soup, or Lucy.

Lack of any of these inputs will have a direct, and negative, effect on Lucy's ability to achieve her goal—some more than others. For instance, if she uses one onion instead of two, the impact would be negligible. Conversely, however, if Lucy doesn't have a stove, and can't use someone else's or come up with an alternative such as a grill, she's dead in the water. She'd either have to change her menu (how about gazpacho?) or figure out another way to heat her soup.

Once she is convinced that she probably has, or can purchase, the necessary equipment, Lucy does the smart thing and asks her chef friend for his favorite wild rice soup recipe and, voilà! she's ready to go!

Now Lucy just has to assess which ingredients she already has and which ones she'll have to purchase, and make sure she understands all the steps involved, or:

3. *The process*. The actions she'll use to complete the job, such as:

- Making a list of ingredients she needs to purchase.
- Traveling to and from the grocery store, selecting and paying for what she needs.
- Reading and following the directions on her recipe.

Lucy's ability to attain her goal depends on a number of different variables such as the quality of the directions she receives; how well she interprets them, and/or her ability to measure the ingredients accurately.

Every time she deviates from the system and compromises the inputs or process—overcooks the rice, fails to double the recipe, or worse, ditches the recipe and decides to "wing it"—she increases the chances that her soup, or output will not live up to her expectations. In any case, she'll achieve a result (soup) but not necessarily her goal (warm, creamy, scrumptious wild rice soup for 13). So Lucy not only needs inputs and processes, she also needs a valid system if she wants to achieve reliable results.

If Lucy ignores the trial-and-error practice and knowledge used to create the recipe and decides to go it alone, she's far more likely to overlook essential inputs and ignore vital processes. And, as they say, the proof is in the pudding (or soup).

Results vs. Goals: The Good, the Bad, and the So-So

Whenever you input resources and complete a series of related actions (processes)—ones with a beginning, middle, and end—you will get a result, or "R."

The challenge lies in doing everything in your power to ensure that your Rs meet or exceed your goals, or Gs!

If R > G, you've managed to exceed your expectations.
If R = G, you've hit the nail on the head.
If R < G, you fell short of your goal.

Our soup analogy aptly demonstrates how these variances can occur, but keep in mind that this uncomplicated example illustrates the concept in its most primitive form. In this instance, Lucy had only one very specific goal that could be completed quickly, inexpensively, and without a great deal of planning.

But what if it was more involved? What if Lucy's ultimate goal was to open a wild rice soup catering business and she was preparing this one pot of soup in an attempt to perfect her recipe? If so, she did not achieve her longer term goal, no matter how her soup turned out.

Rather, her result, or sub-goal, either got her one step closer to her big "G" and she could check the recipe off her list and begin working on other sub-goals such as, looking into a business license, obtaining funding, or finding a location; or it's back to the drawing board for our friend. You get the idea.

And even if Lucy's soup is successful, it doesn't necessarily mean that her process ends there. Rather, if she's smart, she'll continually look for new recipes and ways to improve her product; time-saving methods and systems; cost efficiencies, and the like.

The Four Most Critical Marketing Inputs

There are four essential inputs required for excellent marketing, which when combined with your actions, can literally make, or break, your business. They are:

Mindset: Your philosophies, attitudes, and beliefs.

Assets: Your resources—time, money, people, machines, systems.

Skills: Your talents—financial, managerial, technical, etc.

Knowledge: Your facts and figures—information on your company, competitors, marketplace, industry, customers, prospects, products, and services, etc.

The acronym we use to remind ourselves of this "tool chest" is MASK. Additionally, you'll want to make sure that the system you use to develop your processes is reliable. We use a simple and effective model that we call "PETE." It is a variation of the famous "Plan, Do, Check" quality control system that Dr. W. Edwards Deming introduced to the Japanese after World War II. It contains four elements, which are:

Planning: Forethought and decision making regarding key strategies and tactics.

Executing: Implementing the plan.

Tracking: Benchmarking and the methodology for measuring success.

Evaluating: Analyzing the results and adjusting accordingly.

Figure 4.2 is an illustration of how it works.

As you can see it is an ongoing, circular system that entails building and executing a plan; tracking, measuring, and analyzing results; amending the original plan; implementing the changes; tracking, measuring, and analyzing those results, and so on.

It does not start and stop. It's continual, just like marketing your business.

A good way to begin assessing your own inputs and processes is by asking yourself questions such as:

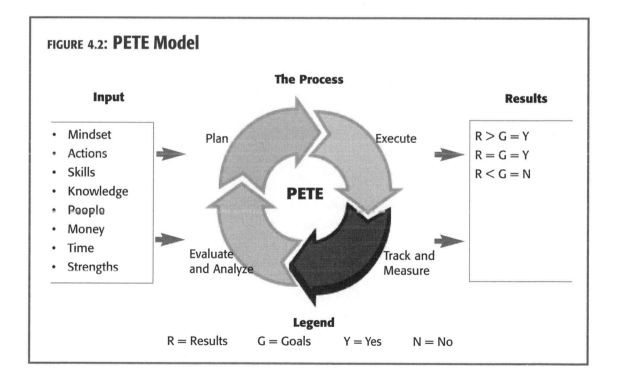

FIGURE 4.2: PETE Model

- Am I really ready to take control of my own business or grow someone else's?
- Am I certain that my existing loyal customers will follow me anywhere?
- Do I have what it takes to make millions?
- How does my experience and expertise compare with others in my industry?
- What education, observations, or experiences make me qualified to effectively manage:
  - Marketing and public relations?
  - Advertising?
  - Lead generation and conversion?
  - Product development?
  - Finances?
  - Internet marketing?
  - Web site development?
  - Human resources?
  - Data management?
  - Business systems?
- What do I know about my:
  - Industry?
  - Competitors?
  - Prospects?
  - Community?

Your answer to these and other vital questions will determine the quality of your inputs, and ability to reach your goals. In the following chapters we'll go into great detail on things you can do to improve in each of these areas.

Marketing Plan Components: Strategies and Tactics

You'll find that there are numerous marketing plan outlines to choose from, and most are perfectly fine to use. Much of your decision will hinge on personal preference, so feel free to select one that meets your needs, as long as it contains the most important sections. Also, we suggest that you avoid using boiler-plate, fill-in-the-blank, one-size-fits all plans—you know, the kind where you just slip in your company's name, address, products, and the like. Samples and templates are wonderful, but your marketing plan will be meaningless if you take too many shortcuts. Don't worry about the words, but pay attention to your inputs.

We like the five-part section plan included in Chapter 13 because it's uncomplicated and easy-to-follow, yet meaty enough for any purpose. The five sections, which we'll discuss in more detail in subsequent chapters, are:

1. Executive summary
2. Situational analysis
3. Marketing strategies
4. Tactics and marketing communication
5. Budgets and measurements

Don't let the official-sounding titles scare you. They're simply commonly used jargon for basic elements. But more on this later.

Marketing plans consist of two main parts: *strategies and tactics*.

What Are Strategies?

We stumbled across a brilliant military definition for the term—one that we've paraphrased here: Strategy involves planning and deploying scarce resources and selecting the tactics and tools necessary to achieve an objective.

This is worth committing to memory because it reminds us that strategies and tactics work together, one cannot be substituted for the other and it recognizes that all business owners have limited resources (time, energy, money, people) that must be *leveraged* for the best possible results.

What Is Leverage?

Quite simply, leverage means control, or advantage. In this case, the goal is to maximize your influence over events so that your *inputs* (work, money, time, effort) result in the highest possible *outputs* (customers, profits, prosperity), as illustrated in the following formula:

$$\text{Lower/Same Input + Maximum Leverage =}$$
$$\text{Highest Possible Output}$$

It's simply another way of rephrasing that old maxim: work smarter, not harder. The strategies section of your plan will, among other things, state your goals; articulate your product and service features and benefits; define your target audience; and communicate your company's

- mission and vision,
- strengths and weaknesses, and
- major opportunities and threats.

In the next chapter you'll define your strategies, and later on, select the tactics for achieving them. So begin thinking about them. What are your bigger-picture goals? A larger customer base? Greater market share? Increased awareness? Improving your average transactional value?

What Are Tactics?

The second main part of your plan is devoted to tactics, your actions and the tools you'll use to support your overall strategies.

It will contain explicit, measurable activities, as well as the specific sales channels, communication vehicles, and other methods you'll use.

This part will also contain your incremental sales and revenue forecasts (the direct impact of your actions); benchmarks for success and how that will be measured; and an itemization of all associated expenses.

 ## Opportunity Costs

As well as calculating direct costs, you should also consider the opportunity costs associated with every action. In other words, everything you do must be weighed against your other alternatives, or what you choose not to do. Huh, you say?

OK, let's say one of your direct sales tactics is to spend every Monday and Tuesday on the road. So, you get in your car one morning, and drive to one of your prospects' location. It takes you two hours to get there; then you spend an hour with your contact and another two to drive home—a total of five hours.

Since none of us gets more than 24 hours in a day, and you've only set aside two days a week for cold-calling, it's best to objectively assess, beforehand, what else you could be doing with that time. For example, you should ask questions such as, "How likely is it that this prospect will become a profitable customer?"; "How many local prospects can I visit in the same amount of time?"; and "Which is a better use of my time?" In other words, in addition to the traveling expenses directly associated with your day-long trip, you must also add up the potential costs of missed opportunities.

In the next chapter we'll begin guiding you through our nine-step process for gathering the information you'll input into your plan. We've broken each one down into manageable pieces with clear directions. But before we begin, we'd like to make you aware of two critical concepts. Understanding these will greatly enhance your ability to create a profit-producing marketing plan. They are the only four ways to grow any business, and how to calculate Customer Lifetime Value (CLV).

Mine Your Own Business

No matter what you may have heard, there are only *four ways to grow any business*. As you build your marketing plan, make sure you develop strategies and tactics that address each of them. The four ways are:

1. *Get new customers.* As we said before, most entrepreneurs focus their time, energy, and money here. The reasons they do so are obvious— new customers add vital sales and profits, take the place of "deserters," and feed the sales cycle. Additionally, if you're a start-up, you have no choice but to focus on stimulating new sales. However, once you've established a base, we advise you to concentrate more of your efforts on the next three growth strategies.

2. *Increase the average transaction amount.* Simply put, if your average transaction amount (or sale) is $10 search for ways to improve it. You'll be amazed at how much slight increases will add to your bottom line. One way to do this is by offering natural add-ons to your products, like the famous McDonald's tactic, "Would you like fries with your hamburger?"

3. *Increase the number of average transactions per customer.* Let's say that your average customer eats dinner at your restaurant once a month. Now, imagine increasing this to twice a month. Ask yourself what types of things you can do to encourage this behavior, such as offering loyalty discounts, creating daily specials, or providing live entertainment.

4. *Improve customer loyalty.* For example, if your average customer does business with your company for six months before they take their business elsewhere, then increasing their "stay" by even a small amount could result in significantly higher gross revenues. That's why, in addition to ensuring that your customers are delighted with your products and services as a standard, it is wise to institute solid retention programs aimed at hanging onto valuable customers.

The following example demonstrates how small increases in average customer behavior can have dramatic effects. Let's assume the following:

You are a widget retailer and have just acquired 300 new customers. Your average customer spends $10 per transaction and makes 2 transactions per month. In six months, your average customer moves on. Expressed in a formula, it looks like this:

300 customers x $10 x 2 transactions x 6 months
= $36,000 in gross revenues

Now what happens if you:

1. Increase the average transaction amount by $1?
   Answer: 300 x $11 x 2 x 6 = $39,600, a 10 percent improvement!

2. Increase the average number of transactions per month from two to three?
   Answer: 300 x $10 x 3x 6 = $54,000, your revenue increases by $18,000, a 50 percent improvement!

3. Increase average length of stay from 6 months to 7 months?
   Answer: 300 x $10 x 2 x 7 = $42,000, a 17 percent improvement!

4. Increase all three factors by one?
   Answer: 300 x $11 x 3 x 7 = $69,300, a 92.5 percent increase!

This is a very simple, but powerful, model. It clearly illustrates how important it is to find ways to grow your business geometrically with the customers you already have.

The Bottom Line
Mine Your Own Business

Customer Lifetime Value—What Does It Really Mean?

As we said in Chapter 3, a company's average customer's lifetime value, or CLV, is perhaps the most important piece of information it has because it is the basis for every marketing decision. Calculating it can be a bit tricky, because every Tom, Dick, and Mary Marketer have done their best to make it more complicated than necessary, but we'll keep it simple.

The hardest part of calculating CLV is figuring out exactly what your average customer's lifetime really is, and the only accurate way to arrive at that number is by getting, storing, and analyzing their information. Period.

Although there are several ways to calculate CLV, the easiest is to multiply:

1. The average length of time a customer stays your customer;
2. The number of transactions that an average customer will have with you during that time; *and*
3. The average dollar amount per transaction.

Once completed, you'll arrive at a useable number. But remember, if your original numbers are inaccurate, your CLV will be also.

Once established, you can use your CLV as a benchmark for developing a realistic budget for customer acquisition (or retention, for that matter). For example, let's say you find out that your average customer:

1. Stays with you for five months.

2. Purchases something from you three times per month.

3. Spends an average of $2 per transaction.

In this case, your average CLV would be $30. Based on this, it would be foolish to spend even $20 to acquire a new customer: you'd be left with little, or no, profit—unless, of course, your margins are outrageously high.

On the other hand, your customers may hang in there for 22 months, spend $20 per transaction and purchase from you more often. Since your CLV would be much higher, you could afford to pay more to gain a new customer. Again, the specifics differ widely and there are many factors to consider. Also note that this does not include any costs associated with preserving this customer relationship. In the real world, these must be included.

Once you've arrived at your CLV, you can break it down into twelve-month increments and compare it against what it costs you to acquire one customer—your other most important business metric.

Getting the Information

Obviously the best way to get accurate information is by inputting your own customer data into a computerized database that can be accessed as needed (and there's no excuse anymore because there are wonderful and extremely affordable web-based programs available).

However, computers are not required! You can hand-write customer information on index cards if you like. The most important thing is to gather as much data as possible about each and every one of your customers.

If you're a start-up it's a bit tougher, but the internet is chock-full of free information on consumers' behaviors, industry trends, economic forecasts, and more.

Following are several web sites that are great resources.

- *U.S. Census Bureau*: www.census.gov/main is loaded with business and demographic data.
- *U.S. Postal Service*: www.usps.gov is great for looking up zip codes, tracking mail, rates, and more.

- *Better Business Bureau*: www.bbbonline.com gives the BBB online reliability seal that inspires consumers' trust, if your business qualifies for it.
- *The Wall Street Journal Center for Entrepreneurs*: www.startupjournal.com is loaded with useful business information.
- *Small Business Administration*: www.sba.gov gives statistics, regulatory information, loan resources, and much more.
- *Biz Stats*: www.bizstats.com has retail benchmarks for most industries.
- *U.S. Chamber of Commerce Small Business Center*: www.uschamber.com/sb/default has lots of good information geared specifically to small businesses.
- *Service Corps of Retired Executives*: www.score.org offers free business advice on all kinds of stuff—taxes, finances, cash flow, accounting procedures, and more.
- *Entrepreneur.com*: www.entrepreneur.com is a treasure trove of great information. It has tons of resources, links, articles, and more.

Now it's your turn. Calculate your CLV using the worksheet in Figure 4.3 as a guide. Once it's filled in, multiply the number in column one by those in column two and three.

We've also included a template (Figure 4.4) to help you get started documenting your customers' spending behaviors. Since you're the most knowledgeable person about your business, feel free to choose the revenue tiers that make most sense, but use this one to help organize your thoughts. You can also customize the headings to better reflect your situation. This template can be repurposed to analyze customer churn by revenue tier as well. If you'd like to download a blank copy of this, go to: www.TheProcrastinatorsGuideToMarketing.com or www.TPGTM.com. Once there, you'll be asked to register and given instructions for downloading.

In the next chapter you'll start gathering the information you'll include in your plan. Try not to skip over parts, they're all related to each other and you'll be far less confused if you take it one piece at a time.

FIGURE 4.3: **CLV Worksheet**

Average time in months a customer does business with company	Average number of transactions per customer monthly	Dollars average customer spends per transaction	CLV
Example: 5 months	3 transactions per month	$2 per transaction	$30

FIGURE 4.4: **Revenue Tiers Template**

Average Monthly Transaction Revenues	Total Customers (Past and Present) at this Spending Level	Product One	Product Two	Product Three	Number of Active Current Customers	Number of Inactive Customers	Average Length of Stay
$0							
$.01–$ .50							
$.51–$1							
$1.01–$ 2							
$2.01–$ 5							
$5.01–$10							
$10.01–$ 15							
$15.01–$ 25							
$25.01–$ 50							
$50.01–$ 75							
$75.01–$100							
$100.01–$200							
$200.01+							
Total:							

Chapter 4 Snapshot

Before moving on to Chapter 5, let's take time to review several of the most important take-aways from this chapter:

- A marketing plan is a written roadmap that documents a company's short- and/or long-term objectives.

- A marketing plan is not a full-blown business plan.

- The single best reason for writing a marketing plan is the journey, not the plan.

- Goal attainment = Inputs + Process.

- A solid system—one that achieves predictable results—consists of quality inputs and well-thought-out processes.

- A system is a standardized and organized method for solving problems.

If a man will begin with certainties, he shall end in doubts;
but if he will be content to begin with doubts, he shall
end in certainties.

—FRANCIS BACON

STEP 1

Defining Your Future and Assessing Your Current Situation

You'll begin building your marketing plan by defining your lifestyle and business goals. Then you'll be asked to assess your current situation to determine if your objectives are reasonable and achievable. Simply put, we'll help you answer the following questions:

"Would you tell me, please, which way I ought to go from here?"

"That depends a good deal on where you want to get to," said the Cat.

"I don't much care where," said Alice.

"Then it doesn't matter which way you go," said the Cat.

—EXCERPT FROM *ALICE'S ADVENTURES IN WONDERLAND* BY LEWIS CARROLL

---

1. Where am I now?
2. Where do I want to go?
3. Can I get there from here?

Your replies will serve as the foundation for your marketing efforts and help you determine the amount of time and effort it will take you to achieve your goals. So, let's begin at the end!

> *If you take responsibility for yourself you will develop a hunger to accomplish your dreams.*
>
> —LES BROWN

Defining Your Future

The purpose of your business is to produce an income that will support the lifestyle you choose. Therefore, define what you want most out of life.

- Do you want to spend more time with your family?
- Do you want to send your kids to private schools?
- Do you want to travel around the world?
- Do you want to support your favorite cause?
- Do you want financial freedom?
- Do you want to use your money to provide your family with a safe environment?
- Do you want to have enough money in the bank so you can live off of the interest when you're 40 years old?

This is where it all begins and before you add a strategy or tactic to your marketing plan, ask yourself this question:

Is this bringing me closer to from my life's purpose?

If not, ask yourself why. The answer to this question should determine whether you move forward or reconsider.

 ## The Three Most Important Life Decisions

The three decisions that will have the most impact on your life are:

1. Whom you marry
2. The five people with whom you associate the most
3. What you do for a living

Every other decision in your life will be influenced by these three. For example, if you've chosen the wrong career—one that provides you little joy—then it will be more difficult for you to achieve your dreams, unless you have the courage to make changes. However, if you have a supportive spouse and friends—ones who share your dreams and believe in your abilities—your road will be much smoother.

Your Personal Vision

Paint a picture of your ideal life, however that looks for you. For instance, "By the time I am 45 years old, I want to own my home, have enough money saved to educate my children, do work that is rewarding emotionally and financially, enjoy fulfilling relationships with my family, have a few good friends, enjoy a healthy body and mind, and have enough free time to read books, take vacations, and smell the roses."

As you create your own vision, try to keep these sage words in mind:

Life best lived is life by design, not by accident, not just walking through the day and reeling from wall-to-wall and managing to survive. That's OK, but if you can start giving your life dimensions and design and color and objectives and purpose, the results can be absolutely staggering." —Jim Rohn, American businessman and philosopher

Now it's your turn. Use the space below to document your ideal future.

_____

_____

_____

_____

_____

_____

_____

_____

Next, use the list below and check off the statements that are true. The more you mark, the better.

❑ This is *my dream*, not one set by anyone else.

❑ My vision is aligned with my beliefs and values.

❑ Achieving this vision is very important to me.

❑ I am physically, mentally, and emotionally ready to begin working on attaining my vision.

❑ My dream is challenging but achievable.

❑ My vision is well-balanced and includes more than monetary goals.

Your Lifestyle Goals

Next, we'll ask you to write down your lifestyle action goals—what you'll do to ensure you attain your vision. In order to jump-start your thinking, we've organized them into logical categories and provided a sample for each. Feel free to include as many as you'd like, keeping in mind a bit of advice from Ben Franklin, "Early to bed and early to rise, makes a man healthy, wealthy, and wise."

Health

Example: I will get adequate rest daily.

1. I will _____

2. I will _____

3. I will _____

Finance

Example: I will live within my means.

1. I will _____

2. I will _____

3. I will _____

Knowledge and Wisdom
Example: I will become a life-long student of business.

1. I will _____

2. I will _____

3. I will _____

Relationships (Family, Friends, Community)
Example: I will be home from work no later than 6 P.M. so my family can eat dinner together.

1. I will _____

2. I will _____

3. I will _____

Fun and Relaxation (Sports, Hobbies, Interests)
Example: I will put aside at least one hour each day to sketch.

1. I will _____

2. I will _____

3. I will _____

Consider these your promises to yourself as you craft your business objectives. They should support, not contradict, each other. In other words, make sure that you're not a victim of conflicting intentions by having a vision that you are not able, or willing, to sustain.

The content of your character will shape your destiny.

—EXCERPT FROM UNIVERSAL PICTURE'S *THE EMPEROR'S CLUB*

If you're still having difficulty coming up with some or all of these, take whatever time you need to think through them carefully. You might try using some of the great goal-setting tools that you'll find at www.mindtools.com/page6.html.

Your Strategic Business Objectives

The next step is to define your strategic goals and enter them into Figure 5.1 on page 75. Ask yourself, "What do I want my marketing efforts to accomplish?" But first, some cautions and guidelines:

- *Take it slowly*. Many marketing plans include a variety of objectives, products and services, target audiences, and the like. But for learning purposes, keep it simple. The techniques that we'll teach you can easily be applied to more complex situations; once you've mastered the basics.
- *Select no more than one or two business objectives if you're a beginner*. At this stage, you should be focusing more on the methodology, not the particulars. If you add too many layers right away, you'll lengthen your learning curve and likely become frustrated. However, if you're a more advanced marketer, choose as many as you'd like.
- *Be sure to include all of your "sub goals."* That is, additional or interim tasks that must be accomplished before you can achieve your main objectives. For example, if your main objective is to sell 6,000 books in 2009, then your sub goals might be to finish writing the book by January, 2008, and have it printed and published by December, 2008. You get the idea.

We have purposely used simple strategic objectives as examples. Additionally we have included the transitional phrase, *"In order to accomplish this I will . . ."* which reminds you to translate your goal into realistic action. For example, your strategic goal might be to increase your customer base by 20 percent. In order to put together a plan to accomplish that, however, it needs to be converted into one or more actions. So it may look something like this:

In order to accomplish this I will . . . add 300 additional new customers to my current base and retain 400 of my existing customers.

Then you'll continue to peel away the onion and decide what products or services you'll sell these folks at what price, and how you'll reach them—or, your tactics.

Your strategic goals may be very different—broader, narrower, simpler, or more complex, but these straightforward examples are sufficient for learning purposes.

Also, if you're already running a business, make sure to consider how much more business you can realistically handle without having to do such things as hire more employees, purchase new equipment, or lease a larger facility.

Here are some handy rules of thumb.

1. You must be able to *craft a marketing plan around these business objective(s)*.
   Like this: In the next 12 months (1/1/08–12/31/09) my strategic goal is to earn $299,250 in revenues with a 25 percent ($74,813) net margin.
   In order to accomplish this I will sell 15,000 T-shirts to new and existing customers at an average price of $19.95 each.
   Not like this: My goal is to have Harry stop coming to work late every morning.

2. Your objective(s) must be *specific*.
   Like this: In the next 12 months my goal is to increase yearly gross revenues from $150,000 to $200,000.
   In order to accomplish this I will acquire 50 new customers who spend an average of $1,000 each.
   Not like this: My goal is to be rich.

3. Your objective(s) must be *measurable*.
   Like this: My goal is to increase market share in my service area from 5 percent to 12 percent by September, 2009.
   In order to accomplish this I will keep 90 percent of my current customer base and add another 1,000 new customers in my service area.

Not like this: My goal is to do better.

4. Your objective(s) must be *actionable*.
   Like this: My goal is to attain 300 new customers who will spend $20 each during the next 12 months.
   In order to accomplish this I will sell 300 additional cookbooks at an average price of $20 each.
   Not like this: My goal is to think about ways to cut expenses and get new customers.

5. Your objective(s) must be *reasonable*.
   Like this: My goal is to sell two additional cars per month (total of 24) at an average price of $20,000 over the next 12 months.
   In order to accomplish this I will plan and execute an advertising campaign designed to attract qualified prospects and turn them into customers.
   Not like this: My goal is to sell 25 additional cars each month at an average price of $30,000 each for the next six months, using only word-of-mouth referrals.

6. Your objective(s) must be *time bound*.
   Like this: My goal is to increase my average sales of 10-ounce jars of vanilla handcream by 5 percent—from 247 to 259 units per month—on or before November 3, 2008.
   Not like this: My goal is to sell 30 new cars.

Business Objective(s) Worksheet

Use the worksheet in Figure 5.1 to document your goals, timelines, and forecasted revenues and gross profit. It is also a useful tool if you have several things you'd like to try, but are unsure which ones, if any, to include or if you have multiple main or subgoals to enter.

If you'd like to down a blank copy of this template, go to: www.The ProcrastinatorsGuideToMarketing.com or www.TPGTM.com. Once there, you'll be asked to register and given instructions for downloading.

Keep in mind the following:

- It's best to begin with a 12-month plan, so pick a realistic date to begin preparations and implementation.

- Customer Lifetime Value (CLV) is a very important consideration for companies that have been in existence a while and are looking for continued growth. However, if your business is a start-up, do your best to make reasonable predictions for the shorter term. The easiest way to do this is by getting advice from established businessowners in your industry. Contact them directly (just make sure they're not direct competitors) or consult trade associations and literature.

- Remember, all of your goals will eventually be translated into profitable sales of your products or services, so you'll want to make sure you calculate them accurately. Therefore, we've included several additional worksheets in the Appendix that will help you calculate gross profits and prioritize your goals.

Directions and Key Elements

Fill in the information requested using this key:

1. *Description.* What are your specific strategic goals for the next 12 months? (For example, 1,000 new customers, $1,000 in additional revenues). Be specific; it will make the rest so much easier.

> Keep your number of objectives small. If you have multiple goals, make sure you list different types separately if they are not part of the same goal. For instance, if your goal is to earn $1,000 in revenue and you plan to do that by selling 100 customers product X at $10 each, you're OK. But, if your goal is to earn $1,000 with product X and earn $500 with product Y, they need to be listed separately.

2. *Timeline.* How long will it take you to accomplish this goal? When will you begin and when will you end?

> Enter exact dates and make sure they're realistic.
>
> Traditionally, marketing plans covered three to ten years. We suggest, however, that you focus on no more than one year, especially if this is your first time. However, you'll still want to make sure that the strategic objectives you include support your business goals three to five years out.

3. *Forecasted revenues.* What are the total gross revenues you'll earn if you achieve this goal?

Here's our sample:

Sample Business Objectives Worksheet

Business Objective(s) Description	Timeline	Forecasted Gross Revenues or Impact
1,500 new customers contributing $34 each	1/1/09–12/31/09	$51,000
100 new customers contributing $75 each	1/1/09–12/31/09	$7,500

A blank worksheet (Figure 5.1) for you to fill out.

FIGURE 5.1: **Business Objectives Worksheet**

Business Objective(s) Description	Timeline	Forecasted Gross Revenues or Impact
1.		
2.		
3.		
4.		
5.		
Total		

These are the strategic marketing objectives that you'll summarize in your plan (Part I: Executive Summary, Section D: Summary of Strategic Objectives and Recommendations on page 267). All of your tactical activities will support these.

Assessing Your Current Situation

Now that you've defined your business goals it's time to objectively evaluate your present circumstances. You'll do this using a brilliant tool called a SWOT (Strengths, Weaknesses, Opportunities,

Never underestimate the power of passion.

—EVE SAWYER

and Threats) analysis, which is designed to help you reduce multiple variables into a manageable number of key issues. This way you'll be able to focus your efforts where they count the most. You'll use your SWOT analysis to:

- Judge the distance between where you are today and where you'd like to go.
- Develop strategies and tactics that play to your strengths and minimize your weaknesses.
- Create contingency plans for overcoming external threats and seizing golden opportunities.
- Enter into Part II (Situation Analysis) of your marketing plan.

Your SWOT Analysis

Remember, this should be an objective analysis of your current situation, and a snapshot of your company's health and capabilities as well as environmental factors that will affect your ability to achieve your business objectives.

Keep the following five major categories in mind as you complete your SWOT Analysis:

1. *You and your company.* Your competencies, funding, resources, personnel, knowledge, culture, goals, reputation.
2. *Your customers and prospects.* Their loyalty, buying habits, size, growth potential, your ability to find and reach your target market.
3. *Your competitors.* Their product and service offerings, tactics and perceptions, relative market share, brand awareness, reputation.
4. *The climate.* Your external political, social, cultural, economical, legal, international environment.
5. *Your collaborators.* Those people and companies who support you such as distributors, contractors, suppliers, and alliances.

Strengths

These are your (or your business's) most positive aspects, or what you do best. They should be internally focused and concentrate on "the now"—not what you did well ten years ago. Here are the types of question you should ask your-self:

What are my top five strengths? (e.g. skills, industry knowledge, personality traits, assets)

1. _____
2. _____
3. _____
4. _____
5. _____

What are my company's top five advantages? (e.g. loyal customer base, his-torical performance, market share, brand recognition, profitability, work force, quality, product selection, reputation)

1. _____
2. _____
3. _____
4. _____
5. _____

What does the public see as my company's strengths?

1. _____
2. _____
3. _____
4. _____
5. _____

How do these compare with others in my industry?

_____

_____

_____

_____

_____

How do these compare with competitors in my service area?

_____

_____

_____

_____

_____

Will they help me achieve the business objectives I've identified? If so, why? If not, why not?

_____

_____

_____

_____

_____

Weaknesses

These are your *internal* disadvantages, the ones that are most likely to inter-fere with your ability to achieve your business objectives. They are your major concerns and the ones you most want to improve. Focus on your mindset, company culture, resources (time, money, people, and systems), knowledge, skills, employees, processes, and the like. Remember, the more *undiscussables* you surface, the better. It's time to face reality by asking yourself:

What are my top five weaknesses? (e.g. skills, industry knowledge, personality traits, assets)

1. _____

2. _____

3. _____

4. _____

5. _____

What are my company's top five problem areas or weaknesses?

1. _____

2. _____

3. _____

4. _____

5. _____

What does the public see as my company's weaknesses?

1. _____

2. _____

3. _____

4. _____

5. _____

How do these compare with others in my industry?

_____

_____

_____

_____

_____

How do these compare with competitors in my service area?

_____

_____

_____

_____

_____

Which weaknesses need to be erased right away?

1. _____

2. _____

3. _____

4. _____

5. _____

Which weaknesses can be avoided in the future?

1. _____

2. _____

3. _____

4. _____

5. _____

What are the most important things I can do to overcome these weaknesses or solve these problems?

1. _____

2. _____

3. _____

4. _____

5. _____

Opportunities

These are external openings that will allow your company to be even more successful. A good idea is to refer back to your strengths and see which ones you can turn into opportunities—take advantage of them!

Ask yourself the following questions:

What are the top five opportunities that are staring me in the face?

1. _____

2. _____

3. _____

4. _____

5. _____

Are there interesting trends that I can take advantage of? If so, list the top five.

1. _____

2. _____

3. _____

4. _____

5. _____

What are the top marketplace changes that can improve the way I do business?

1. _____

2. _____

3. _____

4. _____

5. _____

Are there new technologies available that can save me time and money? If so, what are they?

1. _____

2. _____

3. _____

4. _____

5. _____

Threats

These are external factors that may impact your business in a negative way, such as competitors, the economy, and current events. However, you should also look inside your business because your own weaknesses can become your worst threats!

Ask yourself the following questions:

What are my top five external roadblocks?

1. _____
2. _____
3. _____
4. _____
5. _____

What are my competitors doing better than me?

1. _____
2. _____
3. _____
4. _____
5. _____

Am I facing significant changes in requirements for conducting my business? If so, what are they?

1. _____
2. _____
3. _____
4. _____
5. _____

Does my current financial situation pose a threat to my company? Am I under-financed? Do I have a great deal of bad debt?

1. _____

2. _____

3. _____

4. _____

5. _____

Are my weaknesses serious threats to my business? If so, in what way?

1. _____

2. _____

3. _____

4. _____

5. _____

SWOT Sample

Many people find it easier to create their SWOT using a simple, four-section box. Following is a sample of "XYZ" Company's assessment using this graphic.

Sample SWOT Analysis

STRENGTHS	WEAKNESSES
– Excellent reputation with our customers	– New in the marketplace so have no brand awareness
– Quick response time due to less bureaucracy	– Small staff leaves us vulnerable to outages due to sickness, vacation time, etc.
– Manageable workload allows us time for valuable customers	– Limited cash flow
– Overhead is low so we can offer exceptional value to customers	

Sample SWOT Analysis

OPPORTUNITIES	THREATS
– Growing industry affords us opportunities to expand	– The cost of new technology is prohibitive right now. Will our competitors beat us to the punch and limit our ability to adapt?
– Our local government has asked us to bid on a lucrative contract	– Large competitors may decide to focus on our "niche" and drive us out of business
– Our competitors are bigger and much slower to respond	

Figure 5.2 is a blank template you can use or photocopy. If you'd like to download a blank copy of this, go to: www.TheProcrastinatorsGuideToMarketing.com or www.TPGTM.com. Once there, you'll be asked to register and given instructions for downloading.

Remember, a SWOT analysis is a framework. Its ability to help your company become stronger depends on the information (knowledge) contained within! Before moving on to Step 2, where we'll help you define your company's identity, vision, and mission, candidly assess whether your current situation will make your path smoother or rockier and make the necessary adjustments.

FIGURE 5.2: **SWOT Analysis**

STRENGTHS	WEAKNESSES
OPPORTUNITIES	**THREATS**

 Chapter 5 Snapshot

Before moving on to Chapter 6, let's take time to review several of the most important take-aways from this chapter.

- Developing your marketing plan begins with answering the following three key questions:
    1. Where am I now?
    2. Where do I want to go?
    3. Can I get there from here?

- Your business objectives should support your dreams and lifestyle goals.

- A SWOT analysis is a brilliant tool for helping you connect the dots between where you are today and where you'd like to go.

Take time to deliberate; but when the time for action
arrives, stop thinking and go in.

—ANDREW JACKSON

CHAPTER

6

STEP 2

Shaping Your Identity, Mission, and Vision

In this step you'll describe your business's character and identity and identify the traits that make your company unique. You'll begin by defining your business's reason for being and express it in a vision statement. Then we'll ask you to take a look at where you stand in the eyes of the public, and share your sense of responsibility via a mission statement.

> *The true voyage of discovery lies not in seeking new landscapes, but in having new eyes.*
>
> —MARCEL PROUST

Defining Your Business's Character and Personality

The internal cultural fabrics of all businesses are built around their founders' visions and senses of duty and their ability to communicate them regularly and often. This is the first step in establishing a company's image, or how the public perceives it.

That's why leaders must be careful to develop their business's central purpose and ensure that everyone involved, such as employees, distributors, and suppliers, can articulate it. If employees are confused over their company's position in the marketplace, so will the public be and the business will end up lumping together with every other ill-defined company.

There is none so blind as those who will not listen.

—WILLIAM SLATER

In the first section of your marketing plan, the Executive Summary, you'll be asked to define your company's vision and mission. Once developed (notice we didn't say "devised") you should communicate them often, both verbally and nonverbally, and make sure that your actions are consistent with the brand you've created. If not, you may end up damaging your good name. (See Mary's Lesson Learned on the next page for more on this.)

As you begin to develop your company's core philosophies, keep the following in mind:

- They must be based on honest beliefs, not contrived, overused, or vague platitudes. Phrases such as, "world's best," and "friendly service," are trite and meaningless.
- You must be able to translate your company's philosophies into action; never promise what you can't, or won't, deliver—one of the surest ways to kill a business.
- Never lie, or even exaggerate, especially about the core of your business. Do not underestimate the intelligence of consumers; they know a fake when they meet one.
- Make sure that everyone associated with your company, particularly customer contact personnel, know, understand, and embrace the core philosophies.

Mary's
Lesson Learned:

It Pays to Be Firm, But Kind

In 1999, I co-founded a small, competitive long-distance company. As part of our service consultant training program, we developed standard written customer care policies as well as specific guidelines and scripts for dealing with difficult situations.

Unfortunately, such situations occurred at least once every month when we were forced to terminate some of our customers' services due to nonpayment. Understandably, these folks would phone our call center to express their concerns, anger, frustration, panic, embarrassment, and much more. Fortunately, we were able to work out acceptable payment arrangements with most.

Regardless of the final outcome, our service consultants never used the situation to belittle, chastise, or pressure these customers. Rather, the customers were treated with the utmost respect and we often took great leaps of faith to serve them well, and sometimes we lost a few bucks. But what we gained was far more valuable because this one policy resulted in more positive testimonials than most of our other, more formalized, programs.

Furthermore, a lot of those customers ended up becoming some of our best, and most loyal, because we demonstrated our core beliefs, even when our revenues were on the line.

Did that mean we carried nonpayers indefinitely? Absolutely not! Consistent nonpayers were fired. But no one complained about the way they were treated by anyone in our company and many even recommended us to others.

- Be prepared to demonstrate the attitudes and behaviors that support your core beliefs, and tolerate nothing less from others.

If you'd like help with defining your business's character, use Figure 6.1: Business Personality Worksheet. Check off all the traits that apply to your company's image and fill in the information requested.

FIGURE 6.1: **Business Personality Worksheet**

What words best describe your current company's personality or the one you would like to develop?

❏ Serious	❏ Humorous	❏ Trendy
❏ Traditional	❏ Intellectual	❏ Warm
❏ Cutting-Edge	❏ Homey	❏ Scientific
❏ Supportive	❏ Innovative	❏ Refined
❏ Casual	❏ Official	❏ Natural
❏ Funky	❏ Elegant	❏ Reliable
❏ Professional	❏ Specialized	❏ General
❏ Entertaining	❏ Conservative	❏ Industrial
❏ Informational	❏ Creative	❏ Tasteful
❏ Off-Beat	❏ "Green"	❏ Formal
❏ Young and Hip	❏ International	❏ Eclectic
❏ Low Cost	❏ Top-of-the-Line	❏ Middle-of-the-Road
❏ High-end	❏ Understated	❏ Over-the-Top
❏ Reputable	❏ Flexible	

In the space below, list your top five *core values* (principles, standards, and ethics), *beliefs* (attitudes and viewpoints), and/or *characteristics* (uniqueness, personality, traits)—the ones for which you would most like your business to be known. You'll include these in your marketing plan in Part I, Executive Summary, Section C, Purpose.

1. _____
2. _____
3. _____
4. _____
5. _____

Perception Is Reality: If We Only Knew What They Were Thinking

If you've already been in business a while, you have a pretty good idea of your company's place in the public's mind, so completing the previous exercise (the personality worksheet) may have been quite easy. However, if you're just starting it may have been a little tougher. If so, don't sweat it. Give it the time and attention it deserves and you'll be glad you did.

Having said that, once you've developed it you absolutely must, on a regular basis, double-check to ensure your views match those of the public. For example, even though you think you're communicating "classy and elegant," your prospects may perceive you as "stuffy and boring." Can you see how this misunderstanding could hurt your business?

Or you might see your products as medium-priced, high-quality while your target audience think they're high-priced, medium-quality. Again, this is not a good thing. Worst of all, what if you're a retailer who offers women's stop-quality, trendy, all-natural-fiber, easy-care garments for traveling, and when asked, your target audience says your company "sells clothes?" Yikes!

As we've said many times before, perception is reality—even if it's not factual—and understanding the place your products or services occupy in the public's mind is vital to the success of your business.

 Great Expectations

Many entrepreneurs overlook another important aspect of perception—how well they manage the public's expectations. They fail to consider that each one of their customers has his or her own benchmark—standards for assessing whether an experience was below par, average, or superior. As a result, they don't know whether they're measuring up!

For instance, let's assume that you're shopping for groceries at your local market. At a minimum you might expect shopping carts, wide aisles, fresh produce, canned goods, fresh meats, and dairy products, as well as clerks, cashiers, and baggers.

These, then, are your *realistic expectations*. Upon arriving, however, you discover that there's no milk; the floors are dirty; the cashier overcharges you; no one knows where to find anchovies; you have to pack your own bags; and the lines are incredibly long. You're understandably disappointed and frustrated because your realistic expectations weren't met! *Will you continue to patronize this store?* Probably not, but even if you do, you're sure to complain to friends and family.

Conversely, how would you feel if your shopping experience *exceeded your expectations*? That is, in addition to their great selection of canned and frozen vegetables, they offered locally grown, fresh produce. And you strolled your shopping cart down extra-wide, well-lit, and spotlessly clean aisles. Then, when you asked a clerk to point the way to the anchovies, they escorted you to the right aisle. And to top things off, you waited in line less than a minute, the cashier was enthusiastic and friendly, and the bag packer insisted on helping you put your groceries in your car. What a nice surprise, huh? *Will you go back to this store?* Absolutely! And you're sure to recommend it to family and friends.

The moral of this story is simple: Ask your customers what they expect. Then exceed, do not merely meet, their expectations.

The Perception Map

So, how do you find out if your inside reality matches outside perceptions? The simple answer is: Ask! Gathering prospects and customers is the most time-consuming part of the process, so consider using online or in-person surveys and e-mail or snail-mail questionnaires. You'll find that most people are happy to give their opinions, especially if you offer an incentive (such as coupons, discounts, or free merchandise). Although there are several ways to corral this information, our favorite is using a *perception map*. This is an extremely versatile device that is nothing more than a box with four equal quadrants, containing extremes of two important product or service traits. It is perhaps the most effective tool for understanding your place in the public's mind and how they see you relative to your competitors.

The attributes you measure are entirely yours to choose. However, we suggest that you stick with one or two key dimensions at a time, otherwise it can get pretty confusing. Following is a list of product, service, and brand variables you may want to track:

- Features and benefits
- Pricing
- Convenience
- Guarantees
- Customer service
- Selection
- Expertise
- Quality
- Social appeal
- Brand awareness
- Ease of doing business
- Reputation

Now, here's how to create your own perception map:

- Choose one of your company's products or services, product line, or entire brand to map.
- Pick comparable selections from competing companies.
- Select key attributes/benefits that define your product's place in the public's mind based on a random sampling of consumers' opinions and/or your own.
- Pick two attributes. Put each on an axis, with its extreme manifestations on either end (e.g., high quality, low quality; high performance/sporty and practical family vehicle).
- Ask a random sampling of people to mark where on the map they view your company's selection and/or those of your competitors. (Obviously, the group you select will depend upon the type of information you're seeking, and the validity of your results will depend greatly on the number of respondents.)

- Once collected, place a dot in the area where the majority of the respondents placed theirs. Remember to include your own! This is very important!
- Take a look at the results and ask yourself the following questions:
  - Did you place your product in the same area as the majority of random responders? If not, why not?
  - Where does your product fit relative to others in your industry?
  - Did the respondents position you where you'd like to be? Again, if not, why not?
  - What position do you currently own?
  - What position do you want to own?
  - How will you compete to get there?
  - Do you have the resources to do it?
  - Can you persist until you get there?
  - Do your tactics support your positioning objectives?

In Figure 6.2, you'll find a simple example of how a perception map might look for the auto industry, considering two logical dimensions—style and price—and that the variables range from one extreme to the other: conservative/practical vs. sporty/sexy and least inexpensive vs. most expensive.

As you can see, this offers a quick snapshot of how certain brands might be perceived relative to each other. Additionally, the results may or may not reflect reality (for example, Porsches may be more expensive than Mercedes), but they are still useful because consumers often make buying decisions based on their perceptions, right or wrong, and that's what you want to understand about your product.

Figure 6.3 is a blank perception map that you can photocopy or use here. If you'd like to download a blank copy of this, go to: www.TheProcrastinators-GuideToMarketing.com or www.TPG TM.com. Once there, you'll be asked to register and given instructions for downloading.

An error doesn't become a mistake until you refuse to correct it.

—ORLANDO A. BATTISTA

FIGURE 6.2: **Sample Perception Map**

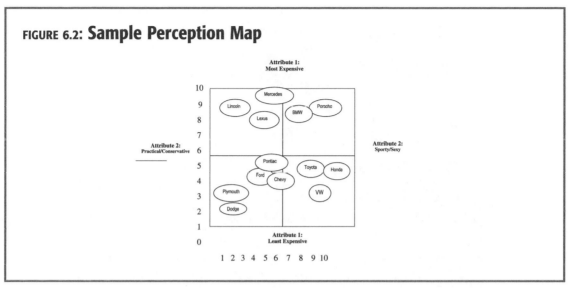

FIGURE 6.3: **Blank Perception Map**

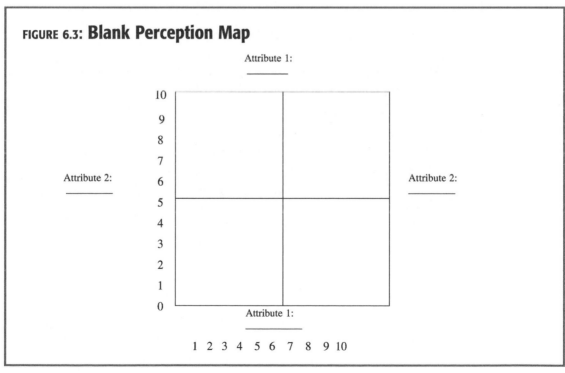

David's
Lesson Learned:
Quality, Flexibility, and Innovation—
Consumers Want All Three

Entrepreneurs should always keep their fingers on the marketplace's pulse by understanding current trends and how they impact their customers' experiences. For example, in the 1980s many companies focused on *quality*, when sales of American-made cars plummeted and imports, perceived as higher quality, were all the rage. In the 1990s companies that demonstrated suppleness and flexibility dominated the business world.

Now in the 21st century, businesses are focusing much time, effort, and money on discovering ways to become more *innovative and collaborative* using emerging technology and systems. This is particularly evident on the World Wide Web where the internet's accessible technologies and fast-growing Web 2.0 culture allow small businesses to compete on level playing fields with the "big guys."

Remember, your business is only as good as your weakest skill, so if you're techno-phobic, get over it! Computers and the internet are here to stay, and if you ignore them much longer, you'll get left behind. Either develop your own skills (there are tons of computer and software classes you can take, easy-to-follow tutorials, and geeks who are willing to educate you), or hire someone who can take over this aspect of your business.

By the way, does this mean that consumers have forgotten quality and flexibility. No, they want it all!

Developing Your Vision Statement

We'll begin with your vision statement, which will provide inspiration. Think of it as a painting that depicts your company's ideal future. Effective vision statements use colorful, vivid, and vibrant yet concise language to:

- Communicate a compelling mental image of the future, such as:

- The gymnast who watches as she accepts an Olympic gold medal.
- The writer who sees himself receiving a Pulitzer Prize.
- The mountain climber who pictures himself on Mt. Everest's summit.
- The florist who envisions Kentucky Derby winners draped in her creations.

• Motivate and inspire others to take action.

• Describe realistic, but challenging, ambitions—usually five to ten years in the future.

• Articulate core values and cultures.

• Present a guiding image of success.

Now, here are some good real and not-so-real examples:

• "XYZ Company will become the nation's number one provider of electronic widgets by 2015."

• "By the end of the decade, we will put a man on the moon." —John F. Kennedy

• "To be recognized and respected as one of the premier associations of HR Professionals." —HR Association of Greater Detroit

• "Year after year, Westin and its people will be regarded as the best and most sought after hotel and resort management group in North America." —Westin Hotels

• "A personal computer in every home running Microsoft software." —Microsoft Corporation

> *A merchant who approaches business with the idea of serving the public well has nothing to fear from the competition.*
>
> —JAMES CASH PENNEY

Now, it's your turn. Write your own vision statement in the space provided on the next page. If you'd like more ideas, go to www.google.com and type the keywords "vision statements" into the search field and hit the enter key. You'll be amazed at the number of resource links you'll receive!

_____

_____

_____

_____

_____

_____

_____

Your Mission Statement

A mission statement is a declaration that outlines the specific actions that will be used to accomplish a business's goals. It addresses *how* the vision will be attained and is therefore narrower in scope.

Remember, it must be an actual representation of your beliefs, not some fancy words on paper. And it's a good idea to develop your statement using input from everyone involved in your business, especially employees. After all, they'll be called upon to make it a reality.

We think the best ones include a company's:

- *Contributions*. What will be done by whom?
- *Intended audience*. Who will benefit?
- *Distinguishing features*. What sets it apart from others in its industry?

Following are several samples of mission statements, all in narrative form. If you're more comfortable using a list format in your statement, that's fine as well.

Courtyard by Marriott

To provide economy and quality-minded travelers with a premier, moderately-priced lodging facility that is consistently perceived as clean, comfortable, well maintained and attractive, staffed by friendly, attentive and efficient people.

Otis Elevator

To provide any customer a means of moving people and things up, down, and sideways over short distances with higher reliability than any enterprise in the world.

Dayton Hudson

To appeal to a younger-thinking, style-conscious, moderate- and better-priced customer by providing trend merchandising and superior service. Trends mean private labels, fast reaction, measured risks; service means warm, friendly, helpful people in a convenient, efficient environment.

Deluxe Checks

To provide all banks, S&Ls, and investment firms with error-free financial instruments delivered in a timely fashion. Error-free means absolutely no errors; timely means a 48-hour turnaround.

Ford Motor Company

Quality is Job 1. (Notice how Ford Motor Company's famous slogan is also their mission statement.)

Use the space below to create your mission statement. Once again, if you'd like more ideas, go to www.google.com, type the keywords "mission statement" into the search field, and hit "enter."

_____

_____

_____

_____

_____

You'll include both your vision and mission statements in your marketing plan, Part I: Executive Summary, Section C: Philosophies.

Chapter 6 Snapshot

Before moving on to Chapter 7, let's take time to review several of the most important take-aways from this chapter:

- Your company's vision statement is a declaration of your character, identity, and long-term goals.

- Leaders must carefully develop their business's central purpose and ensure that everyone involved in their company knows and embraces this philosophy.

- Your reputation can be one of your biggest assets or most damaging flaws.

- Understanding the place your products, services, or brand occupy in the public's minds is vital to the success of your business.

Good management consists of showing average people how to do the work of superior people.

—JOHN D. ROCKERFELLER

STEP 3

Choosing Your Products and Services

Although we assume that most of you are already selling products or services (or both), you may still have questions, such as:

> ### *In the factory we make cosmetics. In the store we sell hope.*
>
> —CHARLES REVSON

- Which ones will I use to achieve the business objectives I'll include in my marketing plan?

- How do I know if my products or services are priced competitively?

- What are the types of product or service promotions that will enhance my ability to achieve my business objectives?

In this chapter we'll help you select the products and services you'll include in your plan, offer very general pricing guidelines, and give you some ideas on the types of pricing promotions you can use to "sweeten the pot."

In order to save room, reduce redundancies, and avoid using the awkward "product/service" phrase, from here on we will use the words "product" and "service" interchangeably, even though we understand that they are technically different. However, when appropriate we will differentiate between them.

Selecting Your Product and Service Offering

Many entrepreneurs erroneously believe that they must promote every product they offer. This couldn't be further from the truth, and quite often results in nothing more than throwing money down a well.

Your job is to select only the ones that will help you get from Point A to Point B most efficiently, effectively, and inexpensively. This means you'll want to consider product variables, such as:

- Popularity among your target audience
- Profitability
- Availability
- Ease of production and shipping
- Seasonal fluctuations
- Recent trends in your industry

If you have multiple products, consider narrowing your selection to two or three that you'll actively promote, especially if you purchase inventory ahead of time. If this is your situation and you'd benefit from guidance, fill in the requested information in Figure 7.1 to thin out your assortment. However, if you have only one product or have already chosen your products, skip this worksheet (although we do suggest that you look at consideration number 3).

Based on your assessment, narrow your selection to two to five products, unless you have an extensive selection. Then, fill in the information requested in the Figure 7.2 the Product Selection Worksheet grid. You'll include this information in Part III: Marketing Strategies, Section B: Products and Services of your marketing plan.

FIGURE 7.1: Production Selection Worksheet

1. List the products that could be used to help you achieve your strategic objectives over the next 12 months.

1. _____	6. _____
2. _____	7. _____
3. _____	8. _____
4. _____	9. _____
5. _____	10. _____

2. List the products with the highest gross profit margins.

1. _____	6. _____
2. _____	7. _____
3. _____	8. _____
4. _____	9. _____
5. _____	10. _____

3. Which of these products are available now, and will continue to be in the foreseeable future?

1. _____	6. _____
2. _____	7. _____
3. _____	8. _____
4. _____	9. _____
5. _____	10. _____

4. List your top sellers.

1. _____	6. _____
2. _____	7. _____
3. _____	8. _____
4. _____	9. _____
5. _____	10. _____

FIGURE 7.1: **Production Selection Worksheet,** continued

5. Do all of these products appeal to the same target audience? If not, group them accordingly. This is an important consideration because you may have to set up multiple tactical plans to address each one.

1. _____   6. _____
2. _____   7. _____
3. _____   8. _____
4. _____   9. _____
5. _____   10. _____

7. Can any of these products be packaged together? If so, which ones?

1. _____   6. _____
2. _____   7. _____
3. _____   8. _____
4. _____   9. _____
5. _____   10. _____

8. Are there other product variables that you should take into account? If so, list them below.

1. _____   6. _____
2. _____   7. _____
3. _____   8. _____
4. _____   9. _____
5. _____   10. _____

Product/Service Grid Directions and Key Elements

    1. *Product/service description.* Here's where you list the specific product(s) or service(s) that you will sell in order to achieve the business objectives you identified in Chapter 5.

2. *Availability*. Fill in when this product will be available and ready for sale. If it's ready now, no sweat. If it's not, make sure you've left enough time to get it ready for sale and execute the action plan.

3. *Regular price*. What is your usual, or forecasted, per-piece selling price for this product, before discounts, sales, or other special offers?

4. *Offer price*. If different from the regular price, what is the selling price you'll use to achieve your marketing plan objectives? If you're not certain whether to reduce or increase your prices, don't worry right now. You can always change these numbers later on. Be aware, however, of the impact that altering one variable may have on others. For example, if you raise your per-piece price you may have to reduce your projected sales or increase your profit margins. Conversely, if you lower prices you may have to reduce your marketing budget or buy more raw materials to accommodate an increase in sales.

FIGURE 7.2: **Product/Service Availability and Offer Price Worksheet**

Description	Availability	Regular Price	Offer Price
1.		$	$
2.		$	$
3.		$	$
4.		$	$
5.		$	$
6.		$	$
7.		$	$
8.		$	$
9.		$	$
10.		$	$

Product Pricing Primer

Service professionals are particularly beset with confusion about how to begin pricing products and gauging whether their products are priced correctly.

This is because there is not one right way to price products due to the many variables that must be considered. Having said that, there are some very basic guidelines you can use to begin pricing your products sensibly, realistically, and profitably. Following are some quick tips to get you started, and a couple of cautions:

- *Never hyper-focus on price*. Yes, it is an important consideration but it's far wiser to concentrate on value and never, ever, use it as your only differentiator!
- *One size doesn't fit all*. There is no good universal pricing strategy because of critical differences between industries, geography, personal and business goals, company size, raw materials, advertising costs, capital expenses, and much more. You (or others directly involved in your business) must consider these factors and fill in the blanks.
- *Consult with an objective financial advisor*. Our advice is limited to its relevance to the marketing process and should be used as a framework only. We strongly recommend that you consult with a financial specialist—one who can provide you with a total picture of your current status and advise you on such things as cash flow management, investment capital, profit and loss statements, balance sheets, and the like.
- *Make sure you've got enough money to weather some storms*. Many entrepreneurs and small businesses struggle and ultimately collapse because they're underfunded from the get-go. It's best to plan ahead and set money aside for unexpected delays, cost over-runs, and slow sale periods.

Ballpark Pricing

Understanding your costs is the most essential component for establishing your prices. It's fairly easy to arrive at ballpark pricing by assigning costs by product. Even better, you can work it either way. Begin with a proposed price and work back, or build methodically from the ground up.

Here's a very simple example of the process using the first approach:
- I manufacture and retail one product: an oak, one-piece picnic table with attached chairs.
- I receive $100 whenever I sell one.
- Each table costs me $44 to produce:
  - $20 for the wood
  - $2 for stain
  - $1 for bolts, screws, and sandpaper
  - $1 for wasted materials (wood, stain)
  - $20 in labor
- Given this scenario, my *gross profit* (the money I'm left with after material and labor expenses) is $56, or 56 percent.
- But that's not all. Now I have to deduct that one product's portion (percentage) of my *administrative* (rent, utilities, office supplies, and management salaries) *and* my marketing expenses (signage, ads, on-hold music, business cards, and specialty ad items). If these come to $10 per table, my *net margin* before taxes is $46, or 46 percent.

How Do You Know What to Deduct from each Product Sale?

Simply divide the total amount you've spent in each category over a specific period of time. Then figure out what percentage of your total budget (for the same period of time) they represent. Deduct that percentage amount off your sales price.

For example, let's say I sold 5,000 picnic tables last year and earned $500,000. When I deduct the $220,000 it cost me to produce the tables, I'm left with $280,000.

Now, let's assume that I spent $50,000 total on administrative and marketing expenses. Since the $100-picnic table accounts for 100 percent of my sales, all 5,000 sales bore an equal percentage of these costs. So, I simply divide $50,000 by 5,000 to arrive at my $10 estimate. Obviously this is much easier in a case like this, since there is only one product. However, you'll use the same methodology to calculate expense percentages regardless of the numbers of products you carry.

Costing Multiple Products

If you market multiple products, you'll need the following information for a given period of time:

1. Each product's average sale price
2. The total number of sales by product
3. The total amount of revenue received by product
4. The total labor and material costs by product
5. Your company's total sales dollars for all products
6. Your company's total administrative and marketing expenses and/or individual marketing expenses by product

Once armed with this information, you can easily assign each product's portion of the load. For instance, if Product A accounted for 50 percent of your sales, then you would assign it half of your administrative costs. And if your marketing dollars were spent equally across your product line, you could safely assign the same amount.

There is hardly anything in the world that some man can't make a little worse and sell a little cheaper, and the people who consider price only are this man's lawful prey.

—JOHN RUSKIN

However, be careful because it can get tricky and is more complex than this simple illustration. Most companies do not spend the same amount of time or money on their marketing efforts for every product, so you must take this into account and adjust your percentages accordingly.

Also, do not assume that the numbers we used here are high, low, or average. Every industry sets their own profitability standards, which vary widely as well.

If you're a new company without historical sales data, you'll have to take an educated guess based on your costs and competitors' prices. Remember, however, that consumers do not buy on price alone so consider the following as well:

• Demand
• Availability
• Your overall marketing strategy

- Government regulations
- Production capability

You should also take into account how your company and products are positioned and make sure that they're included in appropriate perceptual pricing categories.

Perceptual Pricing

A simple way to begin the pricing process—especially for start-ups—is by placing your products, services, or company into one of the following three categories:

1. *Elite companies.* These businesses are considered "upper crust" for their outstanding services, superior products, exquisite environment, and other factors, and their products are priced according to their exceptional quality and the value of their outstanding services.
2. *The A- to B+ businesses.* Their pricing is competitive with others in their industry, whether that's steep, cheap, or somewhere in between. Most small businesses fall here.
3. *The "plain-folk-down-home-workingman" group.* These companies use tactics such as: bare-bones, "warehouse" environments; no-frills packaging; sale of irregular or discontinued merchandise; big lot quantities at big savings, which they pass onto consumers (or at least that's the perception). Although they adopt an "outlet" mindset, their products can be as good, or better, than the ones included in groups one and two.

At first glance these categories might appear arbitrary, but we think it's important to place your company in one of them for several reasons. First, it will give you a jumping-off point if you're just beginning. Second, the category you select will determine your target market selection and the type of marketing tactics you'll use. (Remember, while each appeals to different audiences, they are equally valid and offer comparable value in the marketplace.)

Once you've settled on a group, conduct some research. Depending on your business type, check out the competition in your service area—ones as similar to yours as possible—and place them in one of the categories as well.

Find out whatever you can about their company and its product selection—and prices. Yours should be close. And even though you must never compete solely on price, it is a good idea to reduce your prices on identical products by a very small amount; usually between $1 and $5 is enough.

This is a simple but brilliant way to ensure that you, your customers, and your wallet are thrilled—and you're *not* competing on price!

Mary's
Lesson Learned:
Strive for
Picture-Perfect
Pricing

David and I recently enjoyed a white-water rafting trip in the mountains of Tennessee. It was a wonderfully exciting experience made even more pleasurable by the company's fun and energetic guides, carefully planned routes, and watchful attention to detail. They even placed photographers, armed with digital cameras, along one of the river's first category-four rapids. They snapped at least eight pictures of each raft (average of 4 to 5 guests a raft) and had them ready for viewing at the end of the trip. Great idea!

During the quieter moments on our trip we had an opportunity to discover more about our leader, Craig, and his experiences as a river guide. He enthusiastically shared fun stories and patiently answered our endless questions. We were particularly interested in learning that his company guided nearly 48,000 tourists down this river each season.

As we neared the end of our trip, Craig reminded us to stop by the camp shop to see our pictures before leaving. Since we had neglected to bring a camera we were pleased to learn that our great adventure was captured and eager to buy a photo or two.

After removing our wet clothing we made a beeline to the counter where a computer displayed the digital photos. After we provided the necessary information, the clerk retrieved our group's eight pictures. Each one captured our exhilaration clearly and colorfully. We were ready to buy, so we asked the clerk to clarify the various price and package choices. Our choices were:

- One 8.5 by 11-inch printed photo for $19.95. He suggested we forgo this alternative pointing out that, because of the poor quality paper, the picture would fade in a couple of months.
- One photo on a CD for $21.95
- All eight photos on a CD for $49.95

Our opinion? Their prices were way too high for the value, especially when you added Tennessee's 9.5 percent sales tax! I politely communicated our feelings to the clerk, who replied that we didn't have to buy one, or any, if we thought they were too pricey (after adding that camera equipment is expensive).

The result? They lost a sale. Yet, we were intrigued. After discussing our experience, watching others, and performing some quick calculations, I approached the shop owner. I introduced myself, related my experience, pointed out that I felt his pricing strategy was significantly hurting his bottom line and asked if I could offer him some free counsel. He graciously agreed.

I asked him to verify my assumption that only 10 to 20 percent of the guests bought either the photo or one of the CDs. He nodded, agreeing. And further, since the photos—the most reasonably priced choice—were printed on poor-quality paper (and all were warned!), the only viable choice was the CD. This made his average sale somewhere in the $35 range. When asked if this was accurate he nodded again. I also told him that I felt the best alternative was all eight pictures on one CD. Not only is it a better value, but it would save time, since customers wouldn't have to choose, which resulted in long lines.

Finally, I recommended that he get out a calculator, pen, and piece of paper and do some back-of-the-envelope math. (Remember, the actual numbers are not as important as the overall impact and there is plenty of wiggle-room either way.) Here is a set of assumptions and one scenario:

Current Operating Assumptions
1. 24,000 (out of 48,000) are potential photo buyers each season.
2. 15 percent (between 10 to 20 percent), or 3,600 visitors, currently buy "something."
3. Average transaction amount per customer is $35
4. Current yearly revenues = $126,000

Scenario One
1. 24,000 (out of 48,000) are potential photo buyers each season
2. 75 percent (between 70 to 80 percent) or 18,000 visitors buy something
3. Average transaction amount per customer is $20
4. Scenario One yearly revenues = $360,000 ($234,000 difference)

Scenario Two
1. 24,000 (out of 48,000) are potential photo buyers each season
2. 50 percent (25 percent lower than Scenario One) or 12,000 visitors buy something
3. Average transaction amount per customer is $20
4. Scenario Two yearly revenues = $240,000 ($114,000 difference)

As you can see, the results are obvious and significant. There is a good likelihood that this small business owner is leaving at least $100,000 in earnings on the table every season. What's even more significant, however, is that decreasing his purchase price caused his revenues to climb exponentially, yet his costs remain constant and might even decrease! Here's why:

- It costs nothing more to load eight photos onto a CD (about 19 cents each) than it does to load one—and is cheaper than the paper and ink for one photo.
- They could order larger quantities of blank CDs and therefore receive volume discounts.

> • The company had already invested in the camera equipment and was already paying the photographers to take the pictures. These are fixed costs and don't change, regardless of how many photos they sell!
>
> I don't know the exact numbers, although I believe our estimates are conservative. Once again, it is less about the numbers and more about creating a well-thought-out pricing strategy, one that is developed based on an understanding of consumer behaviors, fixed vs. variable costs, product/service delivery and the like.

Value Pricing and "Dollarization"

The strategies we've just discussed are valid approaches for pricing your products and services because they ensure that you earn a profit and position you appropriately.

> *The cost of living has gone up another dollar a quart.*
>
> —W.C. FIELDS

However, this is only part of the picture, because they don't reflect another vital variable—their value. In other words, *your products should be priced in accordance with your target market's assessment of their worth*, which may, or may not, have anything to do with their true needs or an objective evaluation of their intrinsic value. Many consumers buy on emotion first and justify with logic later. So, understanding and providing products that your target audience wants and pricing them in accordance with their value can make you rich. As one of our mentors, Zig Ziglar, says, "You can have everything you want in life if you'll just help enough other people get what they want."

For example, professional athletes and Hollywood movie stars are paid millions each year, far more than teachers or nurses. Does this mean that the public *needs* actors more than teachers? Or that society *needs* sports heroes more than nurses?

If we measure this objectively the obvious answer would be "No," but that's just the point: Marketplace prices are rarely assessed based on their material importance alone. Therefore, consider your products' emotional appeal as well.

Another more quantifiable aspect of value that you should consider is called "dollarizing." Simply put, it's a great idea to measure—in real numbers—the additional benefits your products provide, and communicate those to your prospects and customers. Here are a couple of simple examples:

- How much is a $10,000 car really worth if it is the only method that Tom can use to travel to and from his $50,000-a-year job? One might argue that it's "true" value is $50,000.
- How much is an $80 miter saw worth if it makes it easier for Lewis to build his own deck? Well, if he saves $600 in labor expenses his saw is worth at least that much. It's worth even more if he uses it for ten years to save money on other projects.
- How much is a new $3,000 air conditioner worth to Tara if her electricity bill is $50 per month less than with her old unit? Why it could pay for itself in five years!
- What's more valuable—a $14 can of paint that requires two to three coats to cover, or a $25 can of paint that needs only one? The answer to this question depends upon the value the buyer puts on their time.

Your goal then is to understand and deliver the benefits that are most important to your target audience, price your products accordingly, and communicate their value *using real numbers*, not vague generalizations.

Here's a great analogy. A high school basketball coach is talking with a big-time college recruiter about his star athlete. Their conversation goes something like this:

Coach: "Boy, have I got a player for you. He's the best forward I've seen in years and he's fast and tall."

Recruiter: "How fast? How tall?"

Coach: "Really fast! Really tall!"

Recruiter: "How fast? How tall?"

Coach: "Like I said, really, really fast. Really, really tall. Why, I bet he's faster and taller than anyone you have so far!"

Recruiter: "How fast is that? How tall is that?"

Coach: "Way fast. Way tall."

And so it continues. You see, the coach never *quantified* his player's characteristics so the recruiter could assess the athlete's worth relative to others. How much more meaningful would this discussion have been if the coach had answered, "He runs a five-minute mile and is 6'8" tall"?

You get the idea. If consumers understand the true value of your products and you can justify your prices using real numbers, you'll never have to worry about falling into the commodity trap—competing on price alone.

We'll talk more about identifying and communicating your products' features and benefits in Chapter 9.

> Be careful how you use promotions. They can be wonderfully helpful as long as they're not seen as gimmicky; this smacks of hucksterism, and you don't want to go there.
>
> Also, promotions are "pricey"—no pun intended! That is, they focus on providing cost deals. Therefore, you must use them carefully and not allow price to ever become your chief differentiator. Use them, but use them wisely and intermittently.

Pricing Specials

Now we'll teach you some of the most commonly used pricing tactics. Use ones that are most appropriate to your situation and business, but don't overdo. Sales promotions are designed to have an immediate impact on sales for a predetermined, limited period of time. They are used to increase customer demand by stimulating the marketplace (examples include coupons, discounts and sales, contests, rebates, and can be directed to the end user, sales staff, distributor, or retailer.

Sales and Discounts

Following are some of the most common types of consumer promotions.

- *Sales*. The word "sale" is so overused that it's become almost meaningless to consumers. Many companies use every imaginable occasion to advertise their latest, greatest price cuts in an attempt to lure the unwary consumer. This may work for a while but will hurt your business in the long run.

  Our advice is simple: if you're going to have a sale, make sure it's legitimate and believable. If not, you risk damaging your credibility and reputation. For instance, a mid-July summer sale is pointless. It's best to give a specific reason for the sale and as many details as possible. The following is an example of an effective newspaper ad:

Wednesday's Inventory Clearance Sale

Everything is 50 percent Off!

We'll be closed this Thursday… *Why*? Because it's our annual inventory day! That means we have to *count every single item in our store*, and the way we figure it, the less there is to count, the sooner we'll finish!

AND

We know how much you'll love taking advantage of our one-day prices!

Wednesday Only–Closed Thursday

- *Price deal/seasonal discounts*. These are temporary price reductions during slow times or seasons. A good example of this discount is the ever-popular happy hour, or how about a Maine beach rental in January?
- *Quantity*. These are price cuts given for large buys. The reason behind them is to earn economies of scale and pass some (or all) of these savings on to customers. In some industries, buyer groups and co-ops have formed to take advantage of these discounts. There are two types:

1. *Cumulative quantity discounts*, or price reductions based on the amount bought over time.
2. *Noncumulative quantity discounts*, or price discounts based on the quantity of a single order. The expectation is that they will encourage larger orders, thus reducing billing, order filling, shipping, and sales personnel expenses.

> *It is our attitude at the beginning of a difficult task which, more than anything else, will affect its successful outcome.*
>
> —WILLIAM JAMES

- *Prompt/early payment discounts*. Use these when cash flow is tight and speedy payments mean greater liquidity. Obviously, you can design these promotions to fit your specific needs. Just make sure the prompt payment is worth the discount. For example, let's assume you invoice your customers once a month and agree that payments are due with 30 days. In this case, you might offer a 2 percent discount if they pay within 10 days.
- *Promotional allowances*. These are price decreases given to a retailer for performing some promotional activity. They include an allowance (fixed sum of money) for creating and keeping a retail display or co-op advertising.
- *Trade-ins*. Traditionally associated with the auto industry, an effective trade-in promotion has many advantages. The buyer's price is reduced by the amount offered for the trade-in, encouraging replacement sales without sacrificing perceived value.

Contests and Sweepstakes

These are great ways to get names for your mailing list and create excitement about your company. They may take several forms, but most often people are automatically entered when they buy a product. If you're thinking about trying one, make sure the prize is something desirable and related to your business.

 Be careful! You must comply with all state and federal laws regarding contests and sweepstakes, and they can be burdensome. So familiarize yourself with these before you consider either one.

Point-of-Sale Displays

These are extra sales tools given to retailers to boost sales. Although there are often discounts associated with the displays, their main goal is to attract attention.

REBATES

Rebates are used as incentives or supplements to product sales. They entitle a buyer (as long as they have a bar-coded receipt) to a fixed refund, which varies according to the product, time, and place of purchase. Although heavily used for advertised sales in a variety of retail stores in the U.S. you'll find them most often in computer components and electronics stores.

Here's an example of how one might work: An item is advertised as "$39 after rebate," even though buyers may have to shell out $79 initially. After purchasers mail in the required documentation they usually receive the rebated amount—in this case $40—in four to eight weeks. They may also pay sales tax on the full $79, instead of the $39! Given a 6 percent tax rate, this adds $2.36 to the price.

While rebate promotions clearly work, we suggest you avoid using them for several reasons. First, it's an administrative nightmare to keep track of who gets what and they're not really appropriate unless you sell higher-priced packaged products.

More importantly, they smack of hucksterism and trickery. Companies know that they can substantially, and legally, increase their sales on a particular item by advertising the after-rebate price. However, they also know that a minority of consumers will follow through and send in their rebate coupon—even if they can do so online. And, you guessed it, they experience the best of both worlds: They get to advertise a much-reduced price, stimulate sales, and actually deliver far, far less.

There are other, less manipulative, ways to help sell your products or services without resorting to these tactics. Our suggestion: If you give a discount, give it right away. Don't make your customers work for it.

GIFT CERTIFICATES

These work well for businesses, especially ones that haven't traditionally used them. Merely adding the line "Ask about our gift certificates" at the top of your communication pieces or signage can lead to thousands of dollars in extra sales per year.

COUPONS

A coupon is a ticket or document that can be exchanged for a product discount. Routinely, coupons are issued by manufacturers of consumer goods or retailers. You'll find them in magazines, newspapers, and all over the World Wide Web.

Internet coupons are becoming increasingly popular due to the ever-growing numbers of online consumers and because they're far less expensive for companies to "issue" since their prospects print them on their own computers. The most popular coupons are:

- *Free standing inserts (FSI)*. A coupon or booklet is inserted into a newspaper or mailed separately and is a great way to target certain locations.
- *On-shelf*. Coupons are available on the products' shelves.
- *Check out*. Customers are given coupons that they can redeem on future purchases.

Now it's time to forecast the number of product sales you'll need in order to achieve your business objectives, and the added revenues and profits they'll generate by using the sample in Figure 7.3. Obviously, you'll want to make sure that your predictions are reasonable and achievable and that you'll have enough money left over to execute your marketing communication's plan and earn a comfortable net profit.

Refer back to Figure 7.2 (Product/Service Availability and Offer Price Worksheet) as needed and make sure you include your products' offer price, if it differs from their regular price, and choose ones that are readily available. Then use Figure 7.4 to predict your sales and revenue forecasts.

Products and Services Sales and Revenue Forecasts
Directions and Key Elements

1. *Business objective(s) description*. List your strategic goals—the ones you identified in Chapter 5—for the next 12 months.

2. *Product(s) or service(s) sales.* List your forecasts for the number of sales you'll need to achieve your objectives and the amount (in dollars) per sale. If you will offer more than one product or service, list them separately.

3. *Forecasted gross revenues.* Multiply the number of sales and amount per sale (column 2) to arrive at the total amount of incremental revenue you'll earn as a result of your marketing activities.

4. *Forecasted cost of goods (labor and materials).* This number represents your total labor and material costs for your forecasted product sales.

5. *Difference (gross profit).* This is the amount you'll have left (deduct the number in column 4 from the number in column 3).

FIGURE 7.3: **Sample Products and Services Sales and Revenue Forecasts Worksheet**

Business Objective(s) Description	Product(s) or Service(s) Sales	Forecasted Gross Revenues	Forecasted Cost of Goods	Difference (Gross Profit)
1,500 new customers who contribute $34 each	Sell 3,000 ABC, QRF, XYZ books @ $17 each (2 books per customer)	$51,000	$15,000	$36,000 (70%)
100 new customers who contribute $75 each	Sell 50 DEF coffee table books @ $75 each (1 per customer)	$7,500	$3,500	$4,000 (53%)
Total		**$58,500**	**$18,500**	**$40,000**

FIGURE 7.4: **Products and Services Sales and Revenue Forecasts Worksheet**

Business Objective(s) Description	Product(s) or Service(s) Sales	Forecasted Gross Revenues	Forecasted Cost of Goods	Difference (Gross Profit)
Total				

Please note: If you'd like to download blank templates go to: www.ThePro crastinatorsGuideToMarketing.com or www.TPGTM.com. Once there, you'll be asked to register and given instructions for downloading. The next chapter will help you locate your target audience.

Chapter 7 Snapshot

Before moving on to Chapter 8, take time to review several of the most important take-aways for this chapter:

- As you develop your marketing plan, be sure to include products and services that will help you get from Point A to Point B most efficiently, effectively, and affordably.

- Whenever you lower or raise prices, be sure to adjust all other dependent variables (projected sales, revenues, profits) accordingly.

- There is no one, universal pricing strategy that's right for all companies and industries due to the myriad objective and subjective variables that must be taken into consideration.

- If you're just starting your business, begin the pricing process based on:
  - What you'd like to earn hourly, monthly, and yearly
  - The value your product delivers
  - Competitive pricing for similar products
  - Perceptual pricing categories

- You are paid for the value you bring to the marketplace. Dollarizing and communicating your products' value with true numbers will help you maximize profits.

- Discounts are designed to have an immediate positive impact on sales for a predetermined, and limited, period of time. Use them wisely.

Remind people that profit is the difference between revenue and expense. This makes you look smart.

—SCOTT ADAMS

8

STEP 4

Identifying Your Target Market

> ### *The aim of marketing is to know and understand the customer so well the product or service fits him and sells itself.*
>
> —PETER F. DRUCKER

Small businesses have been around for centuries. And although they may look quite different, the reasons they exist and the fundamental tenets that they operate under are no different than they were in 54 B.C. Yet we operate in a fast-paced, modern-day marketplace—one dominated by the internet's state-of-the-art technologies that allow us to compete worldwide, expand our social networks regardless of geography, and obtain information and purchase products in seconds. Given this, many of us under-standably focus on learning and applying the hottest marketing tactics, espe-cially as they relate to online systems and tools.

And while we believe that entrepreneurs must have a professional-looking web site, employ time-saving web-based automation software, use the inter-net's vast resources to get more information, products and services, and much more, we also think that we can get caught up in this razzle-dazzle world and lose sight of the basics.

Think of it this way. Many artists spend years learning and practicing the basics regarding such things as color, form, and medium—tried-and-true methods for creating paintings, sculptures, photographs, ink drawings, and the like. This training serves as their foundation, one that acts as a springboard for launching their creativity.

It is much the same in business and marketing. That's why we think it's a good idea to step back from time to time to reiterate the basics, then show you how you can use the power of modern technology to jumpstart your success.

This is particularly relevant as we begin discussing ways to identify and locate your target audience—those people who will help you connect the dots between where you are today and where you'd like to go. At its most basic level, commerce begins when two people exchange one thing of value for another. And in the vast majority of transactions, people turn over their hard-earned money in exchange for products or services they choose. Each receives something worthwhile and the rest is history. Pretty simple, eh?

In theory, yes. In practice, not quite. This whole scenario—one that is played out in various forms millions of time each day—rests on the following two fundamental factors:

1. The seller's product must be something that enough people want and are willing to purchase.

2. The seller must be able to recognize and find these people.

In other words, *do not assume*:

- You have willing buyers, just because you have a product.

- It's OK to build your business around an interest without making sure others are interested as well.
- That just because people say they like your product, they will buy it.

So, it is with these in mind that we begin this discussion. And regardless of whether you've oper-

> *Advertising is a ten billion dollar a year misunderstanding with the public.*
>
> —CHESTER L. POSEY

ated a business for several years, own a start-up company, are merely thinking about opening your own business, or anywhere in-between, we'll show you how to identify and locate those wonderful folks who will help you achieve your business objectives.

The Number-One Best Way to Discover and Locate New Customers

Although we covered this briefly in Chapter 4, it bears repeating, so listen up. *The very best way to find new customers is with old customers!* It's shocking how many small business owners target new prospects based on traits and information that they believe are relevant, rather than facts! Don't fall into this pattern and ignore your own valuable customer information if you have it. If you are just starting out, see the "Locating Your Target Market" section, but don't forget to revisit this section. Those of you who have been in business awhile the following are the three most important "rules of thumb" for locating new prospects.

1. *Rule of Thumb 1.* The best predictor of future behavior is past behavior—not words, not promises, not opinions.
2. *Rule of Thumb 2.* The ultimate goal of targeting new prospects is to turn them into profitable customers who behave ideally. For example, they pay you on time, are loyal, purchase more often, and buy more.
3. *Rule of Thumb 3.* The narrower the target audience, the better. It's easy to find masses of people, but you're not looking for warm bodies, you're looking for those people who are most likely to become your customers.

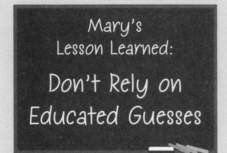

Mary's
Lesson Learned:

Don't Rely on
Educated Guesses

Many years ago, I worked for one of the largest telecommunications companies in the United States. During the early 1990s I was assigned the task of developing sales strategies for optional phone services such as caller ID, call forwarding, and return call (now *69). And because many of these options were fairly new to the marketplace, my colleagues and I were continually looking for new ways to communicate their many benefits, so I was not surprised when I was asked to come up with several great reasons for using "*69," which redialed the last caller.

This was a pretty neat feature way back then. Believe it or not, there was a time when most people had never heard of caller ID; cell phones weighed 15 pounds; very few people used answering machines, let alone voice mail; and MP3 players were merely twinkles in someone's mind.

So, I did what any great marketer would do—not—I went back to my desk and conjured up great reasons for using return call! My two favorite went something like this:

1. "Have you ever experienced the frustration of risking life and limb and running into your house with an armful of groceries to answer the phone, only to have the caller hang up before you get there? Well, now you don't have to . . ."

2. "Imagine this: You're home alone and have just put your two-year-old twins in a bathtub full of soapy water. As you begin to wash them, the phone rings. You think to yourself, "Darn! I bet that's the important call I've been waiting for." But since you would never leave your little ones alone in the tub, and there's not enough time to scoop them up, you miss the opportunity. Now you don't have to . . ."

You get the idea. I was pleased with these scenarios, and figured that even if the circumstances were altered, most people had experienced the frustration of getting to the phone a second too late.

> And the truth is, many people actually did have similar experiences, it just wasn't the reason they purchased return call! However, it wasn't until after my sales strategies flopped that I did what I should have done beforehand: that is, ask our current customers why they bought the product and why they kept it.
>
> *Their answer?* It was fun. Period. No bath tubs. No groceries. No just missing important calls. It was just plain fun to call someone back and say, "Did you just call me?" (Remember, this was back in the Stone Age before 1990!)
>
> *Lesson learned?* Your current customers are the best sources of information about your future customers. Do not assume that you know what drives their purchasing decision, even if it makes sense.

In other words, don't put the cart before the horse by assuming that characteristics such as your target audience's education, zip code, or income make a difference until *you've checked behavior first.* Then, once you've identified your most valuable customers, see what, if any, traits they have in common with each other.

How Can You Identify Your Most Valuable Customers?

A quick way to identify your best customers, if revenue is your only criteria, is by calculating your average customer lifetime value, or CLV (if this doesn't sound familiar, review Chapter 4), and finding out how many and which ones exceed the average by a little or a lot.

Still, in most cases this is only part of the story, because unlike CLV, high-value customer *behavior* is far more subjective and can be measured using many different criteria (even better, you get to decide). However, we advise that you begin by using the "Revenues Tiers Template" in Chapter 4. Once completed, remove customers from the high level tiers if they do not measure up in other areas.

For example, if you have a customer whose overall CLV places them in the highest bracket, but they regularly pay late, then you might remove them from your "high value" tier. *Why?* Simple—because they're not behaving ideally!

Or let's say you have a customer who has done business with your company far longer than is typical, resulting in a higher-than-average CLV, but every month you spend several hours on the phone repeatedly discussing trivial issues. In this case, you might consider removing that customer as well.

However, in order to find out these things, you have to know who they are! If you don't have this information your task is going to be pretty difficult or impossible, unless your customer base is really small and you've got a great memory. This is why it's so important to keep information on all of your current and past customers! And the more data you have, the better.

Once you have the information you can pull out the names of customers who fit your ideal profile and see what they have in common with each other. This is when it's appropriate to consider their *demographics* (gender, age, occupation, and marital status), *geographics* (location), and *psycho-graphics* (opinions, lifestyle, hobbies).

If your customers are other businesses, then you will obviously need to change these categories appropriately. For example, you would be looking for similarities in their size, number of employees, product offerings, and industry type.

Understanding your present customers, then, will help you find look-alike prospects to target. Here is a very uncomplicated example of how this might look in the real world. Let's say that you have completed this exercise and concluded that 10 of your 100 customers (10 percent) act ideally. The next thing you'd want to know is what, if anything, do these customers have in common with each other? For instance, are they:

- Located in certain zip codes?
- Mostly men or women?
- Teenagers or adults?

Use the worksheet in Figure 8.1 to help you organize your thoughts, document your customer data, or begin the planning process for gathering it.

Fill in the information requested and answer the questions as accurately as you can. If you're not sure, do your best. If you're clueless, spend time in the upcoming week looking for the answers.

FIGURE 8.1: **High-Value Customer Worksheet**

1. My company currently has _____ active customers.

2. I consider _____ to be high value, based on the criteria I have established.

3. The types of information that I have readily available regarding my customers are (if you don't have any information, list places where you can get it):

   1. _____

   2. _____

   3. _____

   4. _____

   5. _____

4. The top three to ten things that my very best customers DO that many others do not are:

   1. _____ 6. _____

   2. _____ 7. _____

   3. _____ 8. _____

   4. _____ 9. _____

   5. _____ 10. _____

Examples: They consistently pay me on time; they spend $100 per month with my business; they rarely tie up my phone lines with complaints; they are always pleasant and cheerful; and they remain loyal to my business for six, rather than the average three months)

5. My best customers spend between $_____ and $ _____ in a six-month period as compared to my average customer, who spends between $_____ and $_____ over the same time period.

6. My best customers contribute an average of ____ percent gross profits as compared to my average customers, who contribute an average of ____ percent gross profits over the same time period.

FIGURE 8.1: **High-Value Customer Worksheet,** continued

7. Many of my high-value customers have the following in common:

1. _____   6. _____

2. _____   7. _____

3. _____   8. _____

4. _____   9. _____

5. _____   10. _____

Examples: They live in New York City and upper New Jersey; they are males between the ages of 35 and 45; they work in the computer industry.

The Best Ways for Locating Your Target Market

But where do you begin if you're just thinking about starting a business, or don't have a detailed customer database? Well, fortunately there are several very quick and effective ways for identifying, quantifying, and locating your target audience, so follow along as we discuss our favorites.

How Many People Are Actively Looking for Your Products?

There's no sense in spending a great deal of time creating neat products or services if no one wants them. So it's imperative that you conduct some objective research beforehand in order to answer the questions:

- Are there enough people in the areas I've chosen to serve who are actively looking to purchase my products or services?
- Are they willing to pay enough for me to earn a profit?
- Can I locate these people easily and affordably?
- Is my service area overrun with competitors?
- Can I carve out a powerful niche within this segment?

The absolute quickest way of finding the answers to these questions is to conduct online research (even if yours is a traditional brick-and-mortar business).

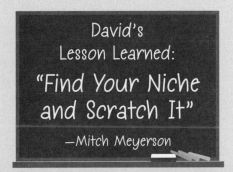

David's
Lesson Learned:
"Find Your Niche
and Scratch It"

—Mitch Meyerson

Today's marketplace is saturated with businesses that try their best to appeal to everyone, a strategy that gets increasingly ineffective as competition heats up. So, we strongly recommend that you look hard within your industry to find smaller segments of people with more specialized wants. It's always better to be a big fish in a little pond, than vice versa. And even though your universe size may be smaller, your prospects will be more die-hard fans than the masses and far more likely to become profitable and loyal customers.

For example, Chelsea is the "social worker who specializes in aiding foreign-born children," and Zach is "the filmmaker who specializes in hot sauce commercials." Smart marketers carve out a position that allows them to stand out from their competitors and they make sure to articulate this often. Niches can be defined in many ways: through a specific target market or a distinct means of service. What's your niche? If your answer is, "I don't know," it's time to begin looking for one.

Here's how:

- Go online to http://inventory.overture.com/ and type in logical words or phrases that describe your product or service into their "keyword selector tool." Make sure you use ones that you think your target audience would type in to find your products! (For example, "books on adult ADD," "beagle puppies for sale," or "writers' software.")
- After you hit "enter" you'll get back a list of the approximate number of people who conducted online searches using that word or phrase (and other related ones) during a specified month.
- Your results will give you an indication of the size of your "universe." Obviously, more general terms such as, "business" (at about 443,023 when we checked) and "tennis" (about 150,712) will return higher

numbers than more narrow phrases such as "business phone systems" (12,528) and "Adidas tennis shoes" (1,401).

But remember, your goal is to get the most highly-focused prospects, not just warm bodies, so more isn't necessarily better. As we said, this is a great tool for gauging the needs of the marketplace, and it will give you a good idea of the numbers of people who are looking for your products relative to others.

Check Out the Competition

Another very easy way to find out if people are looking for your products is to see if other companies are selling similar ones. Again, we recommend that you begin your research online by going to your favorite search engine (www.google.com, www.msn.com, www.yahoo.com, etc.). This time, type in the same logical keywords or phrases into the "search" field and hit "enter."

You'll receive a results list with links to relevant web sites. Visit those sites and see which ones sell products similar to yours. This is also a great way to find out more about your competitors' pricing, selection, packaging, and the like.

Get Industry and Trend Data

Find data that pertains to your industry as well as the latest trends at government agencies, trade magazines, newspapers, and web sites. Here are some of the many useful resources:

- Bizstats.com, www.bizstats.com
- U.S. Small Business Administration, www.sba.gov
- MarketingSherpa, www.marketingsherpa.com
- www.startup.com

See the Appendix for more resources.

Ask Current or Past Customers and Prospects

Check in with those people who may fit your demographics using a short survey or questionnaire.

Find Out Who Your Customers and Prospects Are and What They Have in Common

Once you're convinced that there is one or several groups of people who want your product, your next challenge is to discover who they are. Sometimes the type of product or service you sell will make this simple and other times it will be more involved.

For example, if your product line is devoted to getting rid of acne and minimizing its appearance, then you're probably safe targeting teenagers. At least you can start there. The next challenge might be deciding on whether it's best to focus on young women, men, or both. One strategy might be to appeal to everyone in that age group, but we think it would be smarter to find a much smaller segment within the teen population, one that may be overlooked by other companies, and speak directly to them. The choice is yours.

Simply put, the key to finding your target audience lies in understanding the problem that your product or service solves.

Figure 8.2 is a worksheet designed to help you identify key traits that will move you closer to your best prospects and find those folks who will help you attain your business objectives. If you have several different target audiences, you'll need to complete one for each. Also, be sure to identify sub-segments within your main prospect group.

Change before you have to.

—JACK WELCH

Answer the questions and provide the information requested to the best of your ability. Make note of the questions you cannot answer and work to find out the information. You'll be glad you did.

Now that you've identified the types of prospects you're looking for, you'll want to make sure that there are enough potential customers in your service area.

Quantifying Your Target Market Grid

Once you've selected your final targeted prospects for your plan, it's time to estimate their size and scope. This is a particularly important exercise if your

FIGURE 8.2: **Target Market Locator Worksheet**

My ideal customers share the following characteristics (use this to verify your responses):

1. _____
2. _____
3. _____
4. _____
5. _____

Answer the following as they relate to the prospects who are most likely to purchase your products.

1. What is their age range? _____

2. What percentage are males vs. females? _____

3. Do they live in certain areas? If so, where? _____

4. Are they married, single, divorced, or widowed? _____

5. Do they own or rent their home? _____

6. What types of cars do they like? What types of cars do they drive? (Not necessarily the same thing!) _____
   _____

7. Do they use credit cards? If so, which ones? _____

8. What is their main problem, and what is my solution to that problem? _____

9. What are the top five things they consider when purchasing my products or services? _____

   1. _____
   2. _____
   3. _____
   4. _____
   5. _____

10. What types of things do they read, listen to, or watch? (newspapers, magazines, books, trade journals, particular radio stations/music/shows, television channels/shows, web sites)

   1. _____
   2. _____

3._____

4._____

5._____

11. Do they regularly use the internet to obtain information and/or buy products? _____

_____

12. Are they a part of any group/industry that causes them to read, watch, or listen to specific things? (i.e. trade magazines, newspapers, talk radio shows, music TV, web sites?) If so, which ones?

1._____

2._____

3._____

4._____

5._____

13. What groups (nonprofit associations, chambers, churches, sport teams) do they belong to and what events do they attend (home shows, seminars, local fairs, the theatre, etc.)?

1._____

2._____

3._____

4._____

5._____

14. What other products/services do they buy? Are there local businesses that I can partner with to serve my common base? If so, what are they?

1._____

2._____

3._____

4._____

5._____

service area is limited to your community, metropolitan area, or state, and you don't have the ability to expand your reach with e-commerce sales (something we strongly suggest for packaged goods and informational services).

If this is the first time you've done this, your estimates will amount to educated guesses because you'll be tasked with making broad forecasts. But, do not let that stop you! Keep your predictions conservative and look for as much statistical data as possible; at a minimum you'll have a pretty clear idea if your objectives are reasonable or not. Remember, you can always make changes once you receive actual results.

Figure 8.3: Sample Service Area Worksheet we've used an example of a company that offers facial laser treatments (to smooth out skin discolorations, get rid of spider veins, reduce the appearance of wrinkles, etc.) in Charleston, South Carolina. to help explain the steps involved and show how one might look when completed. We've also provided step-by-step instructions for filling out Figure 8.4: Service Area Worksheet.

So let's get started!

Service Area Worksheet Directions and Key

1. *Product or service description.* The specific product or service you're offering. If you have multiple products that appeal to different target markets, you'll need to complete a separate worksheet for each.

2. *Objective.* What do you want to happen? Remember, it must be specific and measurable. In our example, our goal is 20 new clients.

3. *Service area.* What specific areas have you chosen to serve? As you can see, we've used Charleston County, South Carolina, as our initial service area.

> If you have a brick-and-mortar company you'll want to choose a logical geographical area based on how likely your prospects are to travel to your location and your ability to reach out to them economically. You should also consider how many competitors are operating in this area. Additionally, if you use other sales vehicles such as catalogs, direct-mail, or web site sales, you'll need to include these as well.

4. *Target market.* Who are the people most likely to want or need this product or service? Again, in our example we start out with a very broad group: women, 18 years and older.

> A great resource for obtaining population statistics is the U.S. Census Bureau. Go to: www.census.gov.

5. *Prospect universe.* This is the total number of targeted prospects in your service area. In this case it's the total population of women, 18 years and older, in our service area.

6. *Want or need.* What percentage of this universe wants or needs your product? In our example, we used 20 percent (this is a complete guess, we have absolutely no idea of the true percentage). Once you calculate it, enter the new population number.

   This is where your knowledge of your products and industry is critical. Since these percentages differ widely among business types, it's up to you to ensure that you're up on what's happening in the marketplace.

> Remember, people want things they don't necessarily intend to buy, so there's a big difference! For example, when asked, women might say they liked Kate Spade handbags and want to own one. However, only a small percentage of these women may have the means to buy one or are ready to purchase now.

7. *Ability, means, ready.* What percentage of the previous group has the money, the ability to get to your location, and a desire to purchase your product now or in the near the future? (We took another wild guess and used 5 percent.) Enter the new number.

8. *Know or will hear of you.* What percentage of the previous group is already aware of your company or will hear about you, via your communication plan or word-of-mouth, now, or in the near future?

   Your answer will depend on many variables, such as your budget and ability to find vehicles that target your specific audience. If you have no idea where to begin, pick a very conservative estimate like the 10 percent we used in the example.

The number of prospects in your universe size may, or may not, be the same as the numbers in your reach group. For instance, let's say there are 1,000 prospects in your town when you've chosen to target, and you've decided to run a newspaper ad to spread the word. Even though it's possible that all 1,000 people see your ad, it's not probable.

Your percentage will depend upon such variables as how many subscribe or regularly purchase the paper; the numbers who read the section in which your ad appears; and how many pay attention to the ad.

So what's the right number? We wish we knew! It obviously fluctuates according to the communication type but most media companies can provide you with industry standards.

9. *Take one or more steps.* What percentage of the previous group will pursue the purchase or actually do something? That is, how many will call you for more information, check out your web site, or visit your location, and so forth? Enter the new population number.

Obviously the number of steps involved depends largely upon your products' or services' sales cycle. You can reasonably expect that prospects will spend more time making buying decisions for higher-priced goods.

All direct response communication asks the audience to do something—call or e-mail for more information; visit a location; place an order, etc. Put a stake in the ground by estimating the percentage of your reach prospects who will act as you've requested. Remember, a 1 percent response rate for a targeted direct-mail campaign is considered wildly successful, so it's best to remain conservative and not overly optimistic.

10. *Purchase.* What percentage will actually buy your product or service? In our example, we estimated that 33 percent of the previous group (32 people) would buy, leaving us with 11 new customers overall.

As you can see, this is below our original goal of 20 new customers and is less than 1 percent of the original universe (126,652). Again, this is for demonstration purposes only. We have no idea whether it is accurate. However, it does point to the types of thing you can, and cannot, influence.

For instance, if after completing your service area worksheet, you discover that your objective is going to be difficult to achieve you have several options, such as:

- *Growing your service area.* You can't control the number of people who live in your service area, but you can expand into other locations. In our example below, we added another county (Dorchester), which significantly increased the original population base (from 126,652 to 167,137).

- *Expanding your communication plan.* In other words, increasing the numbers of people who hear about you. We increased the one in the example from 10 to 20 percent.

- *Offering compelling incentives.* This will increase the percentages of people who will take some action and grow your pool of interested prospects, which in turn will result in more sales. You get the idea.

Now it's your turn. Use the blank worksheet in Figure 8.4 to gauge the size of your target market and see how it compares to your goals.

By now you're more comfortable with ways to identify and locate your target market. In the next chapter we'll help you convert your product and service features into customer benefits.

In the space below, write down a description of each of the prospect groups you will target to help you achieve your objectives. You will include this information in Part III: Marketing Strategies, Section D: Target Markets and Segmentation of your marketing plan.

I will target the following _____ market segments during the next 12 months.

1.

2.

3.

4.

FIGURE 8.3: **Sample Service Area Worksheet**

Product or Service Description	Service Area	Objective	Target Market	Prospect Universe	Want or Need	Ability, Means, Ready	Know or Will Hear of You	Take One or More Steps	Purchase
Facial Laser Treatment	Charleston County, South Carolina	20 new clients	Women 18 yrs. and older	126,652 (326,762 x 51% x 76%)	25,331 (20%)	1,266 (5%)	127 (10%)	32 (25%)	11 (33%)
Facial Laser Treatment	Charleston and Dorchester Counties, SC	20 new clients	Women 18 yrs. and older	126,652 + 40,485 = 167,137	33,428 (20%)	1,671 (5%)	167 (10%)	42 (25%)	13 (33%)
Facial Laser Treatment	Charleston and Dorchester Counties, SC	20 new clients	Women 18 yrs. and older	126,652 + 40,485 = 167,137	33,428 (20%)	1,671 (5%)	334 (20%)	84 (25%)	28 (33%)
Facial Laser Treatment	Charleston and Dorchester Counties, SC	20 new clients	Women 18 yrs. and older	126,652 + 40,485 = 167,137	33,428 (20%)	1,671 (5%)	334 (20%)	100 (30%)	33 (33%)

After you complete this exercise we'll move on to Chapter 9 where we'll help you transform features into benefits. Remember, if you'd like to download blank templates, go to www.TheProcrastinatorsGuideToMarketing.com or www.TPGTM.com. Once there, you'll be asked to register and given instructions for downloading.

FIGURE 8.4: **Service Area Worksheet**

Product or Service Description	Service Area	Objective	Target Market	Prospect Universe	Want or Need	Ability, Means, Ready	Know or Will Hear of You	Take One or More Steps	Purchase

Chapter 8 Snapshot

Before moving on to Chapter 9, let's take time to review several of the most important take-aways from this chapter:

- At its most basic level, commerce begins when two people exchange one thing of value for another.

- Your target market is made up of the folks who will help you get from where you are today to where you'd like to go.

- The best way to find new customers is by looking for similar traits among your most valuable past and current customers.

- The more customer information you have, the better.

- Often the product or service you sell will lead you directly to your target audience.

- Never assume that you know anything about your target audience before you conduct research.

Only for the phony is commercialism—the bending of creativity to common utility—a naughty word. To the truly creative, it is a bridge to the great audience, a means of sharing rather than debasing.

—ERNEST A. JONES

STEP 5

Turning Features into Benefits

Now that you've identified your target market it's time to begin thinking about how you'll communicate with them. So, we'll begin this chapter by going over the real motivations behind every purchase decision, and then we'll guide you through the process of translating your product and service features into customer benefits. Once you've completed that exercise, we'll ask you to choose one distinguishing advantage that sets you apart from the rest of your

> *A business absolutely devoted to service will have only one worry about profits. They will be embarrassingly large.*
>
> —HENRY FORD

competitors. And finally we'll have you try your hand at creating your own tag line and "elevator speech."

As you read through this chapter continue to ask yourself the following three questions:

1. What are my prospects' and customers' most pressing problem?
2. How does my product or service solve that problem?
3. Why would my targeted prospects be foolish to do business with anyone other than me?

Why Do People Buy Almost Anything?

Although consumers make their buying decisions based on multiple factors, most experts agree that, at the most basic level, people buy to either avoid pain or gain pleasure. In other words, your customers actually purchase the advantages they receive from your product more than the product itself. If you've ever taken a marketing class, you've probably been asked that passé question, "When someone purchases a drill, what are they really buying?" The answer? A hole. You see, the drill is merely a means to an end. Now the person could try to get the hole another way, but it would be far more time consuming, less accurate, and more frustrating. So, what else does the drill do? That's right—avoid pain.

However, the majority of entrepreneurs and small-business people spend far more time communicating their product or service features and often ignore the very reason their customers purchase from them—a huge mistake.

So let's get this clear before we go any further:

- *Features are the attributes built into your products or services.* This means the stainless steel in your sink; 400-thread count in your cotton sheets; dual power exhausts on your truck; 30 gigs of memory on your hard drive, and so on.
- *Benefits are what your customers experience.* These are the emotional, physical, environmental, or mental gains they experience such as a better night's sleep, sexier smile, less frustration, and fewer headaches.

Although the concept is easy to understand, many people find it difficult to come up with—let alone articulate—benefits. However, it is vitally important that you learn to do this, and do it well. Remember this important thing: regardless of what you sell, or to whom you sell, the end user, company, or organization that purchases your product is concerned about one thing only—*themselves.*

As harsh as it may sound, they could care less about how long you've been in business, how many computers you own, or whether you're "family-owned and operated." Rather, they are asking themselves, *"What's in this for me?"* (Affectionately known in the industry as WIFM.) Your job is to answer this question.

David's Lesson Learned: Benefit-Savvy Home Depot

Home Depot aired a television commercial that brilliantly demonstrated their understanding of why their target customers purchase several of their products. It went something like this:

A man is standing in the tool department holding a drill, while his wife looks on dubiously. He wants to buy it, but apparently expects some resistance from his wife, so in an effort to convince her says, "Don't think of this as a drill, think of this as your new book shelves."

Well, obviously his ploy worked, because in the next scene the same couple is standing in front of the table saws. He smiles at his wife, points to one, and says something like, "And think of this as your new deck!"

The final scene shows the same couple getting ready to purchase a shop vac. Only this time the woman speaks up and says, "And I can think of this as my clean garage!"

Not only do they do a stellar job of articulating their products' benefits, but they do so without mentioning one feature!

Without going into too much detail we'll delve a little bit further into consumers' decision-making processes. But since there are hundreds of studies we could cite, and entire text books devoted to this topic, we will only scratch the surface. However, it's important to note that people make their buying choices based on cognitive evaluations—knowledge and beliefs about a particular product or brand—and "affective responses"—the feelings and emotions they associate or experience with a particular brand or product. And even though marketers must be aware of both—in particular how one affects the other—affective, or emotional, responses are more important because, as we said earlier, it all comes down to avoiding pain or gaining pleasure.

Additionally, please be aware that the phrase "consumer decision-making process" refers to a number of choices people make before purchasing such as:

- Should I shop online or go to a store?
- What company is the best for this purchase?
- Is this ad worth reading?
- Should I let the salesperson help me or will they be too pushy?
- Will my friends think I'm doing well financially if I buy this car?
- Should I pay for this with my credit card or cash?
- Which one of my friends could recommend a good tradesperson?
- Is this worth borrowing money for?
- Could I get a better deal somewhere else?
- Does this jerk think I'm really going to believe this stuff?

You get the idea. There is much more involved and a great many influencers along the way. But for simplicity, let's assume the following:

1. Many people, especially those who live in metropolitan areas, are bombarded with thousands of marketing messages each day. They can only give their attention to and consider a tiny fraction of these at any one time.

2. Consumers will pay more attention to messages that are relevant to their situation (solve their most pressing problem), catch their attention, and mirror their knowledge and beliefs. In other words, we filter

> ### Mary's Lesson Learned:
> ## Honor Thy Reticular Activator
>
> Have you ever noticed that when you're ready to buy something, especially bigger-ticket products—you start to notice things you'd normally ignore?
>
> A year or so ago, David and I were actively looking to buy two new beds—headboards, mattresses, and box springs—for our mountain home. Since we don't buy beds frequently it's not something we think about very often. And let's face it, they're an expensive *and* boring purchase, if you ask me.
>
> Nevertheless, we began the process by looking in our local newspapers for sales and subsequently visiting two retail stores. Before it was all over, we had seen at least 300 mattresses at 10 different locations.
>
> During that time and for about a month later, I noticed every mattress store I passed, ones that I had previously completely ignored. And believe it or not, there's lots of people carting mattresses home on the roofs of their cars! Try it out: you'll be amazed!
>
> The point of the story is that I filtered out mattress information until it became relevant to me. Think of your own experiences. When do you pay attention to car commercials? That's right, when you're thinking about buying one! And, have you ever noticed that you listen up even more if it's a commercial for a brand you're considering? Then when you buy that blue Honda you suddenly start seeing blue Honda's everywhere. Why does this happen? Simple—because of your reticular activator (RA), a part of your brain that heightens your awareness of things that are relevant at that time. So, do your best to find out when your prospect's RA is turned on!

out what's not relevant (remember the hedgehog?) or we'd all go crazy!

Although you'll never learn all of the conscious and sub-conscious reasons behind your target market's buying decisions, you must be aware that at

> *One promises much to avoid giving little.*
>
> —MARQUIS DE VAUVENAGUES

the end of the day it all comes down to their objective and subjective evaluations of the benefits they receive in exchange for their hard-earned dollars.

So, the question you should ask is, "What benefits are most important to my target audience?"

There's a simple way to go about finding the answer. Use Figure 9.1 and start with the two drivers: gaining pleasure and avoiding pain. Then list things that are pleasurable and things that are painful. You're in luck because we've started one for you. Use the empty spaces to add a few of your own!

Your Benefits

Now it's your turn. Take a few minutes to write in Figure 9.3 your own most unique and desirable features, using a simple transition phrase, *"which means that."*

Although you should include your core product and/or service benefits, make sure to include at least one that is focused on the advantages that consumers will realize by doing business with you rather than any of your competitors. For example,

- Our pharmacy is open 24 hours a day, 7 days a week, which means that you'll never have to do without your medicine.
- Place your order by December 23rd and we'll guarantee delivery before Christmas, which means that you'll enjoy peace of mind during the hectic holiday season.

You'll use this to develop your unique selling proposition (USP). If you're not sure, hang on—we'll give you some ideas in the next section.

Remember, it's all about WIFM—What's In It For Me. Also, quality is more important than quantity. Focus on the most important benefits, not the number. Refer to the sample in Figure 9.2. It shows how one might look for an automobile.

Once you have generated this list, double-check how your prospects and customers see your products' features and benefits. Then keep them in a safe

FIGURE 9.1: Pleasure versus Pain Worksheet

Pleasurable Things	Painful Things
Good health	Stress
Success	Financial problems
Wealth	Unhappy relationships
Beauty	Poor health
Fun	Emotional suffering
Acceptance	Getting ripped off
Sex appeal	Losing money
Love and romance	No free time
Popularity	Job loss
Knowledge	Loneliness
Solutions to problems	Lack of acceptance
Instant gratification	Weight problems
Safety	Mistakes and rework
Peace of mind	Insecurity
Value	Shame/embarrassment
Feeling secure	Fear
Confidence	Death or loss
Fulfilling a dream	Watching others suffer
A shortened learning curve	Intimidation
A great, new job	Worry
More free time	Confusion

FIGURE 9.2: **Sample Features into Benefits Worksheet**

Feature	Transition	Benefit
Driver-side and passenger airbags	*which means that*	You and your family will feel safe and secure.
Ergonomic chair	*which means that*	Your back won't become sore on long trips.
Gets 40 miles per gallon	*which means that*	You won't go broke paying for gas.
Sleek styling	*which means that*	You'll look sexy driving your new car.

FIGURE 9.3: **Features into Benefits Worksheet**

Feature	Transition	Benefit
	which means that	
	which means that	
	which means that	
	which means that	
	which means that	
	which means that	

place, because you'll be using them in one way or another in all of your marketing communication.

Unique Selling Proposition (USP)

Hopefully by now your most important advantages are apparent. If so, it's time to express them via a USP, or unique selling proposition. Although the term may be clumsy, the concept is not.

A USP is simply that singular, exceptional, distinguishable initiative that sets you apart from your competition. It can be about almost anything—your guarantee, service delivery, product quality, and much more.

Unfortunately, many entrepreneurs get tongue-tied over questions such as:

- "How are you different from your competitors?"
- "Why would your targeted prospects be foolish to do business with one of your competitors instead of you?"
- "What unique advantage do you have over all of your other competitors?"

If you fall into this category, it's time to do something about it, because if you don't differentiate yourself from the rest of the pack you will at best, get by. Don't forget this, you'll never attract qualified prospects if they don't know you exist! And if they have no way of measuring you against the competition, then you'll be dumped into the same overflowing pot with the rest of them.

"But," you might ask, *"What if there's nothing unique about my business?"*

Great question. Please listen carefully to our answer. If there is absolutely nothing that distinguishes your company from any other you have only two choices, which are:

1. *Invent one.* Do not misunderstand this to mean you should just pick something—anything—and say you do it better than any other company, whether it's true or not.

   Rather this means you should take a long hard look at your company and your products and services. Then try to uncover things that you're already doing well and make them even better—add a unique twist to an existing service, or come up with something completely new and different.

2. *Consider another career.* If there is nothing and never will be anything special about your business, it's time to close shop.

However, if you're willing to work on developing a unique selling proposition, you're in luck. Figure 9.4 is our USP Development Worksheet. Answer the questions as completely and candidly as possible. Who knows? You just may see your USP appear before your eyes!

USP Development Worksheet Directions

Following are some quick first tips to get you started.

1. Want some creative ideas for places to look for unique advantages? How about:
   - *Speed.* Will your customers receive the benefits of your products or services faster? Do you offer free overnight or priority shipping? Can you guarantee 24-hour turnaround times? Do you offer free delivery service?
   - *Simplicity.* Are you doing something that makes it much easier to use your products or services? Are your checkout procedures less confusing? Have you streamlined your ordering process?
   - *"Trialability."* Do you offer a way for your prospects to "test drive" your products or services before purchasing? Do you give away free samples? Offer free consultations or seminars? Can customers use your products for limited periods of time?

2. *Your USP is not unique if other companies say the same thing!* If you're the first to communicate a key benefit (even if your competitors offer the same) it can still be perceived as unique.

   For example, FedEx is known as the company to use when your package "absolutely, positively has to be there overnight," even though UPS and the U.S. Postal Service offer identical (and often less expensive) services.

3. Avoid over-used, trite, and meaningless words and phrases, such as:
   - Friendly service
   - Best
   - Quality
   - Number one

- We'll treat you right
- World's best

4. *Also, steer clear of exaggerated words and phrases that set off the "hooey alarm," such as:*

- Get Rich Now
- Moneymaking
- Fortune
- Incredible
- Outrageous

5. *Remember, it's about them, not you.*

Now it's your turn to work on your own USP, which you include in Part III: Marketing Strategies, Section F of your marketing plan.

> *We have too many high-sounding words, and too few actions that correspond with them.*
>
> —ABIGAIL ADAMS

FIGURE 9.4: USP Development Worksheet

1. List the top five products or services you offer.

    1. _____

    2. _____

    3. _____

    4. _____

    5. _____

2. List the top five problems that your products or services solve.

    1. _____

    2. _____

    3. _____

    4. _____

    5. _____

FIGURE 9.4: **USP Development Worksheet,** continued

3. List the top five benefits that your target market is seeking, whether you offer them or not.

    1. _____

    2. _____

    3. _____

    4. _____

    5. _____

4. Which of the benefits listed in your answer to question 3 do you provide?

    1. _____

    2. _____

    3. _____

    4. _____

    5. _____

5. List the ways these differ from what your competitors provide. Are they better or worse? (If they're worse, now is the time to make changes so the next time you do this, they're all better!)

    1. _____

    2. _____

    3. _____

    4. _____

    5. _____

6. List the top five most distinctive ways that you differ from your competitors.

    1. _____

    2. _____

    3. _____

FIGURE 9.4: **USP Development Worksheet,** continued

   4. _____

   5. _____

7. List the top five reasons why your target audience would be foolish to purchase your products or services from any other company.

   1. _____

   2. _____

   3. _____

   4. _____

   5. _____

8. How will you back up this claim?

   _____

   _____

   _____

   _____

   _____

Once you've completed this worksheet, write your company's USP in the space provided below.

My product/service's unique selling proposition is:

Remember, if you'd like to download a blank copy of this, go to: www.**TheProcrastinatorsGuideToMarketing**.com or www.**TPGTM**.com. Once there, you'll be asked to register and given instructions for downloading.

Look it over and ask yourself this one last question: "Who else can, or does, say this?" If your answer is, "No one," congratulations! If not, it's back to the drawing board!

Remember, very ordinary is very bad.

Create Your Own Tag Line/Slogan and Elevator Speech

A tag line, or slogan, is a shorthand version of your USP with a bit of personality thrown in. It should be no more than one line, and you'll earn extra points for brevity. Your tag line should be included in all communication and express your company's spirit and persona.

Here are some examples of new, and not-so-new, tag lines:

- Anheuser Busch: "This Bud's for you."
- United Airlines: "Fly the friendly skies."
- Timberland: "Boots, shoes, clothing, wind, water, earth, and sky."
- Nike: "Just do it."
- GMC: "Comfortably in command."
- VW: "Drivers wanted."
- Gatorade: "When you're thirsty, it's gotta be Gatorade."
- McDonald's: "What you want is what you get."
- Polartec: "Believe in what you wear."
- Toyota: "Moving forward."
- Subway: "Eat Fresh."

and the best of all…
- Strategic Marketing Advisors: "Influencing outcomes."

So, what's a bad slogan? The following humorous excerpt from Dan Kennedy's *No B.S. Marketing Newsletter* (June, 2005) answers this question much better than we could have:

If by some freak chance you own stock in the old industrial fogey Timken Company, you may want to get out while the getting's good. The big news about Timken is, drum roll please—a new slogan. I'll give it to you as I read it in the newspaper: Timken Company has adopted a new slogan, 'Where You Turn.' The new tag line replaces, "Worldwide Leader in Bearings and Steel." Company officials said it reflects a greater emphasis on finding solutions for customers as well as Timken's broader product line and the rotation of its bearings. Oy vey . . . Just in case you miss the point: slogans don't sell ball bearings, especially when the slogan is completely and utterly meaningless, delivers no hint of a USP or benefit, does NOT represent anything the officials of the company said it does, and could be used by anybody: a car wash, Queer Eye for the Straight Guy *Clothing Stores, a ballet school, or manufacturers of drills, drill bits, oil drilling equipment, tires, etc.*

The Bottom Line
A clever tag line is great, as long as you don't substitute relevancy for wittiness.

Elevator Speech

Most of you have heard of an "elevator speech," that elusive 16-second sound byte meant to say it all. *Sounds easy enough, yes*? No! Especially when the experts tell you it must be: introductory, memorable, benefit-laden, unique, catchy, succinct, meaningful, humorous, and professional. *Geez*, this is a lot to accomplish in 16 seconds!

On the other hand, who knows more about your business than you? Who has more passion and zeal for your company than you? Who has more knowledge and expertise than you? You guessed it: No one.

Inevitably every entrepreneur is asked the question, "What does your company do?" And it's best to be prepared so you don't stand there speechless and tongue-tied, or worse yet, go on incessantly.

So, here are some suggestions for scripting your own elevator speech:

- Let your voice show your enthusiasm, if you love it, it shows.
- Focus on them, not you. (Have we said this before?)
- Begin with a phrase that is humorous or mysterious—make the listener ask for more! Here are a few good ones we found recently:

- IRS agent: *"I'm a government fund-raiser"*
- Private pilot: *"I shrink the globe"*
- Lawyer: *"I empower the powerless"*
- Business consultant: *"I'm a revenue coach"*

• Do not deliver your elevator speech as if you're reading from a script. It should sound relaxed, conversational, and spontaneous, even if that means you have to practice it for hours!

• After delivering your speech it's a great idea to give the listener something that makes you even more memorable and reinforces your message. Now this doesn't have to be something expensive or fancy, just clever. For instance, if you're the private pilot in the example above, you might want to hand people tiny globes, complete with your contact information.

• Try beginning or ending your elevator speech with a question. Often they're easier to develop and they "force" a back and forth between your listener and you.

 ## How Not to Write an Elevator Speech

As we prepared for writing this section, we went online and conducted some research and came upon an interesting web site, owned by a motivational speaker, looking for gigs.

Among other things, he offered advice on writing effective elevator speeches and used his own to illustrate his points. However, this is an example of how an elevator speech should not be written. *Lesson learned?* Be careful whose advice you take! (Clue: count the number of times he uses "I," "we," and "us.")

> I help small businesses and nonprofits tell their story to the people who need to hear it. You see, when someone knows our story, they can't help but like us, and we support and do business with those we like. So, together, we craft your story and start telling it to your employees, the media, potential clients, and to the world. I know it sounds like marketing, but what makes me unique is that first and foremost, I am a storyteller. I

also have a technical art, writing, and design background, which I combine to tell your story in a special, get-their-attention way. I recently completed a sixteen-page publication with an additional 15,000 copies that appeared in the March issue of *Cleveland* Magazine telling the stories of Cleveland's community development corporations. They were so delighted with the outcome that I am now in the process of designing an extensive web site for them.

Here's one of our choice elevator speeches:

We help entrepreneurs and other small- and medium-sized businesspeople create and implement low-cost, high-impact marketing strategies and tactics so they can get and keep more profitable customers.

Now it's your turn. Using what you've learned so far, develop your own tag line/slogan and elevator speech, and when finished, enter them in the spaces provided. Once completed, try them out on family members, friends, colleagues, and customers. Ask them for their honest feedback and suggestions. Better yet, come up with several different versions and ask them to vote for their favorites.

Tag Line(s)

Elevator Speech

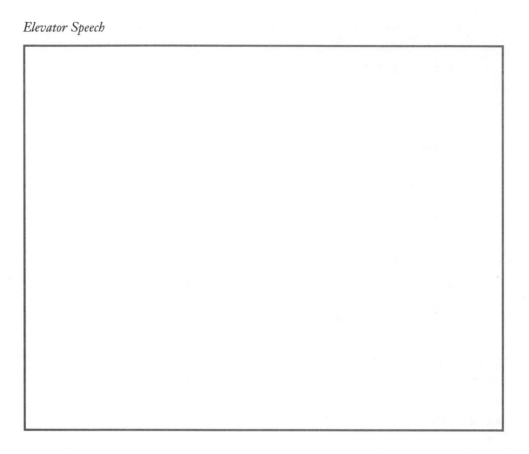

By the way, if you would like to receive our comments about your tag line and/or elevator speech, please e-mail them to: office@StrategicMarketingAdvisors.com.

At this point, you should be more comfortable with identifying the ways in which you stand out from your competitors, and are at least beginning to have ideas for communicating them. Remember, this is a constant work in progress. Everything will not come together at the exact same moment, so don't get anxious if you're still working thorough some of these steps.

The next chapter is devoted to ensuring that you've tended to some of the most fundamental basics of every business. We call them "first-things-first."

Chapter 9 Snapshot

Before moving on to Chapter 10, let's take time to review several of the most important take-aways from this chapter:

- Most experts agree that at the most basic level people purchase products or services to either avoid pain or gain pleasure.

- Features are the elements that are built into your products or services.

- Benefits are the things your customers gain.

- A simple way to turn a feature into a benefit statement is by using the simple transition phrase, "which means that."

- Your unique selling proposition is that singular, exceptional, distinguishable initiative that sets you apart from your competitors.

---

*Losers make promises they often break. Winners
make commitments they always keep.*

—DENNIS WAITLEY

STEP 6

Taking Care of First Things First

We'd like you to think of this chapter as a "getting-ready-for-the-party" checklist. If you've been following along so far, you may remember that in

> *Effective leadership is putting first things first. Effective management is discipline and carrying it out.*
>
> —STEPHEN COVEY

Chapter 2 we described marketing as the "party" and advertising as the "invitation," although you've never been asked, "Hey, a few of us are getting together tonight at my place for a little *marketing*—want to join us?"

However, we used this analogy because so many entrepreneurs focus most of their resources on communicating how great they are to the public. They invite them to do business with their company and often overlook what happens when people take them up on their invitation! In other words, *if you're going to tell the public how wonderful you are, get wonderful, first.*

At first glance, this may seem out of order, after all, we're supposed to help you gather inputs for your marketing plan. But we think this is the perfect place for you to do an assessment of where you are with the basics before you choose your marketing tactics in the next chapter and start writing your invitations in Chapter 12.

Also many of these checklist tactics will cost you little or no money and are extremely effective tools for helping you achieve your business objectives, so you'll want to include some specifically in your plan.

Remember, money has far less to do with excellent marketing than know-how, passion, and resourcefulness.

Getting Started

Unfortunately, many entrepreneurs overlook how powerful seemingly small details are to the success of their businesses. So, please, resist the urge to rush through this chapter before answering the questions we pose—sip, do not gulp; are these, so to speak, the weight-bearing walls of your building. If you ignore any of them you're committing a huge error.

Those of you who have been in business for a while may have moved beyond many of these topics—that is, your company's name is etched in stone; your hours of operation are established; and your logo is a done deal. If so, we still suggest that you use the tips we provide to take a look in the mirror and see how you rate. Maybe you'll pick up some new ideas for ways to improve what you're already doing.

How Does Your Company Present Itself?

We've heard that there are only two types of company names: good ones and bad ones. We agree.

Good business names are:

- Easy to say and spell
- Memorable
- Short and to the point
- Clever, but not overly
- As appropriate today as they will be in the future
- Indicators of the type of work the company performs

Bad business names are:

- Hard to say and spell
- Easily forgotten
- Too similar to another company's
- Exaggerations
- Long and cumbersome
- Faddish
- Potentially insulting or hurtful
- Confusing

Following are a few real life examples of the kinds of name you should avoid:

- *Cricket.* Cute name, but what do they do? Sell crickets? Play cricket? Is "Cricket" the owner's name? Actually, the company is a wireless phones and accessories retailing chain and they'll probably be able to overcome their confusing name successfully via an intensive advertising campaign. But very few small businesses have the resources necessary to do the same.
- *Goin' Postal.* Although some might see this as a clever name for a shipping store, the term was coined after disgruntled employees killed numbers of postal workers. Most people associate the term with senseless violence. The owners may think it's a cute twist on words, but we think they've missed the mark.
- *Kuts 2 Kuts.* We guess this was meant to be a memorable, shorthand name for a hair salon, but it's really confusing and easy to mess up. Is it cuts with a "c" or "k"? Is it "2" or "to"? Why kuts to kuts? It just doesn't

make sense. (By the way, we love the name of the hair salon in the movie, *Steel Magnolias*: "Curl Up and Dye."

Choose your company name carefully and try to find one that implies the type of work you do. Also, if possible, get help from an expert and at least test the name with friends, families, and colleagues, before you settle on it. Once your company is known as "XYZ," it's far more difficult, and expensive, to change.

How Does Your Logo Stack Up?

Your logo is your company's most recognizable symbol, a picture that conveys a thousand words. It expresses your business's culture, values, personality, and purpose, and will either say "professional" or scream "fly-by-night."

It's not just an image; it is your company's face. It should get better with age and stand for a consistent brand identity. This is why logo development is commonly viewed as one of the most difficult areas in graphic design. And while professional-looking logos are not costly, they can be very expensive to change because you may have to reorder stationery, brochures, business cards, and the like. Our advice? Hire a professional to design yours.

Here are a few web sites you can check out. Each offers a variety of affordable and professional design services.

- Filez, www.filezsite.com.ar
- Blipstudios, www.blipstudios.com/
- Retina Web Agency, www.Retina.ro

Simply put, good logos are:

- Distinctive and memorable
- Clear and legible, whether formatted large or small
- Great looking in color or black and white
- Easily integrated into stationery, business cards, web sites, etc.

In general there are five types of logos; each of the five is represented here.
1. Text plus image.

2. Text only.

3. Abbreviation plus image or full name.

4. Abbreviation only.

5. Image only.

How Does Your Letterhead and Stationery Stack Up?

Although your letterhead isn't going to make or break your business, it does emit significant positive or negative clues about it. It shows your confidence, or lack of it. Recently we've seen all kinds of innovative business cards, including mini-DVDs and brochures. While it's great to be creative, we suggest that you save these more expensive varieties for qualified prospects. Also, people in certain service companies should consider using card magnets so they're handy when needed. And don't forget, business cards have two sides—use both of them! Conversely, don't overdo by using excessively expensive or frivolous stock.

How Do Your Business Cards Stack Up?

The days of plain-vanilla business cards with just your name, address, and phone number are over. At a minimum you should use better-than-average card stock; one to two colors; and include your web site's *url* and your e-mail address(es). These are far more important than your fax number!

> *I not only use all the brains I have, but all I can borrow.*
>
> —WOODROW WILSON

Are You Easy to Do Business With?

In this section, you'll review how you interact with your customers, and assess whether your policies and systems make it more, or less, likely that prospects will do business with you.

How Does Your Guarantee Stack Up?

Let's face it, most people are hesitant to take chances, so they are often understandably nervous before purchasing products or services for the first time; handing over hard-earned money in exchange for an unknown experience or product is risky. That's why it's imperative that you remove this potential roadblock from the buying process by developing a no-questions-asked, risk-free guarantee.

Moreover, this is a wonderful way to distinguish your business from others in your industry. Begin by discovering what other companies in your industry put forward, then go one, or more, better!

For example, let's say one of your competitors offers a 30-day, no-questions-asked refund. In this case, you might want to extend yours to 60, 90, or even 365 days! We've even heard of companies that refund the full amount plus five dollars!

Important General Rule

Returns decrease as grace periods increase.

If you're dissatisfied with the amount of returned goods (or service refunds) your company is dealing with, ask yourself the following questions:

- Are you targeting the right audience? (The better the match, the higher the sales satisfaction.)

- How good is your product or service?

- Are you overselling or exaggerating? Are your buyers disappointed with reality?

- Are your return policies too rigid? If so, your customers may be nervous about falling out of the grace period and return the product before they've had an opportunity to understand its benefits.

How Do Your Payment Options Stack Up?

People often assume that partial payment plans are appropriate for larger item purchases, such as appliances, cars, and furniture. However, allowing customers to pay over time—even on low-ticket products—is a wonderful way to generate sales.

This works even better for service businesses, particularly those that send regular invoices. For instance, if you own an accounting practice, why not let your customers pay you a manageable fixed amount each month for an agreed-upon service package?

Then think of other products that add value or are natural extensions to your core offering and allow your customers to buy them directly from you and pay over an extended period of time. Also, make sure you accept all major credit cards, electronic checks, personal checks, and even cash.

How Do Your Phone Lines Stack Up?

Although busy signals are mostly a thing of the past, there are still a few strongholds who refuse to get with the times. If you're one of these folks, it's

Mary's Lesson Learned:
Make It Easy on Your Customers and Prospects

Years ago I worked for a telecom that, due to regulatory restriction, was prohibited from manufacturing or selling telephone equipment. However, we knew that our customers were more likely to buy and keep our optional network services if they used the right phone. So we partnered with another company that sold their equipment directly to our customers. Then we worked out an arrangement whereby our customers' charges were broken up into six equal payments and invoiced on their regularly monthly phone bill. This worked out well for everyone—the customer, our company, and the manufacturer.

time to get out from under that rock. There's no good reason for a busy signal. Period.

A more common experience, however, are companies that have outgrown their phone lines. As a result, callers experience such greetings as, "Dr. Smith's office. Can you hold?" Click. Or, you're still on hold after ten minutes, when someone pops on the line and says, "Are you being helped?" Click. Or, you listen to non-stop ringing until finally someone picks up the line. Or, you're responding to a company's ad that cheerfully invites you to "call for more information," but the lines are jammed and you can't get through.

You get the idea. Don't leave this type of thing to chance. Marketing is about the entire customer experience, and what we've just described does not constitute a good one.

How Do Your Phone Systems Stack Up?

Voice Response Units, also known as VRUs, and more affectionately as "voice jail," rank at the top of consumers' pet peeve lists! Yet, if used appropriately, respectfully, and politely they are valuable tools for small businesses!

They allow you to: provide the public with directions to your location and hours of operation day or night; see that calls get answered by the right person or department; conduct automatic outbound appointment reminder calls; and even help you track advertising programs. Problems arise, however, when companies use VRUs as barriers for talking to real people, so customers, prospects, and suppliers often end up going around in circles, and getting nowhere.

If you're thinking about using a VRU:

- Make sure you seek the advice of a reputable company to design, install, and maintain the system. You'll waste lots time or money if you try to do it yourself.
- A good unit can be pricey but there are many excellent companies that can design a system based on your needs. And although the outlay may seem high, a good VRU is well worth it.
- Make certain the voice is professional, conversational, and friendly. Again, seek wise counsel on this one!

- Keep the number of caller prompts to a minimum! Then, whatever you do, don't ask them to repeat information!

How Do Your Phone Numbers Stack Up?

Except in rare circumstances, we recommend that small businesses have toll-free numbers. At a minimum they are an inexpensive way to encourage prospects and customers to call and—depending on the type of business—can increase inbound sales calls by as much as 30 to 70 percent. And contrary to what you might think, it's not necessary to get a number that "spells" anything because here's what often happens: People see your phone number—1-800-BigBobs. They know they'll remember it, so they don't write it down. Then when it's time to call they think, "Now what was that number? 888BigPete; or 800HugeBob; or 877BobsBig?" So they get frustrated and call one of your competitors.

A better alternative is to get an easy-to-remember (but not that easy) numerical toll-free number. And if you absolutely insist on making your phone number spell something, be sure you include the number-only "translation" with it.

On the other hand, if your company only conducts business locally, there is no need for a toll-free number, and using one might actually hurt you since it's important that your target audience knows you are indeed local! So make sure your exchange(s)—yes, you can get more than one for different parts of towns, cities, states, etc.—and/or area codes are familiar to your prospects. Once again, this is only relevant if you do not conduct business over the internet and your target audience is not located in different regional calling areas.

How Do Your Employees' and Your Attire Stack Up?

Today's business world no longer requires compulsory dark blue suits and white shirts—whew. This doesn't mean, however, that professional, respectable, and suitable attire is not important. Far from it!

Numerous consumer studies confirm that people make judgments about a company's or person's credibility in less than ten seconds after first meeting them or visiting their web site or location. If you pass this initial test, you've made it over the first hurdle. If not, it's all over; you won't get another chance. Given this, wouldn't it make sense to do everything possible to get past this critical milestone? We think so.

Yet, countless businesses allow their employees—even those who deal directly with customers—to look, act, and dress any way they please! Now hear this: over-the-top tattoos; plunging necklines; miniscule skirts; grubby jeans; T-shirts with "Bite Me" emblazoned across the front; and purple Mohawks are perfectly suitable in certain settings and social groups, *but not your business*. This type of attire screams "I'm having fun, hanging out," not "I'm here to serve our customers."

Your employees represent you and your company—so it's up to you to have an appropriate dress policy, then ensure that everyone complies even if you have to buy uniforms. Don't laugh. This has many advantages. Not only does it remove the risk of inappropriate dress, but it provides you with another opportunity to display your company's name and logo. There are many excellent specialty ad companies that sell all kinds of attire and offer advice and design services as well.

Recently we visited a local car wash. All the employees wore simple white shirts, khaki "water" shorts, trendy baseball caps or visors, and rubber water shoes. They looked hip, comfortable, dry, fun, professional, and unified; we were impressed.

Please note: We are not suggesting that you spend lots of money on elaborate costuming and you can choose to pay all, some, or none of the costs.

Obviously this is a far less important consideration for those of you who rarely come into direct contact with your prospects or customers. We love working at home in sweatpants and old T-shirts.

How Does Your Employees' Enthusiasm Stack Up?

Enthusiasm and zest are contagious. If it starts with you, it will positively infect your employees, suppliers, and customers! This may sound hokey, but it's true. Even if you have to "fake it 'til you make it" (smile, sound excited, and

David's
Lesson Learned:
Dress
for Success

I have an acquaintance, Frank, who owns a real estate company. One day I dropped by his office to ask him a question. I was curious: I had recently heard that he purchased a paneled truck that he lent out to customers to help with their move. I was impressed with his innovative marketing tactic and wanted to know how it was working for him.

Upon entering his office I was greeted by his receptionist—a young woman with purple hair who was dressed in a low-cut shirt that didn't cover her belly button, jeans, and earrings everywhere possible. Even worse, when I told her who I was and why I was there, it took her five minutes to figure out that Frank was in a meeting.

So I left and decided to call him back another day. When I finally talked to Frank I commented on his receptionist's lack of professionalism and suggested that he consider how it might be affecting his business.

His reply? "Thanks, Dave, I appreciate you taking the time to let me know that. I value your opinion. And I must admit, we have had many complaints about her, but do you know how hard it is to find good help?" Here was a guy who went out of his way to offer extra value (the truck) to his customers but undid those efforts by ignoring the negative impression his employee left on them.

listen carefully to others), adding a childlike (not childish—there's a big difference) dose of excitement and wonder is always engaging. This is your opportunity to display the passion you feel for your company. By the way, if you have none, you may want to consider a career change. If not, it will show in your attitude toward customers, employees, suppliers, friends, and family, pushing you ever closer to burn-out and extinction. There is nothing more depressing than being around an unhappy person.

How Do Your Hiring Policies Stack Up?

Do you have the right people on the bus, or just warm bodies?

Although human resources is by no means our area of expertise we do want you to consider how important it is to hire employees who are assets to your business. Accomplishing this begins early in the hiring process. If you attract, recruit, and employ people who have the right skills, attitudes, and demeanors, you'll save a great deal of time and money in the long run. This is even more important if you're a service company because customer contact personnel can literally make or break your business. That's why it's important *not* to mistake least cost for *best* cost when it comes to hiring your employees. Unfortunately, many businesspeople believe that they'd be foolish to pay any employee one cent more than they're be willing to accept—but this is not necessarily true.

If you're smart, you'll think this through carefully and do some research. First, consider the potential effect these employees have on your customers and prospects. Obviously, the more direct contact they have, the greater the impact.

Second, take a close look at what you're offering, for example, wages, opportunities for advancement, training and education, health care benefits, and schedule flexibility. Then ask yourself if your policies are hurting or helping you find model employees. If you're hiring less-than-desirable personnel, something is wrong.

Doesn't it make sense to provide a better-than-average incentive to attract like-minded folks? You don't want them working for your competitors, do you?

Even a $1-an-hour wage increase will significantly increase the available pool of potential employees, which means that you'll have an easier time finding exceptional candidates. And in the end, you'll come out ahead financially and culturally because you'll have fewer customer complaints; less employee turnover; reduced churn; and the like. This is also another wonderful way to distinguish your company from others.

All business owners must have written policies and procedures (an employee manual) that clearly sets standards, describes processes, and outlines important procedures. The internet has lots of resources for small business owners who need help developing policies and manuals. We've included quite a few in the Appendix and you can visit our web site: www.StrategicMarketing Advisors.com for more.

How Does Your Customer Service Charter Stack Up?

It is unlikely that your employees will arrive with all the skills they need to help you become a world-class business. That's why you must assess each new employee's abilities and provide the tools and training necessary to make them succeed.

Begin by asking yourself the following questions: Are all my employees aware of my philosophies and goals? Do they know how they are accountable for making them happen? How do I measure their performance? What are my policies for employees who do not demonstrate the needed behaviors?

Do not leave this to chance! Draft a detailed "Customer Service Charter" that includes the following:

- *Mission and vision statements* (see Chapter 6).
- *Specific, measurable customer service standards*. For example, how many times the telephone will be permitted to ring until the call gets answered.
- *Customer expectations and how to meet them*. Remember this important rule about customer service: It is not so much the failure to meet standards that causes major dissatisfaction among customers; we all make mistakes. Rather, most customers become upset because they lack critical information early on; received no apology or explanation when things go wrong; or their issues are not resolved.
- *Systems and processes for measuring*. Your standards must be measurable and you should continue to assess your performance against your benchmarks and communicate the results, internally and externally.
- *Handling customer complaints*. Encourage customers to complain! Why? Because customer grievances are your company's barometer. They tell you how you're doing. Additionally, a recent consumer survey concluded that only one out of ten people voices their dissatisfaction to company representatives, yet will share their experience with at least one or two friends or family members.

That's why it's imperative to capture these complaints so you can offer your sincere apologies, reduce the likelihood that your customers will complain to others, take appropriate corrective action to prevent reoccurrence, and monitor your performance.

How Do Your Employee Training Tools Stack Up?

Successful entrepreneurs understand the importance of weekly sales and service training. It is one of the most impactful and least expensive ways to differentiate your company from the rest. Why? Because few businesses do it, even though it is effective and free!

Additionally, it provides a wonderful opportunity to reinforce your business's cultural values, introduce new products or services, reiterate your commitment to customers, address employee issues and concerns and keep them up-to-date on sales and promotions.

This is especially important if you have employees in multiple locations. If so, consider using technology to your advantage and sign up for a conference calling service. They're extremely affordable and have lots of great value-added features. You can record and download calls, integrate PowerPoint demonstrations, and even add video. They're a wonderful alternative to face-to-face meetings. A good one to check out is at www.MyAccuConfer ence.com.

How Do Your Greetings Stack Up?

Believe us, consumers know when they are, and aren't, being treated well. And the way you say "hello" and "good-bye," whether in person or on the phone, is an extremely telling indication of how much you value them.

If we had to list the ten biggest tactical errors companies make, poor telephone manners would be right there at the top. Happily, it's one of the easiest to fix, so pay close attention, and we'll tell you how to ensure a pleasant phone experience for your customers.

PUT ON A HAPPY FACE

Anyone (including you) who greets the public in-person or answers the phone must smile! Sound corny? Maybe so, but research studies repeatedly confirm that a smile can be "seen" over the phone. If you don't believe us, test it yourself. You will be amazed at the results! It costs nothing and makes such a huge impact! Also, it's a wonderful idea to develop a unique, scripted greeting that everyone can use. This is another no-cost, yet extremely effective, way of setting your business apart from others. For instance, you may incorporate a humorous twist from your tag line like this, *"Thanks for calling Joe's Tire Company, where everyone's full of hot air! My name is, John, how can I help you?"*

We've used iterations of the following greeting and received great reactions: *"Hi, my name is Mary and we're having a great day at XYZ Company, how can I help you have one too?"* A little hokey perhaps, but pleasantly memorable all the same. Recently I called a hair salon and got this message: "Thank you for calling _____, we are busy at the moment, please call back later." This is a great example of what not to do.

Cover Your Voice Mail Basics
Make sure that your voice mail greeting:

- Is short, but pleasant (remember, smile!)
- Tells the caller whether you're on another line, away from your desk, or closed. It's a good idea to change your greeting every day so callers' expectations are managed. For instance, you can begin your greeting with, "Hi, this is David and today is Monday, January 1st. I'll be in meetings all morning, with little opportunity to return calls. However, I will be back in my office by 2 P.M. and will return your call shortly thereafter. If your call is urgent, please call my assistant, Claudia Perkins, at XXX-XXX-XXXX."
- Directs callers to an after-hours hot line for emergencies, if necessary.
- Tells the caller when you'll call back. No customer should wait more than 24 hours—and less is preferable—for a return call. If this isn't possible, find the cause of the problem and fix it.

Also, don't skimp on quality when it comes to your phone systems! Both network service messaging products and/or equipment are inexpensive enough that you no longer have to choose price over quality. There's no reason to exasperate callers with garbled greetings or premature disconnects. In addition to being annoying, it's a good way to make sure you never hear from them again.

Use Scripts

These are particularly important for companies that receive (inbound calls) or make (outbound) lots of phone calls. Consumer studies confirm that companies that use well-thought-out and delivered employee scripts have fewer customer complaints and better-than-average phone sales.

If it's important that something is said correctly—and it almost always is—then don't leave it to chance. Provide your contact personnel with the right words—they'll thank you, and so will your customers.

Place Customers On Hold Infrequently and Respectfully

First, try not to put your prospects and customers on hold, either before or during a call. Also, your callers will appreciate it if your phones are answered by real people. However, if you must place people on hold the following will help:

- *Warn them.* Ask your calls if they're comfortable being placed on hold and tell them what to expect (what they'll hear while on hold—music, talking, or silence), what you'll be doing while they're on hold, and how long it will take.
- *Select your own on-hold music.* Avoid using radio music or talk programs because you'll lose control of the content and even risk airing a competitor's commercial. Use on hold time to relay important information such as new products or services, promotions and sales, and your web site address.
- *Play soothing music.* Studies suggest that many people are calmed by certain music, particularly classical. Check out Baroque-era musical CDs.

 ## Avoid the "Sound of Silence"

In this excerpt from a weekly newsletter that the Guerrilla Marketing Association sends to its subscribers Jay and Amy Levinson explain how important utilizing today's technology can be:

> A typical business receives as many as 100 calls a day and puts callers on hold for over 17 hours each month. A whopping 70 percent of calls are placed on hold for an average of 90 seconds. A depressingly large 90 percent of callers

hang up within 40 seconds if "on hold" means dead silence. And 34 percent of those never call back.

On-hold marketing reduces hang-ups by 77 percent because instead of silence, callers hear marketing messages. It increases telephone on-hold time as much as 230 percent. A full 88 percent of callers say they prefer an on-hold message to music or silence. Best of all, 19 percent of callers buy something when they hear a powerful marketing message while on hold.

Your most unhappy customers are your greatest source of learning.

—BILL GATES

How Does Your Philosophy Stack Up?

Have you adopted a giver-versus-taker mindset? If so, how do you demonstrate it? As we discussed

David's Lesson Learned: Offer a Great Product, then Go One Better

There are two, very similar, apartment complexes located in a large U.S. city. Almost identical in age, size, and design, they are located in the same neighborhood and comparably priced.

The manager of "Building A" was therefore peeved that his complex was never more than 70 percent occupied, while "Building B" enjoyed an occupancy rate of 100 percent, and a lengthy waiting list, to boot! So, she did a smart thing and hired a consultant to look into the matter.

After conducting and analyzing a survey of residents and prospects, her advisor uncovered only one seemingly small, but significant, reason for the difference: Building B provided a free weekly car wash for each resident. This is a wonderful example of how a good product, plus one, can make all the difference in the world! *Can Building B justify the expenses associated with the car washes?* You bet!

earlier in this book, it is important to develop a culture that improves every-one's chances of achieving their personal and professional goals. Some industry experts even maintain that a business's internal environment is the single most important factor in determining its success.

This is a logical theory. New ideas, innovative solutions, and creative concepts are the seeds that begin growing and develop into strong trees—but only if they're nourished. Without sustenance—water, sunshine, and air—they'll die. So it is with stagnant cultures, they do not provide an environment where the seeds of success can flourish. The analogy may be trite and the concept rather simple, but its effect is profound.

One of the most important philosophical principles in creating a healthy culture is the founders' and employees' firm conviction that no matter what type of business or organization they're in—service, manufacturing, retailing, wholesaling, nonprofits, educational institutions, etc.—they are there to serve.

Everyone in your company must embrace this tenet and develop a giver (versus taker) mindset, one focused on solving customers' problems, adding value, and going the extra mile.

How Does Your "Oops" Policy Stack Up?

It's fairly easy to deal with customers as long as everything's hunky-dory, but what do you do when something goes wrong? Are your employees empowered to do whatever it takes to make things right? Or do you make your customers suffer through a lengthy return process?

We believe that every business has a defining moment—that snippet of time when a customer decides whether they'll stay or go. And that split second often occurs when things go wrong.

Developing error-handling guidelines that work well for all concerned can be complicated. Entrepreneurs may feel torn between balancing the needs of the business and satisfying their unhappy customers. So, we'll make this simple with a very straightforward policy that you can, and should, enact immediately:

Every employee must strive to do whatever it takes to thrill your customers and ensure that each and every one of their experiences with your company is delightful 100 percent of the time. Should you fall short of that goal, you will work just as hard to right every wrong, no matter how small.

You'll notice that there isn't a word in this policy about whether the customer is right or wrong, because it doesn't matter. Additionally, you should go out of your way to reward employees who go out of their way to make this happen. Develop and encourage an automatic "Yes I can help you with that" mindset!

Although this is one of the most effective and least expensive policies to enact, many entrepreneurs (and CEOs of large companies) intentionally place huge hurdles directly in the paths of employees who try to "make it right" for customers.

Why? Here's a variation on the answer we usually receive:

I'd be dumb to give my employees any power! I don't allow them to issue credits or approve returns. Trust me, they'd give away the farm and I'd end up broke.

Please understand that this couldn't be further from the truth! As a matter of fact, many experts point to an increase in revenues and profits for companies that adopt and apply this policy.

How Do Your Hours and Days of Operation Stack Up?

Simply put, your target audience expects you to be available when it's convenient for them, not you. So, while we're not advising you to stay open 24/7, we do suggest the following:

- *Conduct a survey of your current customers.* Get their opinions on what days and hours work best for them and schedule yours accordingly.
- *Find out what other successful companies in your industry are doing and use that information to help you plan.* This is especially important for new companies without a large customer base.
- *Make sure that you keep the lines of communication open in some way at all times.* Again, given today's affordable technology, there is simply no reason for anyone to reach a dead end, regardless of the hour or day. This is particularly important for service businesses—physician practices, accountants, utility companies, and the like. You should at least have a

voice messaging system (and, as appropriate, instructions for emergencies), a web site with a search function, e-mail capabilities, and 24-hour fax availability. Depending on your industry you should also consider a 24-hour answering service, hotline, or paging system. Or go one better and install an automated phone or web-based system; (for example, one that allows customers to pay their bills over the phone or make inquiries about their account); after-hours real-person support; or on-call emergency help.

> *You can make more friends in two months by becoming interested in other people than you can in two years by trying to get other people interested in you.*
>
> —DALE CARNEGIE

Remember, consumers now have access to businesses like yours, nationally and internationally, via the internet. There is an ever-increasing population of folks who use the World Wide Web to shop, manage their accounts, and gather information. Put yourself where people are going, and make it easy for consumers to do business with you.

How Does Your After-Sale Contact Stack Up?

Researchers estimate that 68 percent of lost business is due to lack of contact after a sale. Making post-sale communication a vital ingredient of your marketing program suddenly becomes financially imperative when you consider that figure. It costs little and will have a significantly positive effect on your business.

Try this: Thank each new customer by calling them or sending a personal thank-you note or card—no form letters or canned voice messages allowed! And, *do not* try to sell them anything!

After a few weeks, call or write again. This time reiterate how much you value their business and ask for suggestions on ways to improve your products or services. Include information on others that may prove helpful to them based on their previous contact with your company.

After six months, mail your customers a survey and include an incentive for completing it. Then, in nine months, send them information on other businesses that have products or services they may be interested in, and then a thank-you card on their one-year anniversary.

If you have any doubts whether this is worthwhile, please pay close attention to the following formula developed by marketing researchers:

Each time you follow up with one customer—returning a call quickly; contacting them to make sure they're happy with their newly-purchased product or service; sending out requested materials quickly—on average, that person will recommend you to 15 other people.

Four of those will become your customers. Moreover, the recommender will buy from you two times more than an average customer and remain with you at least a year longer!

Do the math with simple numbers suitable for your business. You may be surprised by how it adds up!

Presentation/Location

Have you ever wondered how much more business a roadside gas station would get if they adopted, communicated, and delivered this USP (unique selling proposition, remember?)—"We guarantee that our bathrooms are always spotless"? What does cleanliness have to do with marketing? Lots. How you care for your environment says a great deal about how you care for your customers.

How Does Your Environment Stack Up?

Remember the example of the financial advisor with the messy desk that we used in Chapter 1? The one who couldn't figure out what his unkempt office had to do with monetary counseling, even though he was losing qualified prospects?

Take a minute to look around your location and answer the following questions as appropriate for your situation:

- Is there too much or too little space?
- Have you made the best use of your space?

- Is your reception area well-designed and inviting? Is it well-lit?
- Is your web site (yes, your web site can be your "location") professional looking and easy to navigate?
- Is the décor pleasing and up-to-date?
- Is your environment clean? Are your furniture and shelves dust-free? Are your windows spotless? Are your floors shiny? Are your rugs vacuumed?
- Are your product shelves well-stocked or lonely?
- How about the front door? Does it say "Welcome!" or "Go Away!"?
- Is parking a problem? If so, what are you doing to make it better? Do you warn people ahead of time?
- Do your window displays convey your sense of style, creativity, and attention to detail?
- Does your indoor signage reinforce your audience's decision to buy? Do they provide helpful information and encourage add-on sales?
- Are your outdoor signs easy to read from a distance? Are they eye-catching and inviting? Are they consistent with your company's personality and image?

Are Your Products and Services Up to Snuff?

Now it's time to take a look at your products and service offerings and assess how they're impacting your business.

How Does Your Product Selection Stack Up?

In the same consumer study discussed earlier in this chapter (the one which involved 10,000+ respondents) product or service selection ranked as the fourth most important consideration consumers used when deciding to buy from one company versus another. (By the way, price was not in the top five!)

The goal is to offer enough variety to meet your target markets needs without overdoing it by offering too many things to too many people. Stay focused on what your prospects and customers want—the "niche-ier" the better—and resist the urge to please the masses. It will wear you out, dilute your efforts, and empty your wallet.

How Does Your Quality Stack Up?

If you're in business today, quality is the price of admission. In the same study mentioned above, respondents said quality was the second most important variable that consumers used when selecting companies or products. Unfortunately, however, the word is so overused in today's marketplace that it's become trite and meaningless. Take a look around and count the businesses that use it in their tag lines and ad copy.

What is quality? It's a complex question and the subject of many books and articles. And while it's not appropriate to dissect it here, it is important that you ask others for their definition, especially as it relates to your products and services.

Again, do not underestimate how essential this is! Assuming other elements are similar, consumers will overwhelmingly choose the higher-quality product.

Moreover, as you work to evaluate your company's commitment to quality, keep in mind that it has far less to do with what you put into your products and much more to do with what others get out of them.

Special Consideration for Service Professionals

As we've said before, all companies, regardless of industry, are in business to serve and the marketing approach is fundamentally identical. However, based on the nature of the economic exchange, it is important that service professionals understand that they do face some unique challenges, and then learn ways to overcome them effectively.

Here's why: Clients pay service providers for activities that do not result in ownership. For example, you can't wrap a coaching session in a gift box and take it home, like a blouse or a box of chocolate. Rather, service providers help to promote positive changes in their customers' lives (i.e., guide them toward more physical possessions or intangible assets) by dispensing such things as advice, labor, representation, and information—and then tell their customers when it's been delivered successfully.

In our opinion, the following are the major differences between a packaged-goods company and a service business.

The Heightened Importance of
Service of Contact Personnel

Employees such as customer care representatives, office receptionists, ticket counter clerks, telephone operators, administrative assistants, schedulers, nurses, tellers, and technicians can directly enhance or hurt your business. If your target audience views them as helpful, friendly, and knowledgeable they're one of your biggest assets. If not, you'll lose qualified prospects and valuable customers who will leave without saying a word.

This is such a significant consideration, that if we had to give only one piece of advice to a service professional it would be this: Take a long, hard look at your employees. They are the tangible representations of your values, professionalism, expertise, and beliefs, and if you have even one that doesn't demonstrate your philosophies make the necessary changes or accept that your business has a hitch in its giddy-up. And please understand that we're not suggesting you go on a firing spree. Often, employees miss the mark because they're not certain "how" to behave. That's why it's imperative that you have clearly written guidelines and ongoing customer care training.

Service Professionals Receive Promotional Help

Intermediaries such as manufacturers and wholesalers often play a big role in promoting products to a target audience. This is not the case, however, for service providers. For example, Anheuser-Busch runs promotional specials for products such as Budweiser Lite. In addition to a national ad campaign they send their retailers—places like your neighborhood beer and wine store—signage, floor and counter displays, and literature. Consumers get a deal and their stores sales increase—at least that's the idea.

This is less common in the service world, even though some companies such as travel agencies, airlines, and financial franchisees, do benefit from intermediary help and must compete with other firms and brands in their industry.

This means that a service provider must rely more on tactics such as face-to-face direct sales; effective public relations; informational web sites; free consultations and information; and motivational promotions.

If you're a service professional, we strongly suggest that you assess your own strengths and weaknesses by keeping a journal of your personal consumer experiences. Since a great many of your clients' evaluations are more subjective it's important to take note of how your own consumer experiences affect how you feel and how you react as a result, so you can improve your "bedside manner."

Mary's Lesson Learned:

Marketer: Heed Thyself!

When I was in graduate school, I enrolled in a course titled "Services Marketing." Among other things, my professor required that we students document three positive or negative customer experiences we had each week and answer the following questions:

1. What happened?
2. How did this make you feel?
3a. What should they have done to make your experience better?

or

3b. What did they do that exceeded your expectations?

At first, this exercise was merely another item on my to-do list, but it wasn't long before I counted it among my most valuable learning tools and continue to use it today. I recently pulled out my university journal and here's one of my entries:

What Happened?

This week my boss asked me to buy some "trinkets" (specialty ad products) to give away at an upcoming trade show. And, as luck would have it,
I remembered receiving a catalog from a local company and decided to
give them a try. I found the letter and was impressed. Their ad was pro-
fessionally-designed, and the copy was well written. I was relieved to learn
that the company was close by, hauled out my corporate credit card, and
gave them a call.

I got a busy signal the first two times so figured I had dialed the wrong
number. After double-checking, I redialed. This time "robot man" (or so it
seemed) answered with, "Hi, you've reached Company X. We're not here
now but you know the drill. Leave a message and we'll call you back."

How Did this Make You Feel?

Not good. I felt:

- *Annoyed.* I had to dial their number three times before I even got
  through to their voice mail system.
- *Disappointed.* Their advertisement had created a picture in my
  mind of a professional company dedicated to delivering quality
  products and superior customer service. Obviously they hadn't
  made the connection between customer care and answering their
  phones!
- *Confused.* Why on earth would any business owner spend the time
  and effort involved in creating a first-rate marketing piece only to
  blow it when a potential customer shows interest? It boggles the
  mind.

What Should They Have Done to Make the Experience Better?

Answered their phones. Added more lines. And at a minimum, changed
their voice mail greeting to something like: "Hi! Thanks for calling Company X. Your call is important to us and, although we strive to answer
every call personally, occasionally all of our consultants are busy helping

other customers. However, please leave your name and number after the tone and we will return your call today. We understand that you have many choices, so we're pleased that you decided to give us a try."

The most important take away from this simple exercise is what I did, due to these seemingly small lapses in Company X's customer service. Because I needed the items quickly and didn't want to disappoint my boss, I took our business elsewhere. I was just too nervous about their ability to deliver what they promised in their catalog.

The Bottom Line

Company X wasted money.

Company X lost a sale.

Company X lost a referral.

Company X gained a detractor.

Company X lost profits.

Company X missed the opportunity to get a new customer.

Company X missed their chance for a repeat purchase.

Moral of the story? Never underestimate the power of your own consumer experiences. Whenever you deal with a business ask yourself these questions: How did this experience make me feel? What could, or should, they have done to make it better? or Why was this such a pleasant experience?

Chapter 10 Snapshot

Before moving on to Chapter 11, let's take time to review several of the most important take-aways from this chapter:

- Your logo is your company's most recognizable symbol, a picture that conveys a thousand words about your business's values and personality.

- Offering a no-questions-asked, risk-free guarantee is one of the most effective tools for building solid customer relationships.

- You have less than ten seconds to make a good first impression. Don't leave it to chance.

- Don't underestimate the power of such things as your employees' dress and demeanor, your hours and days of operation, your location and environment, and the way you greet customers in person and over the phone.

- Use your own consumer experiences to gain valuable insights into your service mindset and delivery.

We cannot solve our problems with the same
level of thinking that created them.

—ALBERT EINSTEIN

STEP 7

Selecting Your Communication Tactics

Now that you've attended to your first-things-first essentials, you're ready to choose your communication tools—the vehicles you'll use to contact your target audience and invite them to do business with your company. Also, your reasonable forecasts will serve as relevant backup for achieving your business objectives.

> *Take time to deliberate; but when the time for action arrives, stop thinking and go in.*
>
> —ANDREW JACKSON

Our aim is to jump-start your thinking by presenting a brief, but solid, summary on a variety of tactical

alternatives such as advertising, public relations, acquisition, and retention programs (we lumped a lot of things into this category!), and online marketing techniques. We selected our favorites, the ones we feel are most appropriate for
smaller businesses. Neither time, nor space, allows us to offer more than a brief
glimpse at the many options you have available.

Then we'll guide you through:
1. Working with an advertising agency
2. Creating an ad brief
3. Developing your marketing budget
4. Choosing the right communications vehicles

You'll also find a quick tips guide containing "sound bytes" of information
on specific tactics, including those that are free, low-cost, or pricey. You'll use
this as a checklist for choosing your own. After that, we'll offer you advice on
developing your marketing budget and making sure that you've chosen your
sales channels wisely.

Advertising Overview

Advertising is simply a way to make something known to the public. Kind of
an announcement, it strives to call attention to and arouse public interest in
the desirable qualities of a product, service, or company.

There are two basic types of advertising: *traditional* (also known as institutional or branded) and *direct response*. Entire text books, college courses, and seminars are devoted to an in-depth coverage of the types and purposes of each. That
is not what you'll find in this chapter. Rather, we'll hit the highlights, give you
enough information to guide your selection process, and then provide references
for those of you who would like more information. Additionally, because our target audience is primarily small-business owners, we will pare the subject matter
down even further and limit our discussion to direct response advertising.

We've chosen to do this for one major reason. That is, traditional advertising, which aims at reinforcing a brand's image or creating a positive spin, is
expensive and difficult to measure, which means it's a waste of time and money
for smaller companies. We believe that there are only two exceptions to this

rule of thumb. First, when you've completely saturated a particular market—you've done so well that you've exhaused all growth opportunites—it's a good idea to remind people that you're still around with a well-placed ad, sign, or commercial. However, if you're communicating on a regular basis with your customer base—as you should be—this isn't even necessary.

Second, it's important to support your local and regional communities and charities, so we strongly recommend that you participate in selected grass-roots events and organizations.

Direct Response Advertising

We like to think of direct response advertising as an invitation, one where a company asks its targeted audience—whether they're its products' end users, resellers, or other businesses—to do something in clear and direct language. And, although the ultimate goal is profitable sales, the initial actions requested vary widely and can include: phone calls, web site visits, e-book downloads, course enrollments, location visits, online orders, and appointment scheduling.

You'll notice that we didn't say that your direct response communication should ask for an immediate sale. This is an important distinction, because one of the biggest mistakes that entrepreneurs make is asking for a sale before their prospects have sufficient time to get to know and trust them. Remember, superior marketing involves building healthy relationships, and these take time to grow. People like to buy, but they don't want to be sold. So, your job is to provide your target audience with relevant information and encourage them to take you up on your invitation. Just don't jam it down their throats!

All of your marketing communication should be aimed at engendering trust in you, your company, and the products and services you offer. This has to occur before your prospects will feel comfortable purchasing from you.

 Marketing Is a Lot Like Dating

Mitch Meyerson, my co-author of *Mastering Online Marketing*, came up with a very apt analogy for illustrating this concept. He says, "You know the relationship building process can take months, even years to develop. *It reminds me of dating."* Bingo! Imagine this: You've just met a very nice person, one who has asked you out on a first date. Since you like the person and are quite interested, you gladly say "yes," and off you go to dinner at a lovely restaurant. As you enter, you look into his or her eyes and are immediately glad you've accepted the invitation. However, just after you sit down at your table your date says, "Will you marry me?" If you're like most people, you scream, 'Whhaatt?' then get up from the table, and run as fast as you can in the opposite direction!

This is the same reaction your target audience will have when they're pushed into a sale instead of a long-term relationship.

Whether your goal is to gain more awareness of your brick-and-mortar business, drive traffic to your web site, or increase calls to your center, choose your marketing tactics carefully. And remember, this is not a one-shot deal, so you must adopt a long-term perspective.

Consider this:

- 63 percent of interested prospects take more than three months to become customers;
- 35 percent of interested prospects take six months to more than one year to become customers;

and

- 73 percent of salespeople give up after one or two contacts;
- 90 percent of leads never get followed up after four times.

The Bottom Line
Patience, tenacity, and commitment win this race.

Direct Response Communication Elements
Ideally, the message contained in direct response communication is a straightforward and honest dialogue between a company and its prospects and contains the following basic elements:

- Strong, benefit-laden headline;
- A description of the target audience's most pressing problem;
- The company's solution to that problem;
- The products or services being offered;
- The top three to five product and/or service benefits;
- The advantages of choosing this company over all others;
- Why the target audience should hurry to take advantage of the invitation;
- Pricing information, promotional discounts, and payment policies and methods;
- Multiple options for contacting the company—phone and fax numbers; e-mail and web site addresses; and mailing address;
- Testimonials from other happy customers;
- Directions for next steps, specifically, the action that need to be performed;
- The company's request for their prospects to "act" in one or more specific ways—calling, e-mailing, faxing, visiting their location, etc.;
- Specific directions for completing the desired action;
- Risk-reverse, unconditional guarantee.

> *Advertising is the principal reason why the business man has come to inherit the earth.*
>
> —JAMES RANDOLPH ADAMS

Public Relations (PR) Overview

There are two ways to have your company's information show up in the media: pay to advertise or let the press do it for you. The latter occurs as a direct result of public relations (PR) efforts—actively seeking publicity as a form of marketing communications.

While each of these is valuable, a solid news story can give you a higher ranking on the credibility ladder. *Why?* Because people understand that an ad placed by you is going to be skewed in your favor, at best, and recent consumer studies confirm that most consumers think that advertisements include outright lies and/or misleading information.

> *I'm not doing my philanthropic work out of any kind of guilt, or any need to create good public relations. I'm doing it because I can afford to do it, and I believe in it.*
>
> —GEORGE SOROS

Stories by others, however, are viewed as more objective and thus more believable, (especially if the author has no stake in your company's success or failure).

It's important to understand how this process works, so you'll be able to take advantage of newsworthy opportunities that come your way.

Most newspapers and other media outlets, such as TV and radio, have designated employees, usually called assignment editors, who are responsible for deciding what's news and what isn't. The stories that make their cut are sent to other editors for follow-up and inclusions. Unfortunately, the vast majority, up to 90 percent, end in the rubbish.

This is why it's so important to get it right if you expect to compete with the hundreds of others vying for the same space. Send press releases to all media in your area, no matter how small. If you're an inexperienced writer it pays to hire a professional who knows how to get the media's attention. Web sites like www.elance.com or www.craigslist.com are excellent resources for locating affordable freelancers. It's much easier to get local, rather than regional or national, coverage.

Another great idea is to contact journalists in your town or city and offer yourself as an expert in a particular field, someone they can count on to provide them with accurate and objective information on the subject.

Acquisition and Retention Programs

Programs, or formalized processes, are among the easiest, least expensive, most effective, and yet greatly overlooked methods for getting and keeping customers. And since smart entrepreneurs are always searching for new ways to attract more prospects and turn them into valuable customers, they should be an integral component of your marketing communications plan; the following are some of the most popular methods.

Referral Programs

In the early days of a business, advertising is almost always necessary. After all, the public has to know your company exists. But over time—if you're doing things right—most of your business should come from positive word-of-mouth referrals.

That's why our number-one program choice for all small businesses is referrals, which involves asking your customers—current and past—to recommend your company to others who might benefit from using your goods or services. Think of it this way: your happy customers are already recommending you to family and friends. They appreciate the value of your products and services, so they naturally refer you to their family and friends, when the subject arises or when asked. Let's say you get two new customers every week due to passive referrals. How many more might you get if you instituted a program where you regularly and consistently asked for them? If you do the math, you'll soon realize what dramatic effects small increases can make—even better, they will be immediate.

Remember, it all begins with your philosophies and attitudes. If you respect yourself, your employees, and customers, and admire the value your products/service brings, it is vitally important that others enjoy the privilege of becoming your customer! *Why on earth would you want any other company to serve your target market when you do it best?* When you truly believe this, asking for referrals will become much easier.

However, you must be committed to instituting an ongoing, almost automatic, referral system(s) in order to achieve maximum benefits. After all, you cannot expect your customers to be responsible for remembering to mention your company in every appropriate situation. Your job is to come up with a way to program them so they spontaneously offer to others as long as you do not do this in an overly self-serving way. Here are some other ideas for getting new customers (please also refer to Figure 11.1: Communications Vehicle Reference Table, for more tips on many of these tactics):

- *Bartering.* Try some of the bartering and exchange clubs in the United States and around the world. Simply go to Google, Yahoo!, or MSN and type the words "bartering" or "exchange clubs" into their search fields.
- *Participation.* A successful business owner understands the importance of building and preserving good relationships. Therefore, the more you're involved in your community, the more they'll be involved with you!
- *Causes/affinity groups.* Consumers will buy from a particular company if they know that by doing so, they are contributing to a worthy cause that interests them.
- *Fusion marketing.* This is a new phrase for an old idea—two companies become marketing partners by sharing expenses and, often, rewards.
- *Free services and samples.* These are easy for prospects to agree to. They imply that the company offering the information or products is confident. There will be no pressure or obligation to purchase and the customer is likely to gain valuable benefits.
- *Free samples.* For new products and services, this is a particularly effective tactic.
- *Advertising specialties.* A gift is a great method for promoting your business and can be used in many different ways. The best ones include your business logo, name, and contact information (and for business-to-business sales, the names and logos of past and present comapnies as appropriate).
- *Columns.* Write a regular column for suitable publications. Offer to write it for free if they agree to include your contact information.
- *Articles.* If you don't have time for a regular column, write an article (again, free, as long as they include your business name and contact information).
- *Special events.* These attract publicity and prospects. Special events are activities that can be arranged and presented with other companies and marketing partners.
- *Trade shows.* Trade shows provide you with a wonderful opportunity to talk directly to interested and inquisitive prospects, and when used effectively can dramatically decrease the sales cycle.

Customer Retention Programs

As we've said before, if you're serious about growing and sustaining a profitable business you'll need to do more than focus on getting new customers. One of the most effective ways to ensure that your business continues to flourish is to communicate regularly and often with your existing customers.

The list below contains several superb communication tools aimed at helping you retain your current valuable customer base. (Please also refer to Figure 11.1: Communications Vehicle Reference Table for more tips on many of these tactics.)

- *Welcome letters/package.* Welcome new customers in a sincere way and provide information and instructions they need.
- *No-selling call, letter, thank-you, or survey.* Offer sincere thanks for your customers' loyalty and ask for their opinions on such things as new product offerings and service standards.
- *Safety net (oops!) letter.* When things don't go as planned, turn lemons into lemonade.
- *Newsletters.* This is a great opportunity to follow up, provide relevant information, and regularly stay in touch with your customers.
- *Party/event hosting.* Invite prospects, customers, and members of your community to join you in celebrating something—the weather, your latest product, or a new location. The reason is less important than the event itself. Make sure you schedule it so it's convenient for your attendees and provide refreshments (food is a must) and fun or interesting activities.
- *Networking.* Networking has had a bad rap in recent years because it brings to mind someone with a Scotch in one hand and a stack of business cards in the other, "working" a room full of unsuspecting prospects. However, making genuine connections with like-minded people is one of the most effective and gratifying ways to develop your business. No one says this better than Keith Ferrazzi, author of the best seller, *Never Eat Alone* (Currency, 2005). He's masterfully tackled a subject that no one, since Dale Carnegie, has presented so eloquently. He's also got great networking advice on his web site: www.NeverEat Alone.com.

Online Marketing Overview

Years ago, many businesspeople felt that the most important dynamic in deter-mining a small business's—particularly a retailer's—chance for succeeding was, "Location, location, location." And even though there are many more factors today, there is one location that is a requirement: the internet.

Every business and organization, regardless of size or industry, must have a web site. Period. Web sites are no longer "nice-to-haves." They are "must-haves."

And given all the affordable (some even free), available, and user-friendly development software, web-based programs and templates, there is simply no reason why any company should be without one.

The internet is here to stay and there's never been a better time to take advantage of the far-reaching opportunities that the World Wide Web offers. It is a powerful tool that can help you achieve your business goals and:

- Expand your product and service offerings;
- Create multiple streams of income;
- Share information and ideas with like-minded people regardless of geo-graphical boundaries;
- Exponentially increase your pool of qualified prospects;
- Gain more awareness of your company's products and services;
- Sell supplemental products to existing customers;
- Stay in touch with customers and prospects automatically;
- Interact, real-time, with suppliers, employees, customers, and prospects;
- Keep your finger on the pulse of your target market's concerns, worries, needs, and wants;
- Establish yourself as a subject-matter expert;
- Systematize your business processes;
- Track and manage sales data;
- Conduct research on your industry, target market, strategies, tactics, and much more.

It doesn't matter if your goal is to transform your brick-and-mortar com-pany into a thriving e-commerce business, drive prospects to your location, inform and educate your customers, or anything in between, you need to take advantage of the incredible benefits that the internet affords.

As with all opportunities, however, there are also responsibilities. Nowadays online marketers must do their homework if they want to cut through the clutter and hype; that is, apply sound marketing strategies, use state-of-the-art software and technology to save time and money, and learn effective techniques for attracting qualified web site visitors and converting them to online or offline customers.

Many entrepreneurs mistakenly rush into action and build a web site without giving it sufficient thought, time, or planning. Even worse, once it's up and running, it's ignored completely—even if its purpose is to generate revenue!

Unfortunately, we have only enough space in this book to provide you with a very high-level overview of several online marketing tactics. However, we strongly advise you to get knowledgeable experts to guide the development of your web site and suggest that you, at least, obtain a working knowledge of the types of web sites available, innovative Web 2.0 technologies and culture, web-based automation systems, affordable and free software, and design templates.

Given the ever-growing numbers of online consumers and broadband users, the internet is an incredibly powerful tool—a means to an end, not the end itself. In other words, you should use the same fundamental time-tested strategic approaches on your web site as you would any other communication vehicle—even though you will have to work through its unique "arms and legs" if you plan to develop and maintain a successful web site, whether you measure that with profits, sales, leads, or visitor numbers.

If you want to learn solid ways—not get-rich-quick schemes—to improve all aspects of your web site and how to integrate it into your offline businesses, you should do things such as study other successful internet marketers; enroll in an e-commerce course; ask internet-savvy friends and family for help; and read books on the subject. Ideally, you should hire a trustworthy professional web developer who knows as much as possible about such things as design and navigation, copywriting, search engine optimization, and automation of technology.

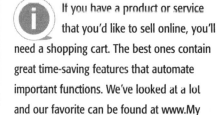

If you have a product or service that you'd like to sell online, you'll need a shopping cart. The best ones contain great time-saving features that automate important functions. We've looked at a lot and our favorite can be found at www.My EasyWebAutomation.com. Check it out.

This is probably the most difficult part of the process since, in our experience, many web developers lack basic, but critical, business and marketing expertise, which can have a significant negative effect on a web site's look, feel, and usability. The good news is that there are also many excellent and affordable companies that can do it all. One of the very best is Brian Austin at www.InternetTips.com.

Slowly, but surely, you will develop and hone your skills and become more confident in your ability to accomplish your online marketing goals. But you'd do well to learn from several of hard-earned experiences.

- Never try a pay-per-click campaign unless you've read and studied it very carefully; you check your results at least once an hour; and test, test, test.
- Web 2.0 is not software. It's a technological and cultural internet movement—do yourself a favor and read up on it. You'll be amazed at how much free or affordable web-based software, programs, and help there is on the World Wide Web nowadays.
- The "build it and they will come" days are long gone.
- There is no way to get rich overnight, on the internet or elsewhere.
- Blogs are wonderful—and inexpensive—alternatives to traditional web sites.
- Internet usage is still in its infancy. To ignore it is to be left behind!

The appendix of this book contains many good resources if you're looking for help with your web site. And for every one we've included, there are potentially hundreds more.

Use Figure 11.1: The Communications Vehicle Reference Table that we've included for some general tips on traffic-generating tactics (e.g., articles, e-zines, pay-per-clicks, and linking) and customer conversion tools (e.g., permission-based marketing, free information, and sales pages).

Advertising is the art and soul of capitalism. It captures a moment of time through the lens of commerce, reflecting and affecting our lives, making us laugh and cry, while simultaneously giving traction to the engine that propels this free market economy forward into the future.

—JEF I. RICHARDS

Your Communication Budget Development, CLV, and Incremental Revenues

Remember, excellent marketing begins with knowledge, not guess work. And one of the things you'll want to know is how well your communication tactics are working. That's why it's important that you understand the concept of incremental revenues first. We'll use the following simple example to explain this concept.

Let's assume the following:

Sally is a widget retailer (does anybody know what a widget looks like?) whose goal is to get 1,000 new customers during the next 12 months. Based on past experience, Sally knows that if she keeps her shop open six days a week for the next 12 months she can reasonably expect to acquire 200 new customers (through word-of-mouth, walk-ins, or phone directory). Therefore, in order to achieve her goal she has to do something more to boost awareness among her target audience. After much consideration, Sally selects direct mail as her primary communications vehicle and sets a budget of $40,000 to "buy" the additional 800 customers.

Sally does her research and learns that according to industry standards, she can reasonably expect that .5 to 1 percent of her targeted prospects will respond (by calling or visiting her store), and that 80 percent of these folks will become customers.

Given this, Sally mailed 120,000 sales letters (which cost her 28 cents each including third class postage). Her total bill for this effort was $33,600, $6,400 below her budget.

After six weeks, Sally evaluates her results, which were:

- 1 percent of her targeted prospects responded (1,200)
- 75 percent of those were converted to customers (900)

And even though her conversion rate was lower than forecasted, she still ended up with 100 more new customers than she forecasted. So, Sally should be happy, yes? No.

You see, Sally failed to consider some very critical elements. First, she didn't calculated her average CLV. If she had, she would have learned that her average customer spends $50 during the time they do business with her company, (over a seven-month period). This means that her 900 new customers will contribute $45,000 in total *incremental* revenues and she'll have to wait seven months to collect that in full.

However, it still looks like she's earned $11,400 in profits, correct? Not necessarily, because the $33,600 she spent did not include her labor and material costs, or administrative expenses.

In the end, Sally either broke even, earned a very small profit or lost money—we just don't know. But we do know two things for certain:

1. She should have known and used her CLV to guide the development of her marketing budget.
2. She should have forecasted and assigned a portion of her cost of goods and administrative expenses to each sale in order to ensure that her project's return on investment (ROI) was sufficient.

If Sally had considered these two critical variables she might have discovered ways to improve her results, such as:

- Reducing the costs associated with creating and mailing the sales letter, such as using one color instead of four; buying lighter weight paper; or mailing postcards instead of letters.
- Beefing up her offer (without increasing expenses) in order to generate more responses and increase sales. These include such tactics as: providing free "bonus" gifts, increasing her senior citizens' discounts, or offering free babysitting while parents shop.
- Increasing her average transaction amount by bundling logical products together or selling supplemental products or services.
- Using other forms of communication to enhance her direct mail campaign such as, joint ventures, e-mail campaigns, newspaper ads, or public relations efforts.

Now it's time for you to work on your marketing communications budget. Keep in mind what you've learned from the previous example as well as the following:

- Your available cash (less what's already promised);

- Seasonal fluctuations that may impact your cash flow;
- Standard response rates by industry or media type
- Past results for similar efforts—the best place to start
- Your current gross profit and desired net profit margins
- The opportunity costs associated with any action
- How much money you feel comfortable spending
- Your average CLV
- Your specific goals (are you focusing on new customer acquisition or current customer retention?)
- How your objectives translate into what you'll sell and to whom

Once armed with this information, you'll be in a good position to select your marketing communication vehicles. After you've decided what you'll spend, write it into the space provided below. Remember to include on-and off-line methods for growing your business. For example, you can use newspaper ads, business cards, or fliers to drive folks to your e-commerce web site. Conversely, consider using your web site to get people excited about your retail store.

> I have set aside $_____ to spend on my marketing communication efforts (advertising, public relations, online marketing and programs) for the time-lines designated in my marketing plan (a consecutive 12-month period). I will choose my tactics based on my ability to reach my goals and stay within my budget.

Don't forget that your advertising medium are the communication vehicles you use to deliver your marketing message; it's important to select ones that use your limited resources to achieve the best possible outcome.

Also, after you've identified your target audience and developed a compelling message, the trick is to select the vehicles, which enhance your ability to reach the right people. For instance, it makes little sense to advertise your retirement community using a fast-paced, loud, radio spot on a hip-hop station, no matter what the salesperson says! So, before you buy, make sure you've correctly identified your target audience and created messages that motivate them. Then select the appropriate advertising medium.

The following are some general tips to help you through this process.

- Unless your target audience is broad, it's best to choose one to two primary advertising vehicles—ones that you can afford to dominate.
- Choose methods according to cost, targeting, and response. Any campaign can be broken down into costs per thousand, and if you're using direct response advertising (which you should), benchmark your success using costs per sale. Your expenses include cost of design (also known as creative), production (producing or printing your ad), and placement (radio, advertisement, list purchase, and postage).
- As a general rule, the more targeted the medium, the higher the cost. In return, however, you should expect a higher response rate, so the cost per response can be lower than less expensive methods.
- Select advertising and publicity methods that are suitable for your target audience. Companies that sell advertising can provide you with a lot of helpful information about various audiences. Also, it's a good idea to look at other types of businesses that continually use specific media, then make sure they're targeting the same audience as you. Bottom line: avoid guesswork by testing before committing to major purchases.

Use Figure 11.1: Communications Vehicle Reference Table to help with your selection. Feel free to choose one, or several, but make sure you consider your target audience for each goal. Before you make your final selection review the checklist we've included next. It contains over 100 tactics—some are revenue generating, others are not. Include any others that are appropriate for your situation.

FIGURE 11.1: **Communications Vehicle Reference Table**

Type	Pros and Cons	Tips

Newspaper Ads	**Most effective for:**
	– Reaching mass audiences inexpensively
	– Advertising locally available services
	– As a booster for other types of advertising
	– Generating traffic to location
	– Announcing sales or discounts
	Drawbacks:
	– Hard-to-target too general niches
	– Ineffective for B2B
	– Low pass–along rates
	– Getting through the clutter
	– Results don't justify rates; use with
	  other media
		Do:
		– Include a strong headline (1 in 10 read text)
		  and subhead, as appropriate
		– Run repeatedly
		– Place above paper "fold" for prime readership
		– Use short sentences (12–15 words)
		– Place coupons in upper right–hand corner
		– Include map/directions to location
		– Try unusual dimensions, i.e., larger than ¼ but
		  smaller than ½ page (also, larger is better)
		– Place in section most read by target audience
		– Buy carefully; prices vary widely

Magazine Ads	**Most effective for:**
	– Perceived prestige and credibility
	– Targeting niche markets
	– Keeping readers' attention longer
	– Products requiring more detailed explanations
	Drawbacks:
	– Can be expensive
	– Long lead times: 1–3 months in advance
		Do:
		– Include graphics or photos demonstrating
		  product being used
		– Add photos of real people
		– Run once and use as reprints and blowups
		– Run in local editions of national magazines
		– Make ad as large as possible
		Don't:
		– Overdo reverse type
		– "Date" ads or include employees' pictures
		– Use horizontal layout–vertical ads pull
		  25 percent better

Classified Ads	**Most effective for:**
	– Two–part processes: e.g. driving traffic to
	  web site or calling for more information.
	– Getting attention inexpensively
		Do:
		– Use as part of two–step process for
		  interested prospects (e.g., place an ad that
		  compels readers to visit web site)

FIGURE 11.1: **Communications Vehicle Reference Table,** continued

Classified Ads (continued)	**Most effective for:** – Growing readership – Immediate sales on higher–ticket items, ones in short supply, specialized merchandise **Drawbacks:** – Breaking through the clutter – May be viewed as less credible	**Do:** – Look for free online classifieds
Yellow Page Ads	**Most effective for:** – Producing inquiries for consumer businesses – Local service companies – Businesses that compete on convenience and/or price – Companies looking for immediate sales **Drawbacks:** – Breaking through the clutter – Yearly commitment means less flexibility and more expense – Not effective for B2B	**Do:** – Include as much information as possible – Make ad stand out from others: must be eye–catching and memorable – Direct prospects to white pages as well– your competitors may not be there – Check rates carefully–they vary widely **Don't:** – Let directory artists design ad–get objective professional help – Assume you have to be in yellow pages; consider online directories instead
Inserts	**Most effective for:** – Including in magazines newspapers, and bills – Businesses looking for inexpensive way to contact target audience – Up–sells to current customerse – Businesses that send regular invoices – Companies with target audiences scattered geographically **Drawbacks:** – Response rates generally lower than direct mail or e-mail campaigns	**Do:** – Use strong headline – Use reverse color or black and white – Check prices carefully, charges vary due to paper weight, dimensions, circulation audience, and distribution method – Buy in volume–you'll save money

FIGURE 11.1: Communications Vehicle Reference Table, continued

Inserts (continued)	**Drawbacks:** – Large percentage of nonbound inserts fall out – Company is responsible for producing insert and delivering to publication	**Do:**
Brochures	**Most effective for:** – Lead follow–ups – Products or services that require detailed explanations, instructions, or information – Companies with multiple products, packages, and pricing – Service professionals **Drawbacks:** – Can be very expensive – Ineffective when design and/or copy are amateurish	**Do:** – Use soft background colors (beige, light grey, pastels) – Use san serif fonts for copy and serif fonts for headlines – Use clear and concise language and keep words to a minimum – Use bullet–pointed benefit statements **Don't:** – Spend time or money on fancy artwork
Posters	**Most effective for:** – Inexpensive and effective signage alternatives – Window displays or as point–of–purchase influencers **Drawbacks:** – Not effective direct response vehicles	**Do:** – Include well–designed art and photos – Incorporate color to attract attention – Use large, readable fonts **Don't:** – Use as standalone advertising – Go overboard with words, keep them to a minimum
Commuter or Traveler Signs (Transit, Buses/Taxis, Commuter Trains, Airport Ads, Company Vehicles	**Most effective for:** – Repeat messaging – Targeting geographically-based markets affordably – Nonprofits or public safety organizations (some companies provide them for no cost)	**Do:** – Include easy–to–remember phone number and web site address – Keep words and copy to a minimum – Use large, legible type – Use bold colors and contrast

FIGURE 11.1: **Communications Vehicle Reference Table,** continued

Commuter or Traveler Signs (continued)	**Drawbacks:** – Cannot control appearance or placement – Not effective for B2B communication	**Do:** – Mount behind plastic (e.g., Lucite) to cut down on graffiti – Make small objects large, not vice versa – Identify product with photos or graphics **Don't:** – Use lots of white space – Place words too close to each other
Billboards	**Most effective for:** – Destination information: restaurants, gas stations, malls, outlets, etc. – Reminders: for radio station call signs, upcoming special events, TV shows, etc. – Branding – Boosting other media results **Drawbacks:** – Expensive – Harder to target niche audiences (unless geographically based) – Difficult to design effectively	**Do:** – Use very few words: nine or less is best – Make headline visible up close and as far back as 400 ft. (20–inch type) – Include easy–to–remember web site address and phone numbers – Use color graphics and photos to grab attention **Don't:** – Make letters any smaller than 12 inches (unless it's for compulsory disclaimers)
Movie Theater Ads	**Most effective for:** – Local service companies and retailers – Companies looking for inexpensive method for targeting niche audiences **Drawbacks:** – Cost of production can be high.	**Do:** – Use attractive visuals that demonstrate product being used – Repeat contact information, including travel directions – Hire professionals to write, produce, and act
Radio Ads	**Most effective for:** – Boosting other media results	**Do:** – Hire professionals to write copy and produce ad

FIGURE 11.1: **Communications Vehicle Reference Table,** continued

Radio Ads (continued)	**Most effective for:** – Products that appeal to niched listening audiences (e.g., teens, inner city, sports fans, etc.) – Campaigns requiring immediate results – Businesses looking for short–term ad commitments and scheduling flexibility **Drawbacks:** – Not cost–effective as standalone direct response ad – Hard for listeners to copy down information –High production costs –More difficult to instill vivid vision in listeners' minds –Speed of delivery makes it harder to convey important information	**Do:** – Tell a story using vivid language –Use sounds to demonstrate how product is used (if applicable) –Choose your listening audiences carefully; active listener stations (e.g., news, sports, religion) draw best (especially for B2B companies) **Don't:** – Use alone; it's rarely cost-effective – Buy or schedule based on station representatives' suggestions; hire an ad agency to purchase and negotiate for you – Bash your competitors
Television Ads	**Most effective for:** – Boosting other media results – Local companies with access to local channels during non–peak hours – Businesses looking for short–term ad commitments and scheduling flexibility **Drawbacks:** – High production and placement costs – Complex buying processes—easy to make mistakes – Hard to control air times	**Do:** – Include testimonials, product demonstrations, attention–grabbing headlines, memorable action – Highlight product, not scenery – Tell a story with a beginning, middle, and end – Include company name, phone number, and web site address – Keep it fresh and up–to–date **Don't:** – Bash your competitors – Make it overly humorous or clever – Schedule or buy yourself; hire reputable ad agency and production company

FIGURE 11.1: **Communications Vehicle Reference Table,** continued

Public Relations (Newspapers, Radio, TV)	**Most effective for:** – Human interest stories – Local and regional publicity – Businesses, people, or industries that are tie–ins to national news or events – Nonprofits, educational organizations, charities, and local businesses – Controversial businesses – Any business that can get good (and free) coverage – Building awareness – Damage control for you, industry, staff, or prior management – Influencing public opinion – Educating consumers about new product, service, technology, idea, or company – Establishing credibility **Drawbacks:** – Difficult to measure results – At mercy of editors and journalists	**Do:** – Edit, edit, edit–typos and other errors are real killers – Meet all deadlines – Include accurate contact information–make it easy to be found – Make content newsworthy and timely – Contact journalist and offer to act as subject matter expert **Don't:** – Write your own press releases–get an expert to help you out – Make it hard for journalist to cover your story–provide back–up information
Participation (Professional organizations, Lead sharing groups)	**Most effective for:** – Businesses whose target audience is primarily made up of local and/or regional businesses – Meeting peers and prospects – Supporting hometown initiatives **Drawbacks:** – Can be time–consuming and results may be difficult to measure	**Do:** – Choose 3–4 trade groups or associations and participate fully – Choose groups that attract your prospects, not necessarily peers – Be sincere and hard–working–provide valuable contributions – Give to local charities – Listen carefully and ask thoughtful questions

FIGURE 11.1: **Communications Vehicle Reference Table,** continued

Participation (continued)	Drawbacks:	Don't: – "Work a room"–if you're insincere, it shows – Overdo–limit the number of your commitments so you can fully participate
Referral Programs	**Most effective for:** – Any business looking to acquire new customers **Drawbacks:** – Must stay on top of program	**Do:** – Tell current customers that you prefer referrals over all other types of advertising – Provide current customers with clear picture of the type of people who will benefit most by doing business with your company – Provide free, expert, no-obligation consultations to anyone referred by a current customer – Offer robust incentives for referrals: bottom-of-the-bill discounts, free merchandise, gift certificates, etc. **Don't:** – Be inconsistent–make it a regular and ongoing part of your marketing tactics – Feel like you're bothering customers to ask for referrals: Happy customers will enjoy recommending your business to others
Welcome Letters and Packages	**Most effective for:** – Keeping current customers – Developing long-term relationships with current customers **Drawbacks:** – Require setting up processes and implementing on regular basis	**Do:** – Welcome new customers immediately. – Use phone call, e-mail letter, or snail mail – Include helpful materials, such as: emergency numbers, product instructions, days/hours of operation, and frequently-asked questions

FIGURE 11.1: **Communications Vehicle Reference Table,** continued

Welcome Letters and Packages (continued)	**Drawbacks:** – Requires time, and revenues are not always immediate	**Do:** – If possible, write handwritten note, or make personal phone call – Automate with special e-mails–particularly if your web site is a large part of your business **Don't:** – Use welcome letter or package to sell–it appears insincere and accomplishes nothing
"Oops" Letters and/or Gifts (Safety Net)	**Most effective for:** – All businesses–particularly ones with higher–than–average in–bound calls from prospects and customers – Service companies **Drawbacks:** – Require setting up processes and implementing on regular basis – Require that all employees understand when to use, and when not to	**Do:** – Empower all employees to give a gift to customers when service is below par (e.g., customer is left on–hold or made to wait in line too long) – Mail apology letter and free gift or offer gift in person – Offer sincere apology **Don't:** – Use this tactic for extremely irate customers
Bartering	**Most effective for:** – Getting products or services you need without spending cash – Spreading word about companies – Testing other products, services, and business relationships for joint venture consideration **Drawbacks:** – Doesn't generate revenues	**Do:** – Use closed-end trade bartering–no one owes anything more when trade is completed **Don't:** – Barter for anything you don't want or need
Affinity Marketing	**Most effective for:** – Companies who can align their products, services, industry, or company with a particular charity or cause	**Do:** – Partner with noncontroversial charities or organizations

FIGURE 11.1: **Communications Vehicle Reference Table,** continued

Affinity Marketing (continued)	**Most effective for:** – Businesses that can work with other nonprofits, such as: credit unions, alumni groups, civic associations, etc. **Drawbacks:** – Can be labor intensive to set up and administer – May be relying on less motivated employees or nonpaid volunteers to generate interest	**Do:** – Align yourself with organizations that reflect your interests, passions, and personality **Don't:** – Align yourself with organizations, companies, or groups that are "anti" any race, religion, or gender, etc.
Free Stuff (Services, Product Samples, Specialty Ad Gifts, Seminars)	**Most effective for:** – Customer acquisition campaigns – Service professionals who can offer free workshops, seminars, consultations, clinics, etc. – Businesses with new products **Drawbacks:** – Can be expensive – Results and ROI may be difficult to track	**Do:** – Offer thoughtful and relevant information during consultations, seminars, workshops, etc. – Include your business name, logo, web site address, and contact information on all specialty ad gifts, service literature, and product samples – Make sure free gifts fit your company's and target audience's personalities **Don't:** – Use free seminars, consultations, and workshops for sales pitches
Trade Shows	**Most effective for:** – Businesses with longer sales cycles – Companies that use direct sales as major revenue generators – Meeting face to face with many prospects over a condensed period of time **Drawbacks:** – Can be costly and labor intensive – Results largely dependent upon external factors	**Do:** – Check everything out carefully beforehand to make sure that your target audience will be represented – Set up appointments with key contacts before the show, if appropriate **Don't:** – Go unprepared—check out everything well in advance

FIGURE 11.1: **Communications Vehicle Reference Table,** continued

| Web Sites | **Most effective for:**
– All businesses and organizations: no exceptions
– Cost–effective option for increasing service area
– Businesses looking for flexibility and passive income
Drawbacks:
– Must be continually maintained and updated
– Can be expensive–but extremely cost-effective if used properly
– Lack of sound strategic marketing knowledge in web development community
– Breaking through the clutter | **Do:**
– Make sure your site is professional–looking, eye–catching, and well–written
– Include company elements, such as: phone numbers, mailing address, photographs, logos, etc.
– Make site simple to use and easy to navigate.
– Use the minimum number of pages to provide necessary information to target audience
– Consider speed–make sure site loads quickly
– Use attention–grabbing graphics, but not too many
– Include your privacy policies and terms of use
– Make sure all external and internal links work correctly
– Take advantage of affordable development and design options
Don't:
– Overdo pictures, graphics, and Flash animation–they'll slow loading times down and can be annoying
– Link with other web sites with offensive material or questionable content |
| **E-Commerce Web Sites** (Direct Sales, Lead Generation) | **Most effective for:**
– Companies seeking online product or service sales | **Do:**
– Follow the same basic design and copy guidelines for all web sites |

FIGURE 11.1: **Communications Vehicle Reference Table,** continued

E-Commerce Web Sites (continued)	**Most effective for:** – Businesses interested in motivating future online and/or offline sales **Drawbacks:** – Involves more robust functionality	**Do:** – Use direct marketing web site with strong sales letter that leads directly to shopping cart for immediate online sales – Provide visitors an opportunity to "opt–in" (provide their name and e-mail address) to build prospect e-mail list – Offer free information or gifts in exchange for visitors' opt–in information – Include a compelling offer; strong call–to–action; attention–grabbing headline; testimonials; site map; benefit–oriented bullet points; reassuring checkout page; obvious "buy now" buttons; interactive, involvement devices; secure shopping cart **Don't:** – Just put up the site and leave it there—it must be maintained regularly and updated often – Use hard-sell tactics – Go overboard with Flash animation, graphics, or video – Ask for a sale on the "first date"–unless your visitors are presold – Do your own designing or copy writing unless you're an expert
Informational, Educational, or Brochure Web Sites	**Most effective for:** – Companies wishing to provide information as lead generation for offline sales, particularly for service professionals	**Do:** – Follow the same basic design and copy guidelines for all web sites

FIGURE 11.1: **Communications Vehicle Reference Table,** continued

| Informational, Educational, or Brochure Web Sites (continued) | **Most effective for:**
– Companies that need to offer back–up information for products or services, such as troubleshooting advice, directions, certification requirements, resources, frequently-asked questions, etc.
– Expanding awareness
Drawbacks:
– Can be expensive to develop a well–designed and easy–to–use web site
– Many web developers lack basic marketing knowledge, which can have negative impact on results | **Do:**
– Include multiple pages, such as home page, contact us, frequently-asked questions, our products/services, testimonials, and the like
– Provide the same types of detailed information contained in traditional brochures
– Offer free content on relevant topics
– Provide multiple ways for prospects to contact company: e-mail address, phone, and fax numbers, location address
Don't:
– Go overboard with words–be clear, but concise
– Put up the site and leave it–maintain it regularly and update it often |
| Blogs | **Most effective for:**
– Finding more about prospects' and customers' interests, worries, and opinions
– Creating quick and affordable online presence
– Sharing ideas and showcasing audio and video
– Main hubs that provide direct links to owner's other sites
Drawbacks:
– Have to be updated often so not a good choice for people who do not like to write or lack writing skills | **Do:**
– Follow the same basic design and copy guidelines for all web sites
– Consider adding a shopping cart or use as purely informational
– Use professional–looking templates available online (free or low–cost).
– Consider replacing full–blown web site with blog–this can save time and money
Don't:
– Develop a blog if your writing skills are below par and/or you don't intend to update it often and regularly |

FIGURE 11.1: **Communications Vehicle Reference Table,** continued

| **Internet Tactics: Driving Web Site Traffic** (Articles, Links, E-Mail Signature, Directories, Pay-per-Click, Tell-a-Friend Scripts, Affiliate Programs, Joint Ventures) | **Most effective for:**
– Increasing targeted traffic to web site
– Publishing information effectively and inexpensively
Drawbacks:
– Have to update and maintain often
– Pay-per-clicks can be complex and money pits for beginners
– Can be labor-intensive without automation software
– The goal is to increase targeted traffic, not just people, which can be tricky
– Takes time to develop and see results in some cases | **Do:**
– Write and submit online articles
– Have your site optimized so people and search engines can find it
– Set up an e-mail signature file with an active link to your web site
– Create relevant inbound, outbound, and reciprocal links to and from other web sites
– Submit articles to more than one site and include a direct link to your web site in your signature file
– Submit web site to appropriate directories
– Write e-zines (e-mail newsletters) and send to your mailing list
– Use pay-per-clicks to obtain instant results on keywords, ad copy, offers, etc.
– Set up referral programs using "tell-a-friend" scripts
– Automate—save time and increase profits by putting web site communication on auto-pilot
– Set up affiliate programs: have other people sell your products and services, and vice versa Join forces with strategic partners
– Use inexpensive desktop publishing software to create newsletters, e-zines, articles, etc.
Don't:
– Link with sites that are unrelated to your product or service, or ones that your visitors may find offensive
– Write articles or e-zines that lack relevant content and are nothing more than sales pitches |

FIGURE 11.1: **Communications Vehicle Reference Table,** continued

Internet Tactics: **Driving Web Site Traffic** (continued)	Drawbacks:	**Don't:** – Plagiarize! Do not copy other peoples' content and pass it off as your own – Submit to directories that require you to link back – Go overboard with Flash animation, graphics, or video
Internet Tactics: **Converting Visitors to Customers**	**Most effective for:** – Any business that seeks immediate online sales or lead generation opportunities for future online or offline sales **Drawbacks:** – Some tactics require more robust web site capabilities – Can be cumbersome to administer without automation – Takes time to develop and see results	**Do:** – Consider adding audio and video to your site to enhance your visitors' experience – Build relationship slowly using permission–based opt–in boxes – Make sure your site is professional–looking, well–written, uncomplicated and easy–to–use – Reassure visitors with your privacy policies and purchasing security measures – Include attention–grabbing graphics – Position opt–in box above "the fold" (visitors can read without scrolling up or down) – Include risk–free and compelling offer – Use interactive involvement devices to increase visitors' interest – Offer product or service bundles, add–ons, and up–sells as appropriate – Send confirmation e-mail and thank–you note to all new customers – Automate–purchase software or web–based solution and put correspondence and list building on autopilot

FIGURE 11.1: **Communications Vehicle Reference Table,** continued

Internet Tactics: Converting Visitors to Customers (continued)	Drawbacks:	Don't:
		– Put up the site and leave it–it must be updated and maintained often
		– Use hard-sell tactics
		– Go overboard with Flash animation, graphics, or video
		– Ask for a sale on the "first date"–unless your visitors are pre-sold
		– Design or write copy unless you're an expert

Tactics Selection Checklist

Figure 11.2 is a marketing tactics and actions checklist that contains more than 150 ideas that you can use as a brainstorming tool for your plan. You'll see that they are not limited to direct-response communication tactics, but contain a wide variety of actions—all of which will have a positive effect on you and your business, either directly or indirectly.

Even though your marketing plan should contain a minimum of two to three measurable direct response activities, you should also include others that will increase your odds of success—even if you're the only one who sees the list. For example, "exercising regularly" may not seem like a marketing activity, but if you're exhausted and stressed because of poor health, your chances of succeeding are certainly lower.

Also, you'll find that our suggestions are "rapid-fire" examples. If you'd like more detailed information on one or more, visit our web site at: www.StrategicMarketingAdvisors.com and enter the appropriate keywords or phrases into the "search" field on our home page. Feel free to add your own ideas—we've left plenty of room at the bottom.

Look this checklist over and check off any that you're seriously considering. Then, if you'd like, enter the following information as requested:

- *Timeline*. When will you start this action and when will it end?
- *Cost*. What will it cost you to complete this action?
- *Owner*. Who is responsible for executing this action?
- *Impact*. How will executing this action positively impact your business?
- *Priority*. What level of importance does this action have? High, medium, or low.

At this point, you've hopefully come up with your own list of tactics and other actions you'd like to pursue during the next 12 months. If so, now is the

FIGURE 11.2: Tactics Selection Checklist

✓	Tactic/Action	Timeline	Cost	Owner	Impact	Priority
	Place a newspaper ad					
	Hand out fliers					
	Create two-sided business cards					
	Design a new logo					
	Produce a radio ad					
	Develop a bumper sticker with your tagline					
	Join your local chamber of commerce					
	Paint the outside of your building					
	Provide discounts for senior citizens					
	Buy subscriptions to your industry's trade magazine					
	Develop at least one robust referral program					
	Set up a direct sales team					

FIGURE 11.2: **Tactics Selection Checklist,** continued

✓	Tactic/Action	Timeline	Cost	Owner	Impact	Priority
	Gather customer testimonials and include them on all your marketing communication					
	Create a company brochure					
	Tie your company to a local or national story and issue a press release					
	Hire a publicist					
	Add a frequently-asked-questions page to your web site and welcome package					
	Collect your web site's visitors' e-mail addresses using an opt-in box					
	Implement programs to reduce customer waiting times					
	Create company T-shirts, hats and name tags					
	Appear on a local radio or TV program					
	Offer to speak at industry events					
	Write and submit articles to on- and offline publications					
	Upgrade your lighting					
	Shop your competitors					
	Develop a customer welcome package					
	Prepare a portfolio of samples and references					
	Add your photo to your web site					
	Add relevant content to your web site regularly					
	Use templates for repetitive work or processes					

FIGURE 11.2: **Tactics Selection Checklist,** continued

✓	Tactic/Action	Timeline	Cost	Owner	Impact	Priority
	Identify tasks that can be outsourced					
	Automate your web site using web-based software					
	Attend industry trade shows or expos					
	Take a marketing class or seminar					
	Personally call and thank five customers each day					
	Hire a business coach					
	Repackage and/or repurpose old products					
	Create a marketing calendar					
	Attend industry conferences					
	Develop a customer-care handbook for employees					
	Place an ad in the local or regional section of a national magazine					
	Let prospects test before they buy— provide free product samples					
	Participate in online forums or blogs					
	Bundle "natural" products or services and offer discounts					
	Use billboards to direct drivers to your location					
	Update the landscaping on the outside of your location					
	Organize your work area					
	Learn ways to master the clock and calendar					
	Create and nurture a network of contacts					
	Hire a virtual assistant					

FIGURE 11.2: **Tactics Selection Checklist,** continued

✓	Tactic/Action	Timeline	Cost	Owner	Impact	Priority
	Continually hone your industry skills to remain a respected expert					
	Minimize stress by exercising daily					
	Learn how to use programs such as Microsoft Excel, PowerPoint, or Adobe Acrobat					
	Get inspired—read, meditate, walk, etc.					
	Develop a realistic marketing budget, and stick to it					
	Collect contact information with peers and prospects and use it to keep in touch					
	Conduct free seminars					
	Offer club memberships and frequent buyer discounts					
	Redesign your web site for easier navigation					
	Hire a cleaning service					
	Redecorate your office					
	Extend your hours/days of operation to better accommodate your customers and prospects					
	Take a computer course to improve your skills					
	Write a column for your local newspaper					
	Convert newspaper or magazine ads into large posters for your showroom or office					
	Use commuter signage—on buses, streets, and subway stations—to advertise your business					

FIGURE 11.2: **Tactics Selection Checklist,** continued

✓	Tactic/Action	Timeline	Cost	Owner	Impact	Priority
	Ask other reputable web site owners to link into yours					
	Communicate your mission and vision statement to all of your employees					
	Develop an automated system for tracking your marketing results					
	Ask customers how they heard about your business and track their answers					
	Join your industry's trade organization					
	Set higher quality-control benchmarks					
	Produce and place a local cable TV ad					
	Analyze the effectiveness of your yellow pages ad and make adjustments					
	Conduct a direct-mail campaign to a targeted list of prospects					
	Develop and send a regular customer newsletter					
	Produce and place a movie ad at your local cinema					
	Submit your web site to appropriate internet directories					
	Assess your location's outdoor signage and make the necessary improvements					
	Develop and maintain strategic partnerships with likeminded people and companies					
	Conduct regular weekly sales training with your employees					
	Create your company's USP, slogan, and elevator speech					

FIGURE 11.2: **Tactics Selection Checklist,** continued

✓	Tactic/Action	Timeline	Cost	Owner	Impact	Priority
	Create and print price sheets and update them often					
	Use vehicle signage to increase awareness					
	Write relevant industry white papers for your target audience					
	Barter for products and services you want or need					
	Add a product discount coupon to your newspaper ad					
	Sponsor a local community or charitable event					
	Create buzz and expand your mailing list using contests					
	Use identifiable mascots to help increase brand awareness for your business					
	Create a product demonstration video and add it to your web site					
	Serve on a local company's or organization's board of directors					
	Organize a local leads group with like minded professionals					
	Host an open house at your business location					
	Provide outbound links from your web site to others					
	Update your computer system every 2 to 3 years					
	Offer free 30-minute "no-sales-pitch" consultations to interested prospects					

FIGURE 11.2: **Tactics Selection Checklist,** continued

✓	Tactic/Action	Timeline	Cost	Owner	Impact	Priority
	E-mail useful tips to your customers and prospects regularly					
	Have your web site optimized for search engines and visitors					
	Place a classified ad that directs readers to your web site					
	Upload a video about your company, products, or services to YouTube.com					
	Replace your traditional web site with a free blog site					
	Offer to teach a class at a local college or university					
	Join your college alumni association					
	Develop and enforce an employee dress code policy					
	Create a perception map to see where you stand with prospects and customers					
	Host a holiday party					
	Give your employees 20 hours of pay if they use that time to do volunteer work					
	Offer discounts to regular customers					
	Create your own online affiliate program and participate in others owned by other web sites					
	Write an e-book					
	Listen to educational tapes or CDs during your commute to and from work					

FIGURE 11.2: **Tactics Selection Checklist,** continued

✓	Tactic/Action	Timeline	Cost	Owner	Impact	Priority
	Re-examine all company processes and systems					
	Send personal, handwritten seasonal, thank you, and birthday cards to your valuable customers					
	Conduct customer polls and surveys					
	Have a super-duper one-day sale					
	Read one good business or marketing book each month					
	Update your phone system to take advantage of new technologies					
	Choose two family members, friends, or colleagues to call or e-mail each day					
	Write a daily to-do list and a not-to-do list					
	Go online and learn more about the Web 2.0 technologies and culture—you'll be amazed					
	Serve refreshments such as soft drinks, popcorn, or coffee in your waiting room					
	Improve your window displays and make sure your windows are sparkling clean					
	Redecorate your office and bathrooms					
	Frame and hang your credentials on your wall					
	Add a shopping cart to your web site					
	Include promotional bill inserts in your customers' invoices					

FIGURE 11.2: **Tactics Selection Checklist,** continued

✓	Tactic/Action	Timeline	Cost	Owner	Impact	Priority
	Offer an automatic payment option to your customers					
	Develop and communicate your company's ironclad guarantee					
	Conduct ongoing "lessons learned" debriefing sessions with employees after completing projects					
	Join a local health club					
	Participate in your prospects' and customers' trade organizations, not just your own					
	Write and implement a strategic and tactical marketing plan					
	Conduct web-based seminars or teleconferences					
	Go to www.skype.com and download their software that allows you to call computer-to-computer for free					
	Join a local Toastmasters International group to improve your presentation skills					
	Offer logical supplemental products or services to your existing customers					
	Do what you said you'd do, when you said you would do it					
	Surprise your best customers with a no-strings-attached gift					
	Reach out to smaller groups (niches) with your targeted market					
	Use internet viral marketing to increase traffic to your web site					

FIGURE 11.2: **Tactics Selection Checklist,** continued

✓	Tactic/Action	Timeline	Cost	Owner	Impact	Priority
	Record and combine soothing on-hold music with useful marketing messages					
	Provide employees with customer care scripts and job aids					
	Offer gift certificates—especially for unusual products or services					
	Host a customer appreciation barbeque					
	Reward employees who demonstrate exceptional customer care attitudes and behaviors					
	Create an enthusiastic and memorable telephone greeting					
	Whenever possible, use environmentally friendly products, services, and processes—go green!					
	Deliver the promised customer experience 100% of the time					
	Encourage a culture where all employees are devoted to achieving your company's number one cause or purpose					
	Donate used equipment to a local charity					
	Institute customer theme days—the sillier, the better					
	Use postcards for your direct response mailings					
	Develop a product or service catalog					
	Enhance your product offerings by adding services such as free delivery					

FIGURE 11.2: Tactics Selection Checklist, continued

✓	Tactic/Action	Timeline	Cost	Owner	Impact	Priority
	Use social book-marking and networking to improve your web site					
	Create and execute a mystery shopper's program					
	Update your voice mail greeting each morning					

time to document your choices and predictions using Figures 11.4 and 11.6 worksheets that follow, just as you've done in previous chapters. Each is preceded by instructions and a completed sample (Figure 11.3 and 11.5).

Action Plan Revenue Forecasts Worksheet Directions and Key Elements

1. *Columns 1 and 2.* Enter the same information as you included in Figure 5.1: Business Objectives Worksheet from Chapter 5.

2. *Column 3, 4, 5, 6.* Enter the same information that you included in Figure 7.4: Products and Services Sales and Revenue Forecasts Worksheet from Chapter 7.

Next, use the following worksheet to forecast your marketing communications expenses and deduct them from your gross profits. The number you end up with is net profit before administrative expenses and taxes. Use this information to plan your activities calendar and benchmark your success.

FIGURE 11.3: **Sample Action Plan Revenue Forecasts Worksheet**

1 Business Objective(s) Description	2 Timeline	3 Product(s) or Service(s) Sales	4 Forecasted Gross Revenues	5 Forecasted Cost of Goods	6 Difference (Gross Profit)
1,500 new customers who contribute $34 each	1/1/09–12/31/09	Sell 3,000 ABC, QRF, XYZ books @ $17 each (2 books per customer)	$51,000	$15,000	$36,000 (70%)
100 new customers who contribute $75 each	1/1/09–12/31/09	Sell 50 DEF coffee table books @ $75 each (1 per customer)	$7,500	$3,500	$4,000 (53%)
Total			$58,500	$18,500	$40,000 (68%)

FIGURE 11.4: **Action Plan Revenue Forecasts Worksheet**

1 Business Objective(s) Description	2 Timeline	3 Product(s) or Service(s) Sales	4 Forecasted Gross Revenues	5 Forecasted Cost of Goods	6 Difference (Gross Profit)
Total					

Action Plan Net Profit Worksheet Directions and Key Elements

1. *Columns 1: Product(s) and Service(s) Sales and 3: Forecasted Gross Profits*. Enter the same information as you did in columns 3 and 6 of Figure 11.4.

2. *Column 2*. Enter the same information as you did in Figure 8.3, column 4.

3. *Column 4*. List each of the vehicles you've selected separately and make realistic forecasts for each one. Make sure you've considered what types of media best suit your target audience's preferences and personalities. Also, don't forget to include all the tactics you'll use to achieve your goal. Regardless of the number you choose, they must all work to get you there. Give yourself a little fudge room, but don't go overboard.

4. *Column 5*. What will it cost you to complete the actions you've included? The best way to obtain estimates is by contacting representatives from various media—online or offline. Explain to them what you'd like to accomplish and ask them for a price quote and make sure they include all charges! For example, if you plan on mailing a sales letter you should include what it will cost you to create, print, and mail. And don't forget to include those channels that require no out-of-pocket dollars.

5. *Column 6*. This is what you're left with after you pay for materials and labor (cost of goods) and communications expenses. It does not include any administrative costs (equipment purchases, rent, office supplies, etc.) or taxes.

To arrive at this deduct the numbers you've entered into column 5 from the numbers in column 3.

Remember, if you'd like to download copies of templates in this book, go to: www.TheProcrastinatorsGuideToMarketing .com or www.TPGTM.com. Once there, you'll be asked to register and given instructions for downloading.

FIGURE 11.5: **Sample Action Plan Net Profit Worksheet**

1 Product(s) and Service(s) Sales	2 Target Market	3 Forecasted Gross Profits	4 Communication Vehicles	5 Communication Vehicle Expenses	6 Difference (Net Profit before Admin. and Taxes)
Sell 3,000 ABC,QRF, XYZ books @ $17 each	Males 30–55 who want information on kitchen remodeling, building a deck and building a water feature	$36,000	– 25 weeks local newspaper 2x/wk. @ $150/ad ($7,500) – Flier in local hardware stores (Home Depot, Lowes) ($500)	$8,000	$28,000
Sell 50 DEF coffee table books @ $75 each	Adults 35–65 who want photo books on State of Connecticut	$4,000	– Brochures in chamber office and Tourist Info. Center ($250) – 5 wks. local newspaper ad 2x/wk. @150/ad ($1,000)	$1,250	$2,750
Total		$40,000		$ 9,250	$ 30,750

FIGURE 11.6: **Action Plan Net Profit Worksheet**

1 Product(s) and Service(s) Sales	2 Target Market	3 Forecasted Gross Profits	4 Communication Vehicles	5 Communication Vehicle Expenses	6 Difference (Net Profit before Admin. and Taxes)
Total		$		$	$

Chapter 11 Snapshot

Before moving on to Chapter 12, let's take time to review several of the most important take-aways from this chapter:

- Advertising is simply a way to make something known to the public.

- There are two basic types of advertising: traditional (also known as institutional or branded) and direct response.

- Direct-response advertising is an invitation extended by a company to its target audience, to do something, such as call, stop in, place an order, schedule an appointment, buy now, or visit a web site.

- All of your marketing communication should be aimed at building a long-term relationship with your customers by engendering trust in you, your company, and the products and services you offer.

I know of a brewer who sells more of his beer to the people who never see his advertising than to the people who see it every week. Bad advertising can unsell a product.

—DAVID OGILVY

STEP 8

*Developing Your Scorecard:
How Will You Measure Success?*

I f you've been using the PETE model we introduced in Chapter 4 to chart your journey, you know that marketing is a cyclical, not linear, process. Just when you think you've completed everything, it's time to begin again. That's why it must be an ongoing component of your daily activities—from the minute you open your doors until close of business.

> *The definition of insanity is doing the same thing over and over and expecting different results.*
>
> —BENJAMIN FRANKLIN

Remember, the goal of direct-response advertising is to achieve an incremental gross profit—a positive return on your investment. If your communication efforts are falling short of this objective, or you're doing better than expected you need to understand why. That way you'll be able to double-up on the things that are working well, and get rid of the things that are not. Otherwise, you'll be operating in the dark. And in addition to wasting valuable time and money you'll find it far more difficult to make informed decisions in the future.

David's
Lesson Learned:
How Seemingly Minor
Adjustments Can Keep
Entrepreneurs on
Course

An aviator's journey is similar to an entrepreneur's—each needs to go from point A to point B, plan a route for getting there, gather the tools they need for the trip and then set off. For example, let's say a pilot wants to fly his jet aircraft from Philadelphia to San Diego in five hours, while maintaining an exact compass direction of 230 degrees during the entire flight, unless he experiences something such as a simple northerly wind, which will blow him off course—a highly likely scenario.

In order to stay on course the pilot would have altered his compass heading, and continue to do so throughout the entire flight, to offset the effects of the wind and other external factors. If not, he might wind up in Mexico.

Even given the sophistication of today's state-of-the-art navigation technologies, pilots must continually monitor and adjust their position to ensure that they arrive at their intended destination. If incorrect data or assumptions were entered into the aircraft's system, the pilot might run out of gas or ignore critical equipment malfunctions—which this ofen results in an unnecessary disaster.

That's why successful entrepreneurs continually correct for the shifting climates of the business world. They look for all of the things that may be standing in their way and adjust accordingly. If monitored and corrected often, their businesses not only survive, but flourish.

Also, keep in mind that your ultimate aim is to travel from point A, where you begin, to point B, your goal. In order to land in the right place at the right time, you must be committed to making small improvements and adjustments every day. If not, you're likely to arrive at an unfriendly place.

Superior marketing is never an accident. It is planned, deliberate, intentional, and calculated. It begins with a healthy mindset and a committment to regularly monitoring all activities and conducting objective assessments of the results. This means honestly and regularly asking yourself questions, such as:

- How am I doing?
- Am I closer to my objectives, or further away?
- How do my forecasts compare to what's actually happened?
- Is my company doing better than I expected? If so, why?
- Am I falling short of my goals? If so, why?
- What actions and processes are working well?
- What actions or processes are draining me and/or my company?
- What external things have or may affect my ability to achieve these goals?
- What minor adjustments do I have to make today to stay on the right path?

If you begin each day with this type of introspection, marketing will become "muscle memory"—an ongoing part of each and every day. And before you know it, you'll be experiencing the many benefits it affords.

So, now that you have selected the marketing communications vehicles that will help you achieve your objectives it's time to decide how you'll track, measure and evaluate your results.

> *Success is often the result of taking a misstep in the right direction.*
>
> —AL BERNSTEIN

Track What? Measure What? Evaluate What?

As we've repeatedly said, good marketers regularly and proactively seek information on all aspects of their business: their customers, target prospects, service area, industry, competitors, and more. Some of this data will be quantifiable, some more subjective. The good news is you can select the types of feedback that are most useful to you like the:

- *Financial advisor* who uses surveys to find out if his clients' service experience met, or exceeded, their expectations.
- *Manufacturer* who regularly collects feedback and suggestions from his products' resellers and end-users.
- *Retailer* who collects and inputs her customers' buying habits and product preferences into her marketing database.
- *Online marketer* who tracks her web site's visitors and the average number of times they return.
- *Marketing director* who surveys past customers to find out why they no longer do business with her company (we've included a customer "churn" tracking worksheet, Figure 12.6, at the end of this chapter).
- *Sales manager* who keeps track of his employees' performances and commission payments.
- *Nonprofit director* who conducts membership surveys to improve his fundraising efforts.

However, you'll need to narrow your focus to more quantifiable data in order to complete your 12-month marketing plan. Therefore, you'll first need to identify and select the actions you'll track, the information you hope to gain, and the tools and methods you'll use to obtain it.

I won 28 games in 35 and I couldn't believe my eyes when the Cards sent me a contract with a cut in salary. Mr. Rickey said I deserved a cut because I didn't win 30 games.

—DIZZY DEAN

Selecting the actions you'll track is the easiest part of the entire process because there's a very simple rule of thumb you can use: If you've chosen Direct-Response advertising or a communications vehicle (direct mail, e-mail campaign, radio, newspaper) that you cannot track or measure, take it off your list.

See how straightforward and uncomplicated that is? Makes the decision-making process that much easier, doesn't it?

Next, review the actions you've included and think about the types of questions you'd like to have answered, ones that will provide the most valuable insights.

For example, would you like to know if you:

- Achieved the response rates and sales that you forecasted in your plan?
- Stayed within your marketing budget?
- Generated the revenues and profits you predicted in your plan?
- Forecasted your various products' or services' contributions to overall sales, revenues, and profits correctly?
- Chose communication vehicles that produced the best return on your investment?
- Selected the right target market(s) for your offer?
- Were successful in upgrading enough current customers to new products?
- Won back a sufficient number of expired clients?

The kinds of information you track is entirely your decision. Just make sure you're prepared to monitor and measure only those metrics that are a direct result of that action and nothing more—otherwise your data will be skewed and unreliable.

> *There is no point at which you can say, "Well, I'm successful now. I might as well take a nap."*
>
> —CARRIE FISHER

How Did You Do?

You'll never know unless you track and measure your results. According to business and marketing expert, Jay Conrad Levinson, "Advertising is an intricate science. Therefore, the best way to be sure that something is, or is not, working is to measure it using predetermined indicators. Gauge the effectiveness of your advertising from the beginning by keeping detailed records on what you did, when, to whom, for how much, and what happened.

The Ten Best Tracking, Monitoring, and Measuring Tools

Admittedly, the results of certain advertising are difficult to gauge. However, if you don't measure, record and analyze them, you may be wasting money and missing the opportunity to make your decisions much easier the next time around. Here are ten of the best tools for measuring your success.

1. Your Ears

Savvy marketers know that their best screening tool are their ears. They've learned to ask the right questions, listen intently to the answers they receive, carefully evaluate their current situation, make informed decisions, and then act.

So, we encourage you to include your ears in your own best-of-the-best marketing toolkit. And we can't think of an easier or more straightforward way to track how well you're doing than by asking this one simple question: *"How did you hear about us?"*

It doesn't matter whether you're conducting business on your web site, retail location, or over the phone. You must vow never to let a prospect or new customer get away from you before you've asked, and documented, the answer to this question.

The well-known marketing expert, Jay Abraham, who has one of the most innovative tactical marketing minds in the industry, says that the usual way retailers greet people who enter their store—"Can I help you?"—is not only unmemorable but actually detrimental to sales. So what does he suggest they do instead? Say, "How did you hear about us?" He claimed that recent consumer research concluded that this question received the best reaction from consumers across the board, and often resulted in higher sales rates.

2. Testing

There are several no-nos to keep in mind before launching a marketing campaign, and they all involve testing:

- Never do anything in a big way until you've tested it in smaller venues.
- Never assume that the headline you use is the best unless you've tested it against others.

- Never assume that your offer, copy, or creative output is the most compelling unless you've tested it against others.

In other words, you must always be testing—but be sure to change only one variable at a time. For example, take your best newspaper ad headline to date and test it against an identical ad with a different headline. Track the results of each. Keep the top performer and get rid of the other. Continue this process indefinitely until you've thoroughly tested all the key elements in your piece.

3. Marketing Calendars

If used correctly, a marketing activities calendar can be one of your business's best friends. It is a wonderful planning tool and a great way to stay on top of things. In addition to charting your communications schedule, it will help you plan your finances, staffing needs, and tracking requirements.

Even better, there is no right or wrong way to create a marketing calendar, although most contain:

- A 12-month snapshot divided into monthly, weekly, or daily views.
- The specific marketing vehicles that will be used during the allotted timeframes, with associated expenses.
- The length of each promotional activity.

We've included a blank marketing activities calendar template at the end of this chapter, which you can use to document your plans.

4. Surveys

These are wonderful tools for understanding what's on the minds of your customers and prospects. You can execute them in one of several ways, such as: sending a questionnaire via snail mail (include a self-addressed stamped envelope); mailing double-sided postcards; or asking for feedback over the phone. Even better, you can instantly create and send an e-mail survey to your prospects and customers, as long as you have their e-mail addresses. If this interests you, check out www.SurveyMonkey.com. They'll allow you to develop and e-mail surveys for free.

5. Ad Trackers

There are many types of ad trackers available and they all work pretty much the same. First, you'll need to purchase ad tracking software (check out www.MyEasyWebAutomation.com) that you can buy as a standalone product, even though many shopping carts now include it. We recommend the latter since it will monitor your web site's click-through rates and calculate your sales and opt-in statistics as well. Google has some great tools as well. Check out Google Analytics at www.google.com/analytics.

6. Codes

It's so easy to add alphabetic or numeric codes on the bottom of any written communication such as direct mail, newspaper ads, or coupons. Create as many as you need (for testing), and when customers contact you ask them to provide the code on their communication piece.

7. Computer Software such as Microsoft Access and Excel

Microsoft Access, Excel, and other similar software programs are wonderfully easy tools for collecting and displaying tracking information. Here are a couple of other resources:

- Marketing Analytics, Inc., www.marketinganalytics.com.
- MarketingPilot Software,www.marketingpilot.com.

8. Dedicated Telephone Numbers

Today it's easy and affordable to use multiple telephone numbers to track call-in response rates from different types of media or channels. For instance, you can purchase multiple toll-free numbers or non toll-free numbers that feed into one, two, or more numbers. This way, when a caller dials the number listed on their communications piece, the network will automatically "document" the call-in number. And since each number is assigned to a different vehicle or channel, you'll know which ones worked best.

9. Web-Based Software

Internet software programs are flexible solutions for your tracking challenges because they can be used to monitor online and offline campaign results. In addition to providing up to-the-minute information, they allow you to put your prospect and customer communications virtually on autopilot.

You can also:

- View and compare individually, or as a whole, the performance of all current marketing campaigns, such as response and sales rates, product and service sales, and leads generated.
- Extract detailed survey and responder data for follow-up marketing and sales purposes.
- Drill down further into individual campaigns to locate information such as a list of responders by campaign, contact information for individuals who responded, and survey results and information.
- Instantly compare all marketing results by media category.
- Quickly calculate the cost of leads by media, helping you refocus your media buying for maximum results.
- View individual survey question data.
- Receive complete survey results in real time.
- Use toll-free numbers and web URLs to track advertising results.
- Add, review, and mange all database contacts, and much more!

Once again, we recommend that you check out www.MyEasyWebAuto mation.com. Another affordable web-based tracking program can be found at http://marketingresultsgroup.com.

10. Customized Tracking Reports

If you're uncomfortable using computer software or web-based programs to track your results, as a last resort, you can always build your own reports and monitor your progress manually. But we strongly advise you to do whatever it takes—enroll in a computer class, ask a friend for help, or hire a consultant—to learn and use state-of-the-art internet technologies to streamline your marketing efforts. They're affordable, relatively simple to use, and incredible timesavers. However, in the meantime, you can use one or more of the tracking templates that we've included at the end of this chapter. And remember, if you'd like to download any of the templates from this book, go to www.The ProcrastinatorsGuideToMarketing.com or www.TPGTM.com. Once there, you'll be asked to register and given instructions for downloading.

Now it's time to select the method you'll use to track and measure your results. Use the space provided below to enter your choices.

Following are tools I'll use to track, measure, and evaluate the effectiveness of my marketing communications plan.

1.

2.

3.

4.

Evaluating Your Results

As they say, knowledge is power. But the effective use of knowledge is even more potent.

Remember, excellent marketing doesn't happen overnight: achieving your vision and big-picture business objectives should be a long-term effort so strive to make measurable progress over a realistic period of time. After you've completed your action steps and collected your data, it's time to assess your results.

Conviction is the luxury of those sitting on the sidelines. For those of us who choose to play rather than watch, measurement is the compass that guides us through our mistakes.

—JOHN NASH'S (IMAGINARY) BOSS SAYS IN THE MOVIE *A BEAUTIFUL MIND*

But don't forget, your ability to make effective changes is dependent upon the accuracy and validity of the data you collected (GIGO—garbage in, garbage out).

One of the easiest ways to find out is by answering "yes" or "no" to the questions in Figure 12.1 after you've executed your communications plan.

FIGURE 12.1: Evaluation Questions

Did I achieve my objectives?	Yes	No
Did I get a reasonable ROI?	Yes	No
Did I generate enough leads?	Yes	No
Did I sell enough products?	Yes	No
Did I earn a respectable gross profit?	Yes	No
Did I earn a respectable net profit?	Yes	No
Did I upgrade or upgrade enough people?	Yes	No
Did I choose the right tactics and tools?	Yes	No
Did I achieve my forecasted response rates?	Yes	No
Did I achieve my forecasted sales rates?	Yes	No

Once you're finished, extract all of the questions that received a "no" answer. Next, use the "Five-Why" system to help you identify the root causes.

 The Five Whys

Made popular in the 1970s, the "5 Whys" is a simple and elegant problem-solving tool designed to quickly answer the question, "What exactly caused this to happen?" (Although it was specifically created to address dilemmas, it can also be used to nail down the reasons for successes.)

The rationale for developing the tool was centered on the theory that asking the question "why?" after a "results" statement will usually prompt another "why?" This continues until enough layers are peeled away and the root cause of any problem is finally revealed. Although it's called the "5 Whys," it may take fewer or more "whys" for you to arrive at the answer.

This is a particularly helpful process for getting to the heart of more subjective challenges such as those involving relationships, decision-making skills, and attitudes.

The Five Whys

Following is a simple example of how you might use this tool.

Question: Did I receive my forecasted response rates?
Answer: No

Question: Why?
Answer: Because a third of the people who received our letter called the wrong telephone number.

Question: Why?
Answer: Because the telephone number displayed on one-third of our letters was incorrect.

Question: Why?
Answer: Because no one caught the error before the letters were mailed.

Question: Why?
Answer: Because the final copy wasn't checked for errors.

Question: Why?
Answer: Because we didn't have the two hours it would have taken for the editor to read it over.

Question: Why?
Answer: Because we were running late and didn't want to miss our deadline.

Question: Why?
Answer: Because we didn't leave ourselves enough time to write, print, and mail the letter.

Question: Why?
Answer: Because we underestimated how long it would take us to complete the entire process.

Question: Why?
Answer: Because we experienced unnecessary time delays due to confusion over who was responsible for what.

Question: Why?
Answer: Because we didn't develop a plan of action beforehand.

As you can see, it took more than five "whys" to find out that the reason for the problem was a breakdown in the process.

The good news is that these types of problems are almost always fixable, when you know the root cause conversely it's nearly impossible to get resolution if you merely state the problem and refuse to investigate further.

Now it's your turn. Use Figure 12.2 (make as many copies as you need) to conduct your own "Five Whys" investigation.

Use the insights and information that you collect through this process to determine your marketing plan's effectiveness and make necessary adjustments, such as:

- Re-evaluating your business objectives
- Finding time-saving short cuts
- Avoiding the actions that didn't work well
- Setting new benchmarks for success
- Developing your marketing calendar

FIGURE 12.2: **The Five Whys Worksheet**

Problem Question: _____

Answer: No

Question: Why?

Answer: _____

Question: Why?

Answer: _____

Question: Why?

Answer: _____

Question: Why?

Answer: _____

Question: Why?

Answer: _____

Question: Why?

Answer: _____

Question: Why?

Answer: _____

Question: Why?

Answer: _____

FIGURE 12.2: The Five Whys Worksheet, continued

Question: Why?

Answer: _____

Question: Why?

Answer: _____

Also, be sure to look for more subtle trends. For instance, are you receiving lots of calls from prospects who need directions to your store? Or, are your customers asking for products you don't carry?

Remember, the best marketing tools are your ears.

In the next chapter, you'll put it all together. That is, use the information that you've gathered and plug it into your marketing plan template.

Figure 12.3: Marketing Activities Calendar is used to track your monthly marketing communications activity.

Figure 12.4: Marketing Activities Results Calendar can be modified to include your marketing activities. This is a great way to keep track of what you've done and how it worked!

Figure 12.5: Monthly Sales by Product Tracking is used to track actual and/or forecasted monthly sales by product.

Customer Churn Tracking Worksheet, Figure 12.6 will help you keep track of the reasons customers leave.

Figure 12.7: Monthly Sales by Communication Vehicle Tracking Worksheet is a template you can use to track total actual and/or forecasted sales by channel. Change the headings to suit your own situation.

FIGURE 12.3: Marketing Activites Calendar

Communication Method	Jan	Feb	Mar	Apr	May	Jun	Jul	Aug	Sep	Oct	Nov	Dec

FIGURE 12.4: **Marketing Activites Results Calendar**

Year:

Month	Marketing Activity Description	Total Sales	DM	DM %	Radio	Radio %	Agent	Agent %	Referral	Referral %	Internet	Internet %
January												
February												
March												
April												
May												
June												
July												
August												
September												
October												
November												
December												
Total												

FIGURE 12.5: **Monthly Sales by Product Tracking**

Product or Service	Jan	Feb	Mar	Apr	May	Jun	Jul	Aug	Sep	Oct	Nov	Dec	Total

FIGURE 12.6: **Customer Churn Worksheet**

From (date):   **to (date):**

Product	Number of Customers Leaving for this Reason	101	102	103	104	105	106	107	108

Code Key Sample *(Customize codes for your business):*

    101   Poor customer service

    102   Price

    103   Competitive offering is better

    104   Product/service did not meet expectation

    105   Billing problems

    106   Moved out of area

    107   Don't need product/service anymore

    108   Other/Don't know

FIGURE 12.7: **Sales by Communication Vehicle Tracking Worksheet**

Month:

Total Sales for all Products:

Product or Service	Total Sales	Direct Mail Sales	Radio Sales	Referral Sales	Internet Sales	Newspaper Sales	Walk-In Sales	Other or Don't Know

Chapter 12 Snapshot

Before moving on to Chapter 13, let's take time to review several of the most important take-aways from this chapter:

- Marketing is a cyclical, not linear, process.

- You must be committed to making small improvements and adjustments every day.

- Superior marketing is never an accident. It is planned, deliberate, intentional, and calculated.

- If you can't track it, if you can't measure it, don't do it.

- Savvy marketers ask the right questions, listen intently to the answers they receive, carefully evaluate their situation, make informed decisions, and then act.

Please note: If you'd like to download any of the templates from this book, go to www.**T**he**P**rocrastinators**G**uide**T**o**M**arketing.com or www.TPGTM.com. Once there, you'll be asked to register and given instructions for downloading.

If at first you don't succeed, try, try again. Then quit.
There's no point in being a damn fool about it.

—W. C. FIELDS

STEP 9

Putting It All Together

If you've followed the steps to this point you're probably more than ready to see your marketing plan take shape. But if you're like many people, you may also feel a bit apprehensive about your ability to take the information you've gathered and include it in one document. If so, relax! The worst is over. You've already completed the bulk of your work. Putting it down on paper is a much less demanding undertaking—particularly since you're not going to be overly concerned with how "pretty" it looks, correct?

> *The best students are ones who never quite believe their professors.*
>
> —JIM COLLINS

Remember this: a written marketing plan substantially increases the odds that you'll achieve your business goals. So, please, organize your data and enter it into the outline we've included or one of your own. The journey that you've taken to get here is far more precious than the words on paper. The insights you've gained—about you, your company, and the marketplace—and the thought process that allowed them to break the surface will serve you well now and in the future. Guidance is a wonderful tool, but in the end the integrity of your plan and ability to reach your goals depend entirely upon your inputs— your mindset, actions, skills, and knowledge.

So, now it's time to begin putting it all together. If you've completed steps one through eight, you'll be able to "cut and paste" your information into the appropriate spots.

But first, here's an overview of what you'll find:

1. *Marketing plan instructions*. A summary of the five main parts and sections of your marketing plan with the types of information to include and references back to the chapters where the topic was covered.
2. *Marketing plan outline*. A very high-level, bare bones outline that you can copy, print, or modify to suit your needs.
3. *Samples*. Examples of plan components for a fictitious business, "Company XYZ"—a Charleston-area firm that sells telephone equipment and services to other companies in their local area.

Drawbacks of this Process

1. *This is but one approach to a marketing plan*. We have intentionally asked that you include plans for 12 months only, even though we strongly recommend that all business owners and managers develop a long-term perspective. That's why everything contained in your plan should support your long-term goals and visions.

   We've chosen this time because things change very rapidly these days and companies must be able to respond quickly. It was fairly easy to plan 10 years out 20 years ago, but that's no longer the case. Because of rapid technological shifts, accurate forecasts that far in the future cannot be reliable. As a result, many companies now use more scenario-related plans that focus on multiple contingencies.

2. *One size does not fit all*. You'll find detailed directions, an outline, and several great samples, but you won't find one boiler-plated paint-by-numbers marketing plan. We've purposely avoided this for several reasons.

> *If you don't know what port you are sailing to, no wind is favourable.*
>
> —SENECA THE YOUNGER, 4B.C.–A.D.65

There is no one version that can fit all needs. We've seen far too many marketing plans that are meaningless fill-in-the-blank documents that required little or no thought, research, or skill to prepare—and it shows. Not only do they lack critical, detailed, and personalized data but also they are simply a waste of time. Trust us, there is no way to write a powerful marketing plan without giving it the time and effort it deserves.

3. *Marketing plans are meant to be flexible* and top-down models such as the one provided in this chapter are more suited to stable companies. Feel free to add, delete, or amend parts or sections to suit your situation. Additionally, we don't expect you to answer every question posed, they're there to jump-start your thinking.

Rules of Thumb

Your marketing plan does not have to be overly formal. Use simple and clear language. If no one but you will read it, don't worry about typos. However, double check all of your numbers, facts, and calculations.

Do not confuse casual with sloppy. If anyone else will be reviewing your marketing plan—especially potential investors—make sure it is well-written and error-free. Avoid:

- *Confusing percentages*—keep them as simple as possible.
- *Bashing your competitors*—provide a realistic assessment.
- *Exaggerations*—it's best to be overly cautious and overestimate expenses and underestimate revenues and sales.

- *Vague justifications*—support your assumptions with specifics.
- *Unnecessary big words, acronyms, or industry jargon*—if someone has to pull out a dictionary, you're in trouble.
- *Beating around the bush*—get to the point, already!
- *Keep readability in mind*—make sure your copy is easy to read and don't overuse fancy type or fonts.

> *There is nothing so useless as doing efficiently that which should not be done at all.*
>
> —PETER DRUCKER

Marketing Plan Instructions

I. Executive Summary

The first part of your marketing plan will lay the foundation for the rest. You'll discuss your purpose for writing the plan, introduce key players, and provide a vivid picture of your company's aspirations for the future. Additionally, you'll summarize important initiatives and final recommendations. *Tip*: Wait to write section "D" last so you can capture relevant data from the other sections.

A. PURPOSE

In this section you'll define the plan's purpose. That is, what do you hope to accomplish by writing this plan? Reasons include:

- As part of your normal planning process
- To include in full-blown business plan
- You're seeking investment capital or a bank loan
- To introduce a new product launch or increased market share

Also include the timeline that the plan covers (in this case, it's 12 months—see Chapter 5).

B. INTRODUCTION AND OVERVIEW

Here you'll introduce your company (including management team if your audience is not familiar with you or your business). You should answer questions such as:

- Why is your company in business?
- Where is your business located?
- What is your company's service area (local, regional, national, international)? Be specific.
- What are your main products and/or services?
- When executed, what effect will your actions have on you company's bottom line?
- What are the long-term goals of your business? (See Figure 13.1.)

C. CORE PHILOSOPHIES

State your company's core philosophies. (See Figure 13.2.) Answer questions such as:

- What do you want your company to be known for? (Chapter 6)
- What is your company's vision for the future? (Vision Statement, Chapter 6)
- What do you see as your company's mission? (Mission Statement, Chapter 6)

D. SUMMARY OF PLAN OBJECTIVES AND RECOMMENDATIONS

In this section, you'll summarize your business objectives for the next 12 months (the ones you developed in Chapter 5—see Figure 13.3). Consider the following:

- Dollar and unit sales
- Gross and net profits
- Market share and/or expansion
- Current customer base
- Changes within your organization
- Streamlining systems or processes
- Training requirements for improving skills and knowledge

II. Situation Analysis

The second part of your marketing plan will contain an objective assessment of your company's current circumstances—its internal strengths and weaknesses and external opportunities and threats (SWOT). Also, you'll include your plan for taking advantage of the positive factors and minimizing or erasing the negative ones. Concentrate on the five "Cs": company, customers, competitors, climate, and collaborators.

The Bottom Line

Describe your current situation—your capabilities and limitations—and explain how they may affect your chances of attaining or surpassing your goals. What are your capabilities? What are your limitations?

See Chapter 5 and Figure 13.4.

A. COMPANY

In this section you'll share detailed information on your company's strengths, weaknesses, opportunities, and threats. You should be internally focused on topics, such as:

- *Resources.* Your cash, funding, employees, subcontractors, agents, equipment, machinery, knowledge, skills, operational efficiencies, internal processes and systems, brand awareness, exclusive contracts—how might these help or hurt you?
- *Culture.* Is it casual or more formal? How does your organization work? What changes are needed, if any?
- *Past vs. Present.* How has your company changed? Do you offer new products or services? Is your business growing, stagnant, or declining? Is your company more, or less, profitable than in the past? How have your sales changed over the last several years? Why? (See Figures 13.6 and 13.9.)

B. CUSTOMERS

In this section you'll share detailed information about your customers. You should answer questions such as:

- Who uses your products and why? How does your ideal customer behave?
- Do your products and services appeal to the masses or more niched markets?

- Who are the key decision-makers?
- How large is the current market you serve?
- What do you know about your current customers? What type of information do you keep on them?
- What are your predictions about the future growth of your customer base and targeted market?
- How long does your average customer stay loyal to your business?
- What are the segments that exist within your customer base?
- Where do most of your customers purchase your products or services?
- What is the buying process? Do your customers buy on impulse or only after careful consideration? How long is your average sales cycle?
- What is the main motivation behind your customers' purchases.
- Are there seasonal factors which increase, or decrease, your prospects' and customers' interest in purchasing your products or services? (See Figures 13.5 and 13.7.)

C. COMPETITORS

In this section you'll share detailed information about your competitors. Answer questions such as:

- Who are your major competitors?
- What are your competitors doing better than you?
- Why would someone choose to do business with your company over one of your competitors?
- How are your competitors positioned in the marketplace?
- What are their market shares relative to your?
- How do their products' and services' features, quality, selection, and price compare with yours? (See Figures 13.8.)

D. CLIMATE

In this section you'll describe your environment and discuss the external factors that may have the greatest positive and/or negative effect on your ability to reach your goals. Consider dynamics such as:

- The political and regulatory environment—government policies and regulations that affect your industry
- Social culture and trends
- The economy—inflation, interest, unemployment rates, and consumers' index
- International issues
- Technological environment—the impact the emerging or future technology may have on your industry or company. (See Figure 13.10.)

E. COLLABORATORS

In this section you'll share detailed information about your collaborators—those people who will help you achieve your goals. They include:

- Distributors
- Suppliers
- Strategic partners
- Subcontractors
- All other people (or companies) who have a direct effect on sales or profits (nonemployees)

III. Marketing Strategies

The third part of your marketing plan is devoted to what you'll say, how you'll say it, and to whom. As we've said many times through this book, your strategies are based on your goals, business objectives, historical customer data, objective research and the opportunities you've uncovered so far. These set the stage for the execution of your tactical plan (Part IV) and create the environment in which you'll operate over the next 12 months and longer (Chapter 5).

A. OVERALL STRATEGY

In this section you'll provide your overall marketing strategy. Answer questions such as:

- What is your strategic focus over the next 12 months? (e.g., new customer acquisition, damage control, customer retentions, investor relations, shareholder value, market share)
- How much of your plan supports your strategic goal of acquiring new customers?

- How much of your plan supports your strategic goal of keeping and getting more out of your current customers?

B. PRODUCTS AND SERVICES

In this section you'll share detailed information about the products and services you'll use to help you achieve the objectives you outlined in this plan. Answer questions such as:

- How do your products and services solve your target audiences' most pressing problems?
- Why do people buy your products (or services)?
- How often do your customers buy your products?
- How long do your products last?
- Can your products be improved? If so, how?
- Do they require any follow-up service? If so, what?
- What do your customers like most about your products? Least? How will you overcome this?
- How do your products compare to others in your industry on such elements as quality, selection, functionality, appearance, price, or overall value?
- Do your customers receive superior service 100 percent of the time? If not, why not?
- How does your service performance compare with that of other companies? Your competitors?
- How will your customers' demands and trends affect you?
- Are there new technologies or materials that might make your product development process more efficient or cost-effective? If so, what are they?
- What are your products' or services' most important benefits? (See Figure 13.11.)

C. PRICING

In this section you'll give more specifics on your pricing policies. Answer questions such as:

- How large a role does pricing play in communicating their value to targeted prospects?
- How do your prices compare with your competitors'?
- What is the gross profit margin of each of your products or services?
- Are your gross profit margins enough to support your marketing expenses? (Chapter 7)

D. TARGET MARKETS AND SEGMENTATION

In this section you'll describe your targeted prospects—those people who are most likely to become your customers. Answer questions such as:

- Who are your ideal prospects?
- Have you defined and identified major segments and subsegments within your target audience?
- What other smaller, but profitable, groups of people can you target?
- Who are the prospects that you will pursue?
- How will you locate your best prospects? (See Figure 13.10 and Chapter 8.)

E. POSITIONING

In this section you'll provide information about your products' and services' position in the marketplace. Answer questions such as:

- What will be the look and feel of your marketing communications?
- How will you position your company relative to your competitors?
- Does your inside reality match the public's perceptions? How do you know? (Chapter 6)

F. VALUE PROPOSITION AND USP

In this section you'll introduce your USP, or what sets you apart from your competitors. Answer questions such as:

- Can you dollarize your products' benefits? If so, how?
- Why should your targeted prospects choose your company over all of your competitors?
- What unique advantage do you have over all of your other competitors?

• How will you communicate your USP? (Chapter 6)

G. MARKETPLACE MESSAGE

In this section you'll present information or exactly what you'll say about you, your company and products—and to whom. Answer questions such as:

- What will you say to your targeted prospects?
- How will you communicate your key values? (Chapter 9)
- Do you have different key messages for diverse prospect groups? If so, what?

IV. Tactics and Marketing Communication

The fourth part of your marketing plan contains a detailed description of the tangible and measurable tactics that will be carried out in order to achieve your business objectives. It also includes associated timelines, service delivery type, and accountable owners for executing each action. You'll also provide your forecasts for what will happen as a direct result of the actions you've listed, and any relevant support data (Chapter 11).

A. CURRENT MARKETING MATERIALS

In this section you'll share detailed information about your current marketing materials. Answer questions such as:

- What kinds of communication pieces do you currently have ready to use?
- Which ones have worked best for you?
- Which ones need to be replaced?
- Do they contain relevant and up-to-date information?

B. ADVERTISING

In this section you'll discuss your advertising plans. Answer questions such as:

- What are your advertising objectives?
- What types of advertising have worked best for you in the past?
- What advertising vehicles will you use to achieve the objectives you've identified in this plan? (Chapter 11)

C. PROGRAMS, PROMOTIONS

In this section you'll summarize information about your program and promotional activities. Answer questions such as:

- What types of programs and promotional activities have worked best for you in the past?
- What programs or promotions will have the greatest positive impact on your ability to achieve your goals? (Chapters 7 and 11)

D. PUBLIC RELATIONS

In this section you'll describe your public relation plans. Answer questions such as:

- What types of public relations activities have worked best for you in the past?
- What public relations tools or tactics will you use to accomplish your business objectives?
- What are you doing to maintain your public image? (Chapter 11)

E. INTERNET MARKETING

In this section you'll outline your internet marketing plans. Answer questions such as:

- What are your goals for your web site and how will you accomplish them?
- What is your web site's major purpose (e.g. e-commerce, informational, branding, etc.)?
- What types of web site tools and tactics will you use to help you accomplish the goals you've identified in this plan?
- What are your linking, SEO, shopping cart, automation, newsletter, and the like strategies?
- Do you have your own affiliate program? Are you an affiliate for other companies?
- How will you collect your visitors' names and e-mail addresses?
- Have you integrated your online and offline strategies and tactics? (Chapter 11) If so, how?

F. Direct Sales

In this section you'll summarize your direct sales methods. Answer questions such as:

- What type of direct sales tactics will you use?
- Do you currently have a direct sales force in place? If so, describe your organization and their sales process.
- What improvements will make your direct sales efforts more successful? (e.g., weekly training sessions, updated materials, increased commissions, etc.—Chapter 11.)

G. Activities List with Timelines and Task Owners

In this section you'll provide a detailed list of actions you'll take, associated timelines, task owners, and forecasts. Answer questions such as:

- What methods, sales channels, and media mix will you use?
- Who is responsible and accountable for various tasks (owners)?
- What are the expected results? Why do you think these forecasts are realistic?
- What are your incremental sales, revenue, and profit forecasts?
- How will these actions impact your company's bottom line? (Chapter 11)

V. Budgets and Measurement

The fifth part of your marketing plan documents your marketing budget and contains an itemized list of expenses for each action included. You'll begin with a brief summary of the tactics you described in Part IV and your incremental revenue and expense forecasts. You should also include cash flow and break-even analyses, for all appropriate activities.

The Bottom Line

Remember, this is not a full-blown business plan and your financial projections should be confined to your marketing activities unless other expenses directly impact your ability to execute your tactical plan.
(Chapters 11 and 12)

A. Marketing Budget

In this section you'll provide detailed information regarding your marketing budget. Answer questions such as:

- Is your marketing budget realistic?
- According to your tactical plan, how much will it cost you to acquire one customer?
- How much revenue ($) will each new customer contribute to your company during the 12-month period covered by this plan?
- How much revenue ($) will each new customer contribute to your company over their lifetime (CLV) as your customer?
- According to your tactical plan, how much will it cost you to retain one customer?
- What is your breakeven point?
- How much will you need and when will you need it to execute your tactical plan?
- What are your fixed versus variable costs? (Chapters 4, 7, and 11)

B. Measurements

In this section you'll outline the types of activities you'll measure. Answer questions such as:

- What will you measure—sales, responses, marketshare, etc.?
- How will you measure results?
- What benchmarks have you established for measuring success?
- How will you know when you've achieved your objectives? (Chapter 12)

C. Tools

In this section you'll describe the tools you'll use to track, measure and evaluate your results. Answer questions such as:

- Will you track your activities using web-based software? If so, which ones?
- Will you develop your own tracking system? If so, describe it. (Chapter 12)
- Will you use automation technology or track your efforts manually?

D. RESOURCES

In this section you'll share detailed information about your resources. Answer questions such as:

- What resources are needed to attain your plan's objectives?
- How much more business can you reasonably expect to handle without having to hire additional employees or subcontractors or purchase new equipment?
- Who is accountable for executing the actions covered in this plan?
- What interdepartmental dependencies are required to successfully implement this plan?
- What resources (time, people, money, and systems) are most critical to your success?
- What type of customer service, operational capabilities, staffing, fulfillments, and the like are required to execute this plan? (Chapter 12)

Marketing Plan Outline

I. Executive Summary

   A. Purpose: How this plan will be used

   B. Introduction and Overview

       1. Company
       2. Employees
       3. Location
       4. Service Area
       5. Product and Service Offerings
       6. 12-Month Business Objectives

   C. Core Philosophies

       1. Beliefs
       2. Vision
       3. Mission

   D. Summary of Plan Objectives and Recommendations

       1. Strategic Goals
       2. Tactical Objectives

II. Situation Analysis (Strengths, Weaknesses, Opportunities, and Threats)
 A. Company
 B. Customers
 C. Competitors
 D. Climate
 E. Collaborators

III. Marketing Strategies
 A. Overall Strategy
 B. Products and Services
 C. Pricing
 D. Target Markets and Segmentation
 E. Positioning
 F. Value Proposition and USP
 G. Marketplace Message

IV. Tactics and Marketing Communication
 A. Current Marketing Materials
 B. Advertising
 C. Programs, Promotions
 D. Public Relations
 E. Internet Marketing
 F. Direct Sales
 G. Activities List with Timelines and Task Owners

V. Budgets and Measurement
 A. Marketing Budget
 B. Measurements
 C. Tools
 D. Resources

FIGURE 13.1

Company XYZ: Overview and Background

Company XYZ is an x-year-old company located in North Charleston, SC. They sell, maintain, service [what]

Although this type of company is growing, its executives want to cultivate more new business; increase the transactional dollar amount per customer; and maintain their outstanding customer retention rate.

Here is a list of the company's x employees/executives and their major responsibilities:

- *Name, Title*. Oversees running of entire company and conducts field visits with clients

- *Other Name, Title*. Supervises office staff; oversees and manages customer service policies and personnel; accounting duties; occasional sales

- *Name, Manager*. Manages technicians; handles dispatch, schedules, orders, and invoices

FIGURE 13.2

Company XYZ: Core Philosophies

It is important to communicate our company's core business and marketing philosophies since they serve as the foundation of our business's most fundamental values, beliefs, and actions. They are:

- Our company is in the marketing business, and our goal is to get and keep profitable customers.

- Marketing is not another word for advertising and/or public relations. Rather, it is the heart and soul of this company and involves all aspects of our customers' experiences.

- We will "dance with the guy who brought us" by focusing more and diversifying less. We will never try to be all things to all people.

- Strategy is the deployment of scarce resources and the selection of tactics and tools to achieve an objective. We will apply this concept to our planning process.

- Excellent marketing will provide our company with increased leverage, or control. We will maximize their influence over the events that impact our company so that our inputs (work, time, money, effort) result in the highest possible outputs (customers, profits, prosperity).

- Business success will be measured by profits, not revenue or sales.

FIGURE 13.2, continued

Company XYZ: Core Philosophies

- Our company will develop written standardized systems and processes that are communicated and followed by every employee.

- All company employees, suppliers, subcontractors, and/or agents will be paid according to the value they deliver.

- Opportunity costs of all activities are a vitally important consideration for our company.

- We are responsible to our clients—that is, we are obligated to provide the highest quality professional advice and deliverables in the least amount of time, regardless of our customers' ability and/or willingness to pay more.

FIGURE 13.3

Company XYZ: Business Goals

Within the next six months we will accomplish the following:

1. Add 60 new clients (10/month). Since we currently average 3-4 new clients per month (strictly by word-of-mouth), we could reasonably expect to acquire 21 new customers with little, or no, additional effort. Therefore, we are looking for an incremental gain of 39 new clients (average of 6.5/month).
   Company executives estimate that each new client contributes an average of $5,000 in initial revenues (equipment purchase) and $200 per month thereafter (maintenance contract). This would result in a total immediate incremental revenue gain of $195,000 (equipment) plus $93,600 over the next two years.

2. Increase current maintenance-contract clients by 20 percent.

3. Launch soft switch Voice Over Internet Protocol (VoIP) and unified messaging products to residential customers. Within the next 6 to 12 months, our goals are:
   - Add 90 new clients (revenue assumptions remain the same as above)
   - Hire and train one new sales person and technician
   - Purchase one new company vehicle
   - Complete detailed written employee training manual, to include customer care instructions and policies; escalation and troubleshooting procedures; our company mission, vision, and founding principles.

FIGURE 13.4

Company XYZ: Situational Analysis: Strengths, Weaknesses, Opportunities, and Threats

Key Strengths and Opportunities

The following list contains assessment of our key strengths—ones we'll develop, maintain, and communicate. Although there are more, we believe the following are playing, and will continue to play, the largest role in our current and future success.

- *Technical Expertise and Knowledge*. The exceptional knowledge base and skill level of our employees.

- *Word-of-Mouth Referrals*. Our company has grown solely on positive word-of-mouth referrals. This is an extremely positive indicator of our ability to retain customers. We will take advantage of this by instituting at least one robust referral program and requesting and publicizing customer testimonials.

- *Outstanding Customer Retention Rates*. Our company's customers are extremely loyal. Their churn rate is essentially non-existent (particularly unusual in the telecommunications industry where companies experience some of the highest customer churn rates of any industry). As a matter of fact, we have never lost a customer to a competitor in our over five years in business.

Key Weaknesses and Threats

The following list contains our evaluation of our company's major weaknesses and threats—the things that could have the most detrimental effect on our ability to achieve our goals, and ones we will correct, amend, or eliminate as soon as possible.

- *No Brand Awareness*. Our company is fairly new in the marketplace and has built no brand awareness in our service area. Many of our most qualified prospects do not know we're in business, allowing our competitors to "beat us to the punch."

- *Vulnerabilities Associated with Employee Size*. Our staff is small leaving us more susceptible to outages due to sickness, vacation time, etc.

- *Lack of Written Plan*. Currently our company has no strategic and/or tactical plan in place (i.e. mission and vision statements; core philosophies; stated company goals and objectives, etc.) resulting in lack of focus, "brain clutter," duplicative efforts, missed opportunities, wasted time and money, and rework.

FIGURE 13.5

Company XYZ: Situation Analysis: Current Customers

Small businesses currently account for approximately 60 percent of our customer base, with the remaining 40 percent split evenly between medium and large companies.

According to information contained in our database (and supported by equipment manufacturers' data) sales companies and service professionals involved in the following industries account for the largest number of our current customers:

- Construction
- Educational and health services
- Health care and social assistance
- Motor vehicle and parts dealers
- Legal services

They may also be companies that:

- Have out-grown their current telecommunications equipment and/or software
- Require immediate help for non-working telecommunications equipment and/or service
- Are looking for ways to increase their productivity
- Have employees who are out of their offices frequently but need to remain accessible

Target Market

Prospect/Customer Industry Niches

- Real Estate Brokers
- Sales Professionals
- Attorneys
- Physicians
- Professional Warehouse Managers
- Car Dealers

Customer Lifetime Value (CLV)

Our average customer contributes $715 in yearly revenues and is loyal to our company for three years, making our CLV equal to $2,145.

FIGURE 13.6

Company XYZ: Situation Analysis: Service Area

Our company is able to sell our products/services anywhere in the U.S. That is, there are no regulatory or other restrictions. However, for now we have chosen to focus our efforts close to home in and around South Carolina's "low country," (although we would like to open additional offices in Savannah, GA, and Florence, SC, within five years). These include, but are not limited to, the following South Carolina areas:

- Summerville
- Charleston
- West Ashley
- North Charleston
- Moncks Corner
- Goose Creek
- Aiken
- Myrtle Beach
- Beaufort

FIGURE 13.7

Company XYZ: Situation Analysis: "Ideal" Customer Behavior

Our "ideal" customers regularly exhibit at least two of the following behaviors. They:

- Pay their bills on time
- Purchase our maintenance contracts (which provide additional, ongoing monthly revenues)
- Recommend our products/services to others
- Are pleasant and easy to work with
- Are not "high maintenance" (i.e., frequent complaints, hand-holding, etc.)
- Contribute $1,215 in yearly revenues as opposed to our average of $715

Characteristics/Traits that Company XYZ "Ideal" Customers have in Common

After further research, we have identified one significant trait that our best customers possess. That is, businesses with at least 20 phone lines are most likely to behave "ideally."

Although this is an important finding, we will conduct more in-depth customer research to verify this and/or look for other similar characteristics. We will also use this information to target new prospects (those that have the highest probability of becoming high-value customers) and develop tiered retention programs for current and future customers.

FIGURE 13.8: **Company XYZ Competitive Analysis**

Company XYZ: Competitors

The following companies represent our top three competitors. This was established based on similarities in:

- Current customer base
- Customer "type" (i.e., business vs. residential)
- Target audience wants, needs and /or problems
- Location and service area
- Product/Service type

In each case, we identified key similarities and differences based on objective research and our own opinions and observations.

Company Name, Service Area and Location	Products and Services	Strengths	Weaknesses
Competitor 1 www.website.com Charleston Office: 10 ABC St. Charleston, SC 29407 (843) 555-0000 *"More than Just Talk"* *"Local company with the muscle of a major player"*	– Structured cabling – Consulting – Relocation – Voice over internet protocol – Technical support – Telephone system service – Local and long distance) (dial tone)	– Clear messaging–they "want to become you phone company," good differentiator – Offer a wide range of products, including dial tone – Provide most telecommun- ications and data services to small businesses–focusing on niche while still offering multiple services	– Web site is cluttered and not easy to navigate (have to double-click twice on every link to move to next page) and missing important functionality (e.g. online bill payment) – Contact page is clumsy and onerous, suggesting that they may be more mired in bureaucracy than us

FIGURE 13.8: **Company XYZ Competitive Analysis,** continued

Company Name, Service Area and Location	Products and Services	Strengths	Weaknesses
Competitor 1 www.website.com	– In business for 23 yrs.	– Dealer partners with the following: • Toshiba • Panasonic • Avaya • 3Com • Teleco Inc • Active • NEC • Nortel • Bell South	
Competitor 2 www.web site.com Charleston Office: 1 Oak St. North Charleston, SC 29406 (843) 555-5555 *"Our commitment is to your peace of mind."*	– Telephone equipment and packages, such as: • Telephone systems • IP-based systems • Internet equipment • Video conferencing systems • Customer premise networking equipment – Dial tone, Long distance – Data and internet services – Conferencing – Voice mail	– Good online customer service options – 100 yrs. old – 40 locations throughout SE with 2,000 employees— suggests "deeper pockets" and more brand awareness – Focus is on telecommunications and data only Publicly traded – Offer leasing options – Well-designed web site	– Losing money: $50.9 million in 2005 – No clear differentiation

FIGURE 13.8: **Company XYZ Competitive Analysis,** continued

Company Name, Service Area and Location	Products and Services	Strengths	Weaknesses
Competitor 3 www.web site.com Charleston Office: 2 Main St. North Charleston, SC 29405 (843) 555-1111	– Voice Products and Services • Business and hospitality • Tailored phone systems • IP telephony • Voice mail systems • Call accounting • Unified messaging • Video conferencing • Conference bridging • Call logger/Call recording • Local & long distance services • Automated attendants • Message on hold • Paging – Data Products and Services • WAN (Wide Area Network) and LAN (Local Area Network) • Computer systems • Network management • Wireless applications • Structured wiring solutions • High speed internet service • Systems integrator and networking value-added reseller – Cable Products and Services • Structured wiring solutions	– Web site design is excellent – Safety net program/service– trademarked and proprietary – Provides total service – In business 15 yrs. with more than 3,000 customers – Strong business partner alliances	– Web site has virtually no customer service capabilities and pages lack detailed information (e.g, FAQs and Careers) – No clear differentiators

---

FIGURE 13.9

Company XYZ: Situation Analysis: Resources

- *Time*
  Although our company is anxious to make our business more profitable, we are not operating under a "do-or-die" timeline and are willing to allocate the resources necessary to achieve our goals in a logical, prioritized fashion.

- *Money*
  To date, we have not developed or set aside specific funds to execute the recommended strategies. Since this is a critical component of the planning process, we will do so immediately to ensure that marketing, advertising, and public relations efforts are prioritized, reasonable, and cost-effective.

- *People*
  Currently we feel that we can comfortably service our forecasted customer-base increase during the next six months without hiring additional employees (although we are are planning to add two more employees—one sales person and one technician—sometime during the next 12 months).

FIGURE 13.10

Company XYZ: Marketing Strategies: Prospect Size and Business Climate

Our 1–12 month goals (150 new clients) mean we must achieve a less than .5 percent market share in our current service area. In our opinion, this is very realistic based on the following facts and/or assumptions:

- Since Charleston County, South Carolina, our main service area, is home to more than 34,000 small- to large-sized firms (Source: 2004 US Census), there are more than enough business prospects available.

- Even when the list of potential prospects is "scrubbed" to eliminate non-targeted segments—e.g., companies who don't have one or more of the stated criterion—there is still more than enough businesses left, assuming our standards remain the same (for example, we can choose to expand into other South Carolina counties or add residential customers to our targeted prospects).

- We operate in an area that has maintained an average new business growth of over 2 percent per year and a forecasted increase of at least the same until 2010.

- A recent 6.3 percent increase in the Charleston area population (583,472), forecasted to increase by 5 percent by 2010 (613,470) (Source: 2006 Center for Business Research study).

- Comfort, availability, and growing demand for state-of-the-art technology solutions particularly among the younger population.

- Berkeley, Charleston, and Dorchester Counties (our service areas) businesses currently employ more than the state's average number of workers (forecasted to rise) in several of our targeted industries (Source: Charleston Regional Development Alliance, Third Quarter, 2004; Center for Business Research) necessitating the need for more advanced telecommunications equipment/software. For example:

  - Professional and Business Services: 31,148 employees

  - Educational and Health Services: 50,648 employees

  - Leisure and Hospitality Industries: 33,974 employees

- The Charleston region (Berkeley, Charleston, and Dorchester Counties) is home to a disproportionately high number of top South Carolina employers in our targeted industries, making it fertile ground for growth.

FIGURE 13.11

Company XYZ: Core Product/Service Offerings

XXX Telecom BBB Office Systems: 500 (small- to medium-sized office), 800 (medium-sized company), 3000 (large company), 4000 ("mission critical" for large enterprises requiring highest traffic capabilities and reliability)

Features

- One-number accessibility

- Wireless capability and simultaneous ringing for multiple call types—if call is not answered, it directs the call transparently into the BBB voice-mail system

- Text to speech capabilities

- Very high quality parts and systems

- System works with landline or wireless phones

- Answering machine emulation

- Audio help integrated voice mail

Benefits

- BBB Product helps provide increased peace of mind by permitting maximum flexibility for businesspeople and customers (allows for immediate communication anywhere)

- Fewer missed opportunities—greater call completion reduces the loss of time-sensitive calls to sales people

- Improved productivity and quicker time to sale—enables sales staff and mobile professionals to respond to questions and make decisions immediately

- Increased customer satisfaction—eliminates long on-hold times and "phone tag" by simultaneously ringing desk phones and remote destinations

Because of its popularity among our target audience, profitability to our company, and availability we will focus our marketing efforts on increasing the sale of this product by 35 percent over the next 12 months

Wrapping Up

Congratulations! If you've come this far, you're already ahead of 90 percent of businesses. Even better, you can count yourself among the top 5 percent of America's entrepreneurs who "get it"—those who understand the importance of planning and then taking action.

Now it's time to celebrate! Take a hard-earned break, pat yourself on the back, and bask in the brilliance of a job well done.

We've enjoyed being part of your trip and wish you great success. Feel free to check out the additional templates and references we've included in the Appendix. Also, please visit our web site, www.StrategicMarketing Advisors.com, often and become a part of our online community of life-long marketing students and don't forget you can download for free all the templates and worksheets included in this book (and lots of other great time-savers) by registering on our web site: www.TheProcrastinatorsGuideTo Marketing.com or www.TPGTM.com.

The reward of a thing well done, is to have done it.

—RALPH WALDO EMERSON

ADDITIONAL RESOURCES AND TEMPLATES

One of our goals for writing this book was to help you learn to ask the right questions and understand what to do with the answers you receive. But now we'd like to provide you with some additional resources for obtaining those answers. That's why we've included the following list of web sites and books that we've found particularly useful. These are but a small sample of what's available so continue to search on your own and compile your own list.

We've grouped them in logical categories, but as you'll see many overlap with others. Also, we've personally checked out all of the web sites and books on this list, but things move quickly, particularly on the internet, so some may have changed. You can also go to our web site: www.StrategicMarketingAdvisors.com, where you'll find updates on these and other resources.

Moreover, at the end of this chapter you'll find some additional templates and samples. We've included several letter examples and budget and processes planners. We hope you find them useful.

Business and Marketing Web Sites

www.StrategicMarketingAdvisors.com. This is our web site, where you'll find lots of great resources and updates.

www.marketingprofs.com. Company specializing in strategic and tactical marketing know-how.

www.MarketingSherpa.com. Articles, case studies, best practices, newsletters, and reports.

www.TheProcrastinatorsGuideToMarketing.com. Again our web site where you can download worksheets and templates.

People and Business Finder Web Sites

www.anywho.com. Up-to-date directory for locating people and businesses.

www.bigyellow.com. Online yellow pages with business, as well as residential, listings, including e-mail addresses.

www.info.com. Directory assistance and lots of other stuff. It's really more like a search engine.

www.knowx.com. Affordable way to conduct a background check on a potential employee or to find information about other businesses.

www.whoishe.com. Flat-fee ($39–$75) based basic, criminal/civil and/or comprehensive background checks.

www.tracerlock.com. Inexpensive monthly subscription web monitoring and clipping service.

www.hoovers.com. Subscription site for researching companies, industries, and people.

www.researchbuzz.com. A collection of items on search engines, online databases, and other information resources.

www.publicrecordfinder.com. Contains free people-finder links—very helpful!

www.inter800.com. Another great directory, this one for toll-free numbers.

www.dnb.com. Buy affordable reports on companies locally or worldwide— their small-business owners' section particularly useful.

http://usptogov.com. This is the U.S. Trademark's official database. Use it to obtain a list of any federally registered trademark including who filed it, when/where it was filed, and a description of the product or service.

www.1800ussearch.com. Use it to find almost anyone although there isn't much in the way of free or easy-to-obtain information.

Web Site Development and Design

www.internettips.com. The best web development company on the planet! They'll help you design, optimize, write copy, and much more. Reasonably priced and extremely trustworthy.

www.superstats.com. Traffic counts shown as graphs and totals, visitor locations, and times (hourly and daily), and destinations, and more.

http://retinawebagency.com. Customized web site design services.

www.bizjournalsdirectory.com. Register your web site here.

www.memail.com. Good web marketing and writing information for beginners and the more advanced.

www.globalpromoter.com. Some great free search engine optimization tools here.

www.blipstudios.com. Offer all kinds of design services.

www.morevisibility.com. Search engine marketing and optimization company.

www.addme.com. Allows you to submit your web site to the top 14 search engines.

www.paypal.com. Serve as a commercial credit card processing center for buisnesses without merchant accounts (or in addition to).

www.filezsite.com.ar. Affordable and professional logo design.

Free Group Mailing and E-Zine Directories

Following are several e-zine directories that you may want to check out.

- http://groups.yahoo.com/
- www.topica.com
- http://groups.google.com/
- http://emailuniverse.com/
- www.ezineseek.com
- www.liszt.com

Search Engines

www.dogpile.com. The search engine for search engines.

www.ask.com. Ask questions in plain English and get helpful answers.

www.google.com, *www.msn.com*, *and www.yahoo.com*. The big three with Google on top.

www.searchenginewatch.com. Search site with great starter guides, and free software and tips.

Business Basics

www.britannica.com. The complete, 32-volume encyclopedia online—lots of great search choices.

http://www.mindtools.com. Great site for anyone wanting to improve their business skills.

http://somedaysoon.brooklynpubliclibrary.org/s1/gs.asp. A wonderful resource for start-ups—focuses on New York but tips can be applied almost anywhere.

http://www.marketingcentral.com. Offer on-demand, web-based marketing automation tools.

http://www.census.gov/main/www/cen2000.html. Invaluable research tool with information on demographics, markets, etc.

www.usps.gov. U.S. Postal Service's web site—great for looking up zip codes, track mail, obtain rates, etc.

www.bbbonline.com. Check out online businesses that have received the Better Business Bureau's reliability seal.

http://www.startupjournal.com. The *Wall Street Journal*'s Center for Entrepreneurs.

http://www.sba.gov. Small Business Administration—lots of information, advice, and resources.

http://www.bizstats.com. Great retail benchmarks for most industries.

www.uschamber.com/sb/default. U.S. Chamber of Commerce Small Business Center.

http://www.va-interactive.com/bankofamerica/resourcecenter. Bank of America's Small Business Resource Center.

www.howstuffworks.com. Find out what makes things tick.

www.hungryminds.com. For learning just about anything free courses available as well as ones your pay for!

www.genimperative.com. Marketing research web site.

www.kinkos.com. Printing help.

http://www.bcentral.com. Small business help—great web site with all kinds of free tools and information for small businesses.

http://www.score.org. Service Corps of Retired Executives—free business advice on all kinds of stuff.

http://www.homebusinesscenter.com. Start-up loan information, forms, and worksheets.

www.officeme.com. Help for running your own small business—forms, news, package tracking, shipping rates, domain names, etc.

http://www.freeworks.com. Free tools and templates for creating human resource and finance reports.

http://www.office.com. Lots of subject matter including business and financial news, research reports, management advice, etc.

www.bplans.com. Contains useful tools to help you create your own business plan.

http://www.businessknowhow.com. Lots of helpful information on a wide variety of topics.

www.ncoe.org. National Commission on Entrepreneurship.

Business Software

www.smartdraw.com. Process mapping with SmartDraw—a must-have if you want to illustrate business processes or systems.

http://www.crypto-central.com/html/timekeeper.html. Software that helps you track how you spend your time during the working day.

www.roboform.com. Software that fills in passwords and your personal information on web sites—a great time-saver.

www.shortkeys.com. Software that allows you to type in one or two letters for common words, phrases, and paragraphs and it fills in the rest.

www.mindjet.com. Great piece of software (MindManagerPro) for taking notes, brainstorming, planning, and keeping track of tasks.

www.gyronix.com. Great compliment tool for Mind Jet Manager software—lets you expand its capabilities.

www.reallyeasyreader.com. Program to help you get through all the wonderful reading material you have on your plate.

http://www.quirk.biz/searchstatus.com. Firefox search tool that provides useful data about web sites, like Alexa score, PageRank, link structure, and more.

www.desktop.google.com. Download to your computer and use it to find documents, files, and e-mails quickly and easily.

www.typeit4me.com. Autotype software for Macs.

www.homebusinessresearch.com. Offers research software and access to business newsgroups—specifically designed for homebased businesses.

Internet, Business, and Personal Security

www.verisign.com. Provides secure encryption to safeguard your web site's visitors' personal information.

www.ripoffreport.com. Nationwide web site that gathers complaints about companies.

http://www.scambusters.org. Keeps you informed about internet scams.

www.fraud.org. Includes information on consumer scams.

www.consumer.gov/idtheft. Tips on preventing and stopping identity theft.

www.spamcop.net. Free service for reporting spam and feeding spam filtering services.

www.MyAccuConference.com. Featuring conference calling and a whole lot more.

www.MyEasyWebAutomation.com. Complete one-stop fully automated shopping cart for selling products and services online.

Free Stuff and Downloads

www.adobe.com. Allows you to view and download pdf files exactly as the author designed them.

www.download.com. Free downloads for Windows operating systems.

www.gotoast.com. Three free tools including a search engine index rating, recommendations for online advertising options, and an auto bid simulator—a good one!

Training

www.90dayproduct.net. Training that helps you produce products for resale.

www.freeskills.com. Free pdf formatted manuals for all kinds of online training—you'll need Adobe Acrobat (www.adobe.com) to download.

www.worldwidelearn.com. Provides an overview of internet training topics found on the web.

www.trainingtools.com. Free software program training courses in FrontPage, PhotoShop, and Dreamweaver. Great time-savers!

www.headlight.com. Source for finding software training courses.

www.MyJimRohn.com. Great personal development site.

Tax Help

www.turbotax.com. Allows you to prepare, electronically file and print federal and state tax returns.

www.taxprophet.com. Tips for planning capital gains, business classifications and much more—also contains interactive tax applications.

www.unclefed.com. Complete online resource for tax relief.

www.irs.ustreas.gov. Income tax forms, instructions, publications, regulations, and other helpful stuff.

www.webtax.com. IRS tax return preparation and filing and lots of good information.

Domain and Hosting Web Sites

www.godaddy.com. Great site for checking out the availability and purchasing and registering domain names, and buying other web products.

www.my1and1.com. Domain registration and web hosting—one of the best.

www.icann.org. Find all kinds of information about domain registration.

Web Site Building Tools

www.brave.net. Offers web sites many free tools for webmasters and fun bells and whistles.

www.luckymarble.com. Affordable and professional-looking web site templates and much more.

www.bigwebmaster.com. Same as above.

www.RocketTheme.com. Web site templates designed to be used with Joomla's free content management system (CMS).

www.joomla.org. A free open source CMS (Content Management System)—a must for anyone who wants to control their own web site and its content.

Business and Marketing Books We Recommend

Here are some of our other favorite marketing books.

Bossidy, Larry and Ram Charan. *Execution: The Discipline of Getting Things Done*, (New York: Crown Publishing Group, 2002).

Carnegie, Dale. *How to Win Friends and Influence People*, (New York: Simon and Schuster, 1981).

Clason, George S. *The Richest Man in Babylon*, (New York: Signet; reissue edition, 2004).

Collins, Jim. *Good to Great*, (New York: HarperCollins, 2001).

Covey, Stephen R. *The 7 Habits of Highly Effective People*, (New York: Simon and Schuster, 1990).

Ferrazzi, Keith with Tahl Raz, *Never Eat Alone: And Other Secrets to Success, One Relationship at a Time*, (New York: Currency Doubleday, 2005), www.nevereatalone.com.

Gerber, Michael. *E-Myth Revisited: Why Most Businesses Don't Work and What to do About It*, (New York: HarperCollins, 2001).

Gittell, Jody Hoffer. *The Southwest Airlines WAY: Using the Power of Relationships to Achieve High Performance*, (New York: McGraw-Hill, 2003).

Gladwell, Malcolm. *Blink*, (New York: Little, Brown and Company, 2004).

————. *The Tipping Point: How Little Things Can Make a Big Difference*, (Boston: Little, Brown and Company, 2000).

Hill, Neopolean. *Think and Grow Rich*, (San Diego, CA: Aventine Press; revised edition, 2004).

Kim, W. Chan and Renée Mauborgne. *Blue Ocean Strategy: How to Create Uncontested Market Space and Make the Competition Irrelevant*, (Boston: Harvard Business School Press, 2005).

Kiyosaki, Robert. *Rich Dad's Guide to Financial Freedom: The Cash Flow Quadrant*, (New York: Warner Books, Inc., 2000).

Kotter, John P. *The Heart of Change*, (Boston: Harvard Business School Press, 2002).

Levinson, Jay Conrad. *Guerrilla Marketing: Third Edition*, (New York: Houghton Mifflin Company, 1998).

Meyerson, Mitch with Mary Eule Scarborough. *Mastering Online Marketing*, (Irvine, CA: Entrepreneur Press, due for release January, 2008).

Miller, John G. *QBQ! The Question Behind the Question: Practicing Personal Accountability in Work and Life*, (New York: Putnam Publishing Group, 2004), www.QBQ.com or 1-800-774-0737.

Rohn, E. James. *The Five Major Pieces to the Life Puzzle*, (Dallas, TX: Great Impressions Printing and Graphics, 1991).

Spector, Robert and Patrick D. McCarthy. *The Nordstrom Way: The Inside Story of America's #1 Customer Service Company*, (New York: John Wiley & Sons, 1995).

Tracy, Brian. *Million Dollar Habits: Proven Power Practices to Double and Triple Your Income*, (Irvine, CA: Entrepreneur Media, Inc., 2004).

———. *The Way to Wealth: Success Strategies of the Wealthy Entrepreneur*, (Irvine, CA: Entrepreneur Press, 2007).

Welch, Jack and Suzy. *Winning*, (New York: HarperCollins, 2005).

Safety Net (Oops!) Letter

This is one of the most useful retention tools we've used. It is a wonderful way to turn lemons into lemonade. Remember, the most telling moments of truth in any business is when things don't go exactly right.

Caution: This is not the type of letter that is appropriate to send to customers who are irate—the I-want-to-speak-to-the-owner-of-this-lousy-company-right-now type. Hopefully, you'll never experience this!

COMPANY LOGO/LETTERHEAD

Date

Dear [Mr. Smith (*very important to personalize*)]:

It came to my attention that you recently [called/wrote/visited] us and received a less-than-perfect service experience. Please accept my sincere apology.

Every employee at [your company] works hard to ensure that each customer contact is delightful, 100 percent of the time, but "to err is human" and we sometimes fall short of our goal. However, we will continue to work even harder to develop and offer exceptional [your product/services], backed up by world-class customer service. You have my personal promise.

We have deposited [$0000 dollars (coupon/gifts/whatever you choose)] into you're your company name account—our gift to you. You and your family can use them to [describe how to use gift].

We hope that you like your gift and use it to enjoy [describe gift benefits]. I'd love to hear from you! My email address is: [janedoe@aol.com]. Thanks for being such a great—and patient—customer!

Sincerely,

Name and Title

High-Value Customer Letter

The following is a sample letter that you can use as a guide for your own letter to your high-value customers. It's a good idea to give a "gift" that's flat and lightweight so packing and postage costs aren't onerous.

COMPANY LOGO/LETTERHEAD

Date

Dear [Mr. Smith (*very important to personalize*)]:

Wow, time flies! It seems like only yesterday that we opened our doors/web site/offices/whatever for the first time, but it's been more than [three months/years]! During that time our [company/practice] has grown and prospered–we now serve over [10,000 customers/clients/patients] and have added [product to our product/service mix]. This would not have been possible without great customers like you! And now is our chance to let you know how much we value your business.

Therefore, please accept the enclosed [coupon/voucher/gift card] as a sincere token of our appreciation. Simply send it in with your next payment [or whatever the directions are] and receive an immediate savings off of your bill. We hope you use it to treat yourself to something special–on us!

And I'd love to hear from you personally with any comments or tips you may have for us. We are always looking for new ways to improve our service. My email address is: [somebody@aol.com] (tip: add an alternate email address so you're able to keep these separate from others) or you can call me at [000.555.5555].

Thanks again, and enjoy!

Sincerely,

Name, Title

Affinity/Cause Letter

Below is a template for a letter that you can use to introduce a partnership with another company, organization or non-profit association. To better illustrate the point, this letter assumes that the writer is an alumnus of the university.

COMPANY LOGO/LETTERHEAD   UNIVERSITY LOGO

Date

Dear [Ms. Smith (*very important to personalize*)]:

As a graduate of [University Name] and owner of [Company Name], I am proud to announce our partnership with [University Alumni Association].

Our company, a [type of company] offers [types of products and services]. We invite you to enjoy what other [University Name] alumni in your area have already experienced [your USP] all backed up by our world class customer service.

Even better, as an alumnus of [University Name], you will receive our special [price/offer/discount/added] services, and [5 percent] of every transaction will be donated to our alumni association, helping to support our many projects.

Call us toll free at: [1.800.555.5555] and mention this ad or shop online at: [www.sss.edu/alumni] and [enter code 8888] to obtain your special gift.

We look forward to serving you.

Sincerely,

Name, Title

General Sales Letter

This is a very generic sales letter template that can be easily modified to accommodate your specific needs. This is an example of a B2B sales letter.

COMPANY LOGO/LETTERHEAD

Address

Date

Chamber Name

Address

Address

Dear [Ms. Smith (*very important to personalize*)]:

I'm writing to you because my company, [Company Name], has conducted several profitable seminars for a number of chamber and organizations like yours. Our innovative workshops have helped them raise substantial extra money while increasing their members' commitment to their chamber!

We've been able to accomplish this by developing and presenting pertinent, well-thought-out seminars specifically designed to what for small to medium-sized businesses. We understand the unique challenges that most companies face daily and have the experience and expertise to offer them what.

Even better, our seminars are COST and RISK FREE to your organization!! How do we do it? Simple. [Company Name] will donate a full [20 percent] of the gross revenues we generate back to your organization, immediately! I've enclosed detailed information for you to review.

I'll be in your area next [day of week and date] and would like to meet in order to discuss how we can work together. I have a window of time available at [0 P.M.] Let me know if that works for you. I'm eager to make this happen!

My contact information is [contact information here].

Sincerely,

Name, Title

Customer Welcome Letter

This is an example of a customer welcome letter that you may find helpful to use as a guide.

COMPANY LOGO/LETTERHEAD

Date

Dear [Ms. Smith (*very important to personalize*)]:

Welcome to [company name] your new choice for your [product/service] needs.

We take great pride in offering you the very best in [your products/services] which means that you [list benefits].

We've enclosed a list of "Frequently Asked Questions." We hope you find this information helpful. We are committed to making each and every experience you have with our company delightful 100 percent of the time, so please let us know when we have, and when we haven't!

You can reach me personally at: [000-000-0000 ext. 000] or by e-mail at: [janedoe@aol.com]. I'd love to hear from you!

Thanks again for choosing [your company name].

Sincerely,

Name and Title1

Winback Letter

You can use this letter template to send out to customers who may have moved on.

COMPANY LOGO/LETTERHEAD

Date

Dear [Mr. Smith],

It came to my attention that you have not [called/wrote/visited] us in a long time. If we've done anything to displease you accept my sincerest apology and we hope you'll reconsider your decision.

Every employee at [your company] works hard to ensure that each customer contact is delighted—100 percent of the time—but "to err is human" and we sometimes fall short of our goal. However, we will continue to work even harder to develop and offer exceptional [your product/services]—backed up by world-class customer service. You have my personal promise.

We're committed to earning your business every, so feel free to contact me personally with suggestions on how [your company name] can serve you better.

I can be reached at the number above or e-mail me at: [janedoe@aol.com].

I hope to hear from you/see you soon!

Sincerely,

Name and Title

Step-by-Step Process Checklist

This tool is a written checklist that clearly and simply outlines key process steps, materials needed, accountability, and timelines. Again, it can be used for any business or marketing process.

Provide the following information in the appropriate areas:

1. *Name the process.* What action is being performed? (For example, opening up your shop in the morning.)
2. *Materials.* What resources are needed to complete the process.
3. *Standards.* What rules apply to anyone performing this task? (For example, what time of day must the store be opened, how many employees must be present when opening, who is responsible for opening, etc.)
4. *Steps.* Actual steps involved in completing the task.
5. *Accountability.* Who is responsible for performing each step?
6. *Due by.* When the task must be completed, if applicable.

Here's an example of one that might be used to open up a store in the morning. You'll find a blank one on the next page for your use.

Process: Opening up the Store

Standards

1. One manager and one employee must be present for store opening
2. All "openers" must read and sign Security and Confidentiality Agreement prior to opening
3. Openers must arrive no later than 8:30 A.M.–store open to public no later than 9 A.M.

Materials Needed

Keys, Alarm Code, Computer Password, Opening Cash

Steps	Accountability	Due by
1. Manager to open front door locks with appropriate keys	1. Manager	1. 8:30 A.M.
2. Deactivate alarm	2. Manager	2. 8:30–9 A.M.
3. Open register	3. Manager	3. 8:30–9 A.M.
4. Start computer, dust, roll up shades, etc.	4. Manager/Assistant	4. 9 A.M.

Process: _____

Standards

1. _____

2. _____

3. _____

Materials Needed

_____

_____

_____

Steps	Accountability	Due by

Sample Six-Month Budget Planner

Expenses	Month 1	Month 2	Month 3	Month 4	Month 5	Month 6	Total Months 1–6
Wages, Salaries, and Benefits							
Raw Materials							
Contract Labor (if applicable)							
Training							
Office Supplies							
Office Furniture							
Office Equipment (Phones, Fax, Printer, Scanner, Computer, Software, Cell Phones)							
Rent							
Office Build-Out/ Renovation							
Utilities (Electricity, Water, AC, Phone Service)							
Insurance (Liability/Other)							
Association Fees							

Sample Six-Month Budget Planner, continued

Expenses	Month 1	Month 2	Month 3	Month 4	Month 5	Month 6	Total Months 1–6
Marketing Advertising							
Travel							
Legal and Professional							
Miscellaneous Expenses							
Taxes							
TOTAL							
Gross Revenues							
Less Expenses							
NET INCOME							
YTD Cumulative							
Assumptions:							
1.							
2.							
3.							

INDEX